THE FATE OF NAZI GERMANY'S JET ENGINEERS

THE FATE OF NAZI GERMANY'S JET ENGINEERS

THE ALLIES' RACE FOR TECHNOLOGY IN 1945 AND INTO THE COLD WAR

REINER DECHER

FRONTLINE
BOOKS

First published in Great Britain in 2024 by Frontline Books
An imprint of Pen & Sword Books Ltd Yorkshire - Philadelphia

ISBN 978 1 03611 100 7

A CIP catalogue record for this book is available from the British Library

Typeset by Lapiz Digital Printed and bound in the UK by CPI Group (UK) Ltd, Croydon, CR0 4YY.

Printed on paper from a sustainable source by CPI Group (UK) Ltd, Croydon, CR0 4YY

Pen & Sword Books Limited incorporates the imprints of Archaeology, Atlas, Aviation, Battleground, Digital, Discovery, Family History, Fiction, History, Local, Local History, Maritime, Military, Military Classics, Politics, Select, Transport, True Crime, Air World, Claymore Press, Frontline Publishing, Leo Cooper, Remember When, Seaforth Publishing, The Praetorian Press, Wharncliffe Books, Wharncliffe Local History, Wharncliffe Transport, Wharncliffe True Crime and White Owl.

For a complete list of Pen & Sword titles please contact

PEN & SWORD BOOKS LTD
47 Church Street, Barnsley, South Yorkshire, S70 2AS, England
E-mail: enquiries@pen-and-sword.co.uk
Website: www.pen-and-sword.co.uk
or
PEN & SWORD BOOKS
1950 Lawrence Rd, Havertown, PA 19083, USA
E-mail: uspen-and-sword@casematepublishers.com

CONTENTS

List of Plates vii
Acknowledgements xi
Prologue: Introduction to a Many-Sided History xiii
Abbreviations xxi

Chapter 1 The War is Over: Now What? 1
Chapter 2 Get What You Can! 11
Chapter 3 The Operation Paperclip List..... 25
Chapter 4 War and Economic Aftermath 30
Chapter 5 The French Connection..... 39
Chapter 6 Accommodations and Life in Central France 51
Chapter 7 Turboméca – Another French Story 59
Chapter 8 Operation Osoaviakhim 63
Chapter 9 The Pflügel Book 69
Chapter 10 Journey to the Volga 75
Chapter 11 Upra (or Uprawlentscheskij Gorodok)..... 87
Chapter 12 Kuybyshev – the City 102
Chapter 13 Our Assigned Task..... 105
Chapter 14 The Buildup to Start Work 109
Chapter 15 Leadership Personalities..... 115
Chapter 16 The Workday 118
Chapter 17 Other Aspects of Life ... and Death 123
Chapter 18 The German Community 137

Chapter 19 The Waiting Years 143
Chapter 20 On Separate Ways 154
Chapter 21 To Berlin without Father....164
Chapter 22 Happy Endings 170
Chapter 23 The Names 173
Chapter 24 Technology Transfer Endings – West and East 178
Chapter 25 Brunolf Baade: Endings "between" East and West....183
Chapter 26 Askania Talent on Hold 188
Chapter 27 Ferdinand Brandner 201
Chapter 28 Out of the Ashes....204

Epilogue – The Role of the US Army 208
Appendix: Reunion in Samara after 47 Years....211
Bibliography 219
Index 222

LIST OF PLATES

1. Anselm Franz (left) and Hans von Ohain in the 1970s.
2. The Pinder Barracks in Landshut where the German dependents as well as "Paperclip" engineers transported from the East were housed. (Photo credit: www.usarmygermany.com.)
3. The Lycoming engineers from Junkers. (Lycoming image C7506005-7)
4. The 104 German scientists and engineers at Fort Bliss, Texas in 1946. (NASA).
5. Herman Oestrich, ca. late 1940s. (Espace Patrimoine Safran)
6. Brunolf Baade (left) and Heinrich Hertel in 1942 enjoying a light moment.
7. An aerial view of Decize with the Cité Voisin caserne building array in the top center of the image.
8. Decize looking to the bridge over the dry (north) arm of the old Loire. (Photo: S. Decher).
9. The German technical people in Decize, ca. 1947.
10. General view of the Cité Voisin residence buildings. (Photo: Karsten Eggers)
11. Wood delivery from the French government to the men before the arrival of families, winter 1947. (Photo: Karsten Eggers)
12. A modern image of the platform sign from which Kurt Pflügel and his family started their forced journey to Russia.
13. Kurt Pflügel about 1972. (Photo: Christa Pflügel)
14. Sigrid (Karkavelas) Pflügel during her time in Russia. (Photo: Christa Pflügel)
15. Sigrid's floorplan sketch of the apartment in Upra, residences no. 28 and 16.
16. The sanatorium on the hill and the fishing village near the shore of the Volga. (Photo: Karl Breuninger)
17. Map showing the location of Kuybyshev (today Samara) on a modern map of the elbow turn of the Volga. (Map data from https://opentopomap.org, CC-BY-SA OpenStreetMap contributors)

18. The Volga River valley, view from near the sanatorium. (From the Haida-Clan website with permission)
19. A sketch map of the Upra complex made by Helmut Breuninger. (Courtesy Karl Breuninger).
20. Two images of Houses 35 and 45. (From the Haida-Clan website with permission and Karl Breuninger)
21. The wooden houses. (Photo: Karl Breuninger)
22. A Finn house in summer with its outhouse. (Photo: Karl Breuninger)
23. (Unidentified) residents of Haus no. 13. (Photo: Karl Breuninger)
24. Brandner (fourth from left) with unidentified members of one of his technical staff sections. (Photo: Karl Breuninger)
25. Ferdinand Brandner as depicted in a Russian book entitled "German Flight Specialists in the City of Kuybyshev in the First Postwar Years (1946-1953)," Samara 2010.
26. Nikolai Dmitrievich Kuznetsov (1911–95).
27. Two views of the Kuznetsov NK-12 engine on a static display of a Soviet Tu-95 bomber. From the website http://culturaaeronautica.blogspot.com/2011/10/kuznetsov-nk-12-o-mais-poderoso-motor.htm
28. The East German Baade 152 airliner prototype.
29. Conference between F. Brandner (l), B. Baade (c), and G. Bock (r). Photo Archive Holger Lorenz. Photographer unknown.
30. The German cemetery with boundary stones and crosses (Photo: Karl Breuninger). The right-hand image was taken in 2007 and shows the addition of Russian gravesites surrounded by traditional fencing. (From the Haida-Clan website with permission)
31. The cross for the German POWs who died in (probably) prison camp no. 5. (From the Haida-Clan website with permission)
32. The Breuninger family (Mathilde, Karl, Dr. Helmut) in Upra in 1947.
33. The East German-built houses for small families.
35. Sketch of the "Special Compound 100" in Tushino.
34. The Clubhouse in Tushino, not unlike the one in Upra.
36. A picture of the newer Magazin. (Photo: Karl Breuninger)
37 and 38. Views of the stone and wooden houses as they appeared in the 2000s. (Photos: Haida-Clan website with permission, Kurt Breuninger)

To Karl and Helmut Breuninger, Hermann Oestrich and Kurt Pflügel

This story belongs in large measure to these men. I met Karl via correspondence and, by his words, his father Helmut Breuninger through the research for this book. I might have met Hermann Oestrich because he sold our family a well-loved dachshund puppy when I was eleven years old. I did not know Kurt Pflügel and now feel I know him in a narrow way. It is the discovery of his writing that precipitated the writing of this book. Having written it, I also know him a little better. If I could turn back the clock, it would be a pleasure to meet the elder of these men who have passed away to learn more details for this story. It also belongs to my father, Siegfried Decher, whose life (and mine) was entangled in the events described here. I would have enjoyed talking more deeply with him about this time in his life with both of us on the same, albeit impossible, level.

To these men, a heartfelt thanks with my sincere hope that I did right by you.

Finally, to the thousands of men, women, and children who spent seven, some as many as eleven, miserable years in the Soviet Union as slave workers and sometimes even longer as captives of the Deutsche Demokratische Republik. May their stories be remembered.

ACKNOWLEDGEMENTS

Material of the kind exposed here is mostly in the German language, sparsely distributed in archives, and difficult to find. Fortunately, there are a few websites maintained for the purpose of keeping the history alive. I am especially grateful for the opportunity to connect with some of the individuals who manage these websites to obtain clarifying details relevant to this story. Email "conversations" with Horst Zoeller of the cited website regarding Ferdinand Brandner were very useful and appreciated.

I sincerely appreciate the insight and images provided by the "Haida-Clan" (Upra Kinder) website noted in the Bibliography. This website commemorates the Russian experience and is dedicated to the memory of Hedwig Haida who was among the abductees. The photographs posted on the website taken in Russia during the detention period and by visitors much later were helpful in supplementing the descriptive text. The photographers are not identified so that credit cannot be ascribed, at least as this is written. If the reader can find the book by Friedemann Singer (in German), it parallels the Pflügel story from another perspective with the addition of a large variety of photographs.

I am especially grateful for the support and encouragement provided by Kurt Pflügel's daughter Sigrid Karkavelas. Conversations with her enriched my understanding, as did the images she provided. I found her name and that of her older sister Christa in the listing of the children in the Haida-Clan website. Their married names were given there. A search of the internet located them with listed telephone numbers. In January 2023, I reached Sigrid. That was the beginning of a very interesting and happy discussion of the book written by her father and the events described therein as she remembered them. Sadly, I also learned that her older sister had passed away just months earlier.

Happily, contact with Sigrid led to correspondence with Karl Breuninger, another of the Upra children, who was kind enough to identify references, links, information, and images related to the Russian abduction. He shared with me an annotated text to presentations he made to interested audiences about his family's experiences in the Soviet Union. His contribution to my understanding through his writing is heartily appreciated. Karl was the child (b. 1944) of Helmut Breuninger, who worked (on gyroscopes for guidance systems) at the DVL in Rechlin and was later part of the Askania group in Russia.

I wish to express gratitude to Pierre Mouton, a retired jet engine control systems engineer at the French jet engine company Safran, for providing the Oestrich manuscript and related documentation. Pierre also brought the Turboméca experience to my attention and provided additional details about parts of that history.

No manuscript is ever good enough when first written with the general ideas bared as if piled in a box of trinkets. It requires readers with editorial and grammatical comments to improve it. To these brave souls I extend a warm "thank you" for suffering through my English that betrays my German roots when it comes to sentence structure. The three heroes on my pedestal are my wife Mary who can never read anything I write without a pencil in her hand and kind words to soften the impact. The second person is Gwenyth Bassetti, a keen editor, outstanding cook and baker, and a wonderful friend. Finally, a big thanks for a thorough review to another good friend, editor, and translator, Yvonne Vogele.

The fact checking help from Tom Fey of the Aircraft Engine Historical Society was very helpful as were the maps drawn by Andreas Illert.

I feel very fortunate in having lived through parts of this time and story and that I avoided being swept up to spend the years described here in Kuybyshev. I learned German from my parents, French when I lived in France, and finally English (American actually!) when I became an adult and a serious student of aircraft engines in the United States. My linguistic breadth allowed me to read much of the documentation related to this writing in the original languages. Do I regret not knowing Russian? Not really, the documentation is likely sparse and skewed.

PROLOGUE: INTRODUCTION TO A MANY-SIDED HISTORY

This book is, in part, the work of individuals who experienced the mayhem at the end of WWII and lived to continue their work with aircraft jet engines in the years that followed. The written words they left behind were meant to be a historical record of the events in which they participated. My role was to pull the record available together into a narrative.

Kurt Pflügel (1903–81) spent seven years in the Soviet Union establishing a jet propulsion development center as an involuntary German engineer. He was repatriated to Germany in 1954. Dr. Helmut Breuninger (1911–2008) was an expert in control systems for flight vehicles who worked with the Askania team abducted to Russia and released to West Germany in 1958. Dr. Hermann Oestrich (1903–73) successfully led the jet engine development effort for the firm SNECMA (today Safran) in France. My father Siegfried Decher worked at Junkers on jet engine control systems and lived to escape the Russian experience described by others. He worked in France under Oestrich, and later emigrated to the United States. Pflügel, Hemut Breuninger, Oestrich, and Decher (1912–80) were members of the previous generation and have passed away leaving behind what you read here. Last, but by no means least, is the light shined on the historical events by Margaret Conner, author of a biography of Hans von Ohain (1911–98). Additional insight to this story is provided by the writings of the controversial and complicated Ferdinand Brandner (1903–86) who led the German team in the Soviet Union during the years of their helotry.

The translated text is by the men who experienced it or reported on it. My own experience is limited to that of a child with access to my father's and other relevant material. The available writings probably fall short of doing justice to the men's emotional states and to descriptions that wives or children might have contributed. It is very sad that few words from the latter are recorded and available. It is, or was perhaps, (mostly) a man's world and the entire story is centered on what men did for a living, what they did to cope, and how they viewed their experiences. Finding facts about private lives in public records is nearly impossible so that the focus must be on the men. The women and children were secondary players, very important ones nevertheless, to the individual men.

As a member of the generation that followed these men, I am interested in questions about the lives of these families because they grew up in environments that differed substantially from those known by their own parents. They experienced new cultures, some entered in shock. Generational continuity usually serves as a model for adults to follow in raising their own young. In this case, the turmoil associated with war and its aftermath was a severe disruption of norms. It made for a time in when the social and schooling environments for the children were uncharted territory for everyone involved. Some of us children were playmates, and in most cases, our paths separated. Making generalized statements about how we were affected is close to impossible, but the history allows some degree of introspection. The years have also taken a toll and continue to reduce our numbers. What remains may ultimately vanish from memory just as we don't know who our nth-great grandparent really was or what he or she did.

Scope

This book is not intended as a scholarly contribution to historical literature. For that, the reader might wish to consult the book by D.L. Augustine in the bibliography. *Red Prometheus* is a description of the political and economic circumstances as these influenced the evolution of what became East Germany where part of this story will end. Rather, this story is a collection of experiences by some of the engineers who were central to the development of jet engines in Germany during the war and their fates in Allied hands after VE-Day. It is also not about jet engine technology nor about Nazi criminality. For a reader interested in the entirety of the industrial structure of Nazi Germany, of which the jet engine is a small part, the well-researched book by Renneberg and Walker may be of interest. The Allies took advantage of winning the war to direct the captured people and their knowledge of aviation technology into their own quarters. This is a part of the story of how they did it.

The totality of the story is much larger than these few pages because a very large number of individuals and institutions were involved in this very large war. Nevertheless, the people named here were some of the giants of their fields at that time. The story of the consequences of the technology transfer at a personal level that is at the heart of this writing have not been thoroughly described to English language readers. While the official American story is relatively well known, or at least available, the French and Russian stories are less so and might be of interest to historians and to people generally interested in aviation and WWII.

My role as author of this book was to put the American *Operation Paperclip* into context with related material associated with transfer of German technology to Russia and France. By doing so I hope to show how American activities at the end of the war played a central role in the broader history of jet engines in the next decade. Others speak in their own voices about their unique experiences. I translated their German text as accurately as I could. The political innuendos are not papered over because they are important as elements of the larger picture. I added supplementary information obtained from referenced sources identified in the Bibliography, editorial comments for context clarity, available images, and maps. The map overleaf should be helpful in locating places cited in various sections of the text.

Outline

This story is divided into sections dealing with the major Allied powers, the Americans, the British, the French, and the Soviets. The British part of this story is brief, but the others are more detailed. The events involved will take the reader to the mid-1950s when the technology transfer associated with the end of WWII had run its course. The road taken by the returnees from Russia will take us to the 1960s with a spectacular dead-end in communist East Germany, the so-called German Democratic Republic or GDR.

A wide philosophical, political, and economic chasm existed between the Soviet Union under Stalin and the Western Allies. That divergence soon developed into the Cold War that followed WWII and had a way of rapidly diluting the German contribution to jet engine technology. It also accelerated jet engine development at the hands of all Allied engineers in their respective countries. The political relationship between Russia and the divided Germany and Berlin was established by the Allied Occupation, the East Berlin uprising in 1953, and the construction of the Berlin Wall in 1961. It profoundly changed again in 1989 with the fall of this wall and by the collapse of the Soviet Union a couple of years later. Changes also occurred in the West since economic and political forces are always in play. The institutions in the West adapted, evolved, and, on the whole, thrived

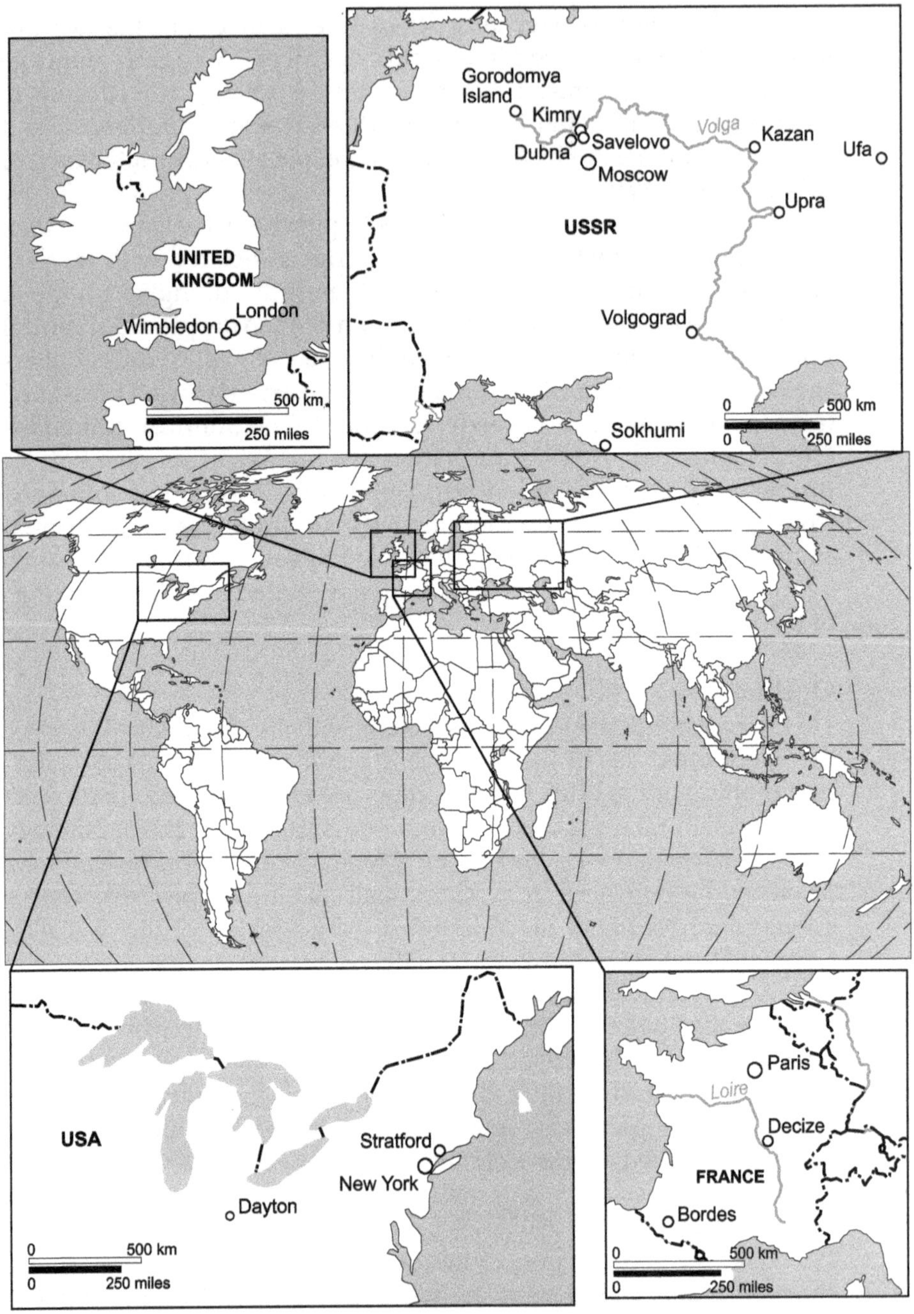

Map 1: World map showing the locations to which the German jet engineers were scattered after 1945. Sokhumi is located off this map about 200 miles southeast of noted location. Map by Andreas Illert.

while those in the Soviet Union changed in their own controlled way. East Germany, i.e., the GDR, disappeared altogether into a larger Bundesrepublik Deutschland, the BRD (also known by the English language acronym FRG, the Federal Republic of Germany) as a result of German re-unification.

This story is illustrated with a few images of people, localities, a few artifacts, maps, and, to the degree that it is possible, images taken by the Germans abducted to Russia. Representative copies of pages from the source material are included, as they were produced in the German language.

To gain a wider perspective on the experiences in Russia, specifically those in Kuybyshev, I consulted memoirs written by other abductees and by POWs interned there at the time. They were helpful in providing other views and fact confirmation about the postwar period in Russia, in Kuybyshev in particular. Such memoirs are not light reading; hence they do not enjoy wide readership and may be hard to find. Such writing is part the historical record and should be preserved as such.

Major Sources

The book by Kurt Pflügel was not copyrighted and is not reproduced in its entirety here. His daughter Sigrid Karkavelas was kind enough to grant permission for her father's book to be used in the manner that I have. The material selected herein is meant to paint a picture of how the Russians handled the technology transfer and the people they needed to execute it. His book includes additional details about the final days of the war, that the reader might wish to learn, but sadly, copies of his book are not likely to be easily found. Pflügel intended for others to read about his experiences and those of the many others who shared them. His self-published book is the basis of much of the text used here. Attempts at locating individuals with an interest in the subject so that it can be described more broadly have been challenging and partially successful. I sincerely hope that this publication will find others with an interest in the experiences described. It is getting late; the children of all the men who went to the countries of the former Allies are well into their eighties or may have passed away by the time of this writing endeavor.

The writing of Hermann Oestrich is an informal memo produced for the record at the company (SNECMA) where he worked as "Technical Director." It is clear from the writing that publication of that memo may not have been intended for general readership, yet it paints a picture of the Allied handling of the German engineers. The firm French Safran (formerly SNECMA) is gratefully acknowledged for sharing Oestrich's text.

Since I am the son of one of the engineers who were central to the development of the jet engine in Germany, I wrote a biography of my father, a quiet man, who participated in the postwar turmoil and found his way to France and later to the United States. His influence on the industry was substantial, although he would never have talked about it in terms of self-promotion. It takes a son, with access to the records he kept, to tell that story. Unexpectedly and happily, readers brought new material to my attention for the present book.

Other Sources and Shameless Commerce

The reader may wish to explore other aspects of this story, namely slightly more technical aspects of aircraft engine developments for commercial aviation described in layman's terms. Such an exposé is available, *Powering the World's Airliners* (2020, see bibliography) where I describe the history of aircraft engine evolution from the Wright brothers to the present day. It covers, among other events, the simultaneous and competitive realization of the jet engine for aircraft propulsion by British and German engineers. Additional printed source material is noted in the Bibliography of this book. Several internet websites were very useful in providing substantiating information.

The *Powering* … book deals specifically with some of the persons who had a strong and decisive hand in the realization of the jet engine. Frank Whittle and Hans von Ohain are generally given a pivotal role in that history. A question that often arises in connection with the jet engine is "Who invented it?" My view is that the two individuals cited above as well as the chief engineers in our story, Anselm Franz and Hermann Oestrich were all present at the time of history where the necessary and available ideas were made into functional hardware. These men deserve the roles assigned to them by history. Their roles were not solitary, however. The ideas that needed to be pulled together into the jet engine were developed earlier and by many others, some of whom understood that a jet engine might be buildable but also believed that a practical engine might not be possible … given the state of the art at the time. The jet engine requires several design aspects to perform well. The necessary improvements in these aspects were pursued and realized by many so that there came a time when a practical engine could be built. The men cited above did it. The ideas were older. See, for example, the extensive review by Eckardt noted in the Bibliography.

The notion of "inventing" anything involves developing an idea and building it in relative isolation. The jet engine as an idea preceded these men and what they built was not in isolation. I credit these men with having the wisdom to know that the jet engine was ready to be built and they did it.

The word "Specialists"

The focus of this book is the fate of the German people involved in undertakings where technology plays an important role. The titular description of such people is challenging because several words apply. In the literature, especially in the British, German, and Russian documentation of the day, the word used to describe a person of interest is *specialist*. This word should be taken as a shortening of *technical specialists*. Its use is fair, but I tend to prefer *engineer* to refer to the people involved in the development of jet engines and airplanes. For an English-language document such as this one, the word *engineer* is often more appropriate, but I will retain the word *specialists* in places where others are speaking in their own voices and where the word is used as a more global descriptor for people who may rightly be classified as *scientists* or *technicians*.

Disclaimer

References to Russia and to the Soviet Union may be viewed as interchangeable in this context because Russia was the principal agency in the Soviet Union (also known as the USSR (1922–91)). The names of Russian locales described here may or may not be standard or uniformly accepted transcription of the names in the Cyrillic writing, but hopefully are clear and acceptable.

Reiner Decher
Bellevue, Washington
November 2023

ABBREVIATIONS

AOZ, BOZ, SOZ, ZOF	Occupation Zones: American, British, Soviet, French
BBC	Brown, Boveri, & Cie. (Swiss power machinery firm, today ABB) also British Broadcasting Corporation
BMW	Bayerische Motoren Werke
BRD	Bundesrepublik Deutschland (see FRG)
CIA	US Central Intelligence Agency
DDR	Deutsche Demokratische Republik (see GDR)
DDT	A powerful insecticide (Dichloro-Diphenyl-Trichloroethane!)
DTI	Directorate of Technology and Industry (French)
DVL	Deutsche Versuchsanstalt for Luftfahrt (German Flight Research Institute)
FDJ	Freie Deutsche Jugend. Communist youth movement
FRG	Federal Republic of Germany (see also BRD, West Germany after 1949)
GDR	German Democratic Republic (also Ostzone and DDR)
HP	Horsepower
JIOA	(US) Joint Intelligence Objective Agency
Jumo	Junkers Motors
KGB	Committee for State Security (in Russian)
NATO	North Atlantic Treaty Organization

NKVD	The People's Commissariat for Internal Affairs, a predecessor of the KGB
NSDAP	Nationalsozialistische Deutsche Arbeiterpartei. Nazi Party in Germany
OKB	Russian acronym for "Experiment and Design Bureau"
POW	Prisoner of War
R	Soviet ruble currency
SAG	Sowjetische Aktiengesellschaft (Soviet company in the SOZ, 1945–6)
SED	Sozialistische Einheitspartei Deutschlands, Communist Party in the GDR
SNECMA	Societé Nationale d'Etudes et de Construction de Moteurs d'Aviation), today Safran
USAAC	US Army Air Corps
USAF	US Air Force
USSR	Union of Soviet Socialist Republics (also Soviet Union)
VEB	Volkseingener Betrieb (GDR state-owned enterprise)
VE	Victory in Europe (over Germany)
VJ	Victory over Japan
WC	water closet (a toilet)

Chapter 1

THE WAR IS OVER: NOW WHAT?

April 1945

The times had been rough in Germany: daily bombings and ever-present shortages of many of the necessities of life. The lives of the engineers who designed and built jet engines were profoundly affected by these circumstances. In a way, they were fortunate to be working on projects that served the German air force, the Luftwaffe, and thus escaped being conscripted to participate into the armies fighting on the Eastern and Western Fronts and becoming part of the carnage that is war, that war specifically. Staying isolated from that violence was neither easy nor simple. The Luftwaffe demands were hard, the schedules tight, and the resources available were meager. There was always the unspoken threat that if this project failed, worse days were in your future and, perhaps, not very many of them.

Late in the war the Luftwaffe's unrealistic hope was to turn the tide with fighter airplanes powered by jet engines to repel the bombing by American B-17s and British Lancasters. The development of jet engines was begun much earlier, before the war, in both Germany and Allied countries. In Germany, the start was a hesitant one, for manpower, resources, and time would be required before a practical airplane using such a new engine can be put in service. The military priority was that this "short" war had to be won first! It was time for "all hands on deck!"

Visionaries who believed in the potential of jet propulsion within the Luftwaffe managed to prevail against then current priorities and convinced the powers that be that the development of a jet engine might help the cause of the war and, amazingly, they agreed. While the initial efforts in 1939–40 were broad,[1] the realities of the war quickly reduced the effort to that of just two companies to produce at least one workable jet engine type for fast fighters and bombers. The companies were the "nationalized" firms Junkers Flugzeug und Motorenbau based in Dessau and BMW in Berlin-Spandau (later in Stassfurt) with the latter headquartered in Munich. BMW is the Bayerische Motorenwerke that is the same company we know today making automobiles.

A third company, Heinkel, the builder of many military aircraft was also active in the pursuit of the jet engine. Construction of a jet engine capable of powering an airplane was the goal of Dr. Hans Pabst von Ohain. Working with Ernst Heinkel's enthusiastic support he succeeded in building such an engine. Together, they built the world's first jet-powered airplane (Heinkel He 178) that flew in the summer of 1939 (27 August). The collaboration between these two individuals continued during the war but was not sufficiently well supported by the Air Ministry for Heinkel to succeed in mass producing jet engines for the Luftwaffe. They tried and proposed many good ideas during the early years of the development but never gained the necessary support. An airplane of Heinkel's design would be scheduled to fly with BMW jet engines. Von Ohain reappears in our story but that of Heinkel jet aircraft ends in 1945, albeit with a notable record. Also cited in our story are the two individuals at the Luftwaffe responsible for pushing it to fund the jet engine development by the Air Ministry: Helmut Schelp and Hans Mauch.

The jet engine production facilities and people were located in the eastern half of Germany. The location of the Junkers Works was in Dessau 80 miles southwest of Berlin. While the Junkers engine facilities were in Magdeburg, the jet engine builders were in Dessau where the production focus was on airplanes. The reason for this location had to do with internal company politics. The BMW engine building facilities were initially in Spandau near Berlin but were relocated to a safer site during the heavy bombing in 1944. The new locale was Stassfurt, about 20 miles south of Magdeburg and 30 miles west of Dessau. All locations where jet engine work was performed were in the state of Sachsen-Anhalt. Importantly, both Dessau and Stassfurt were west of the Elbe River running diagonally across eastern Germany. The river made for a good line for American and British armies to stop and await the conquest of Berlin by the Soviet army. Significantly, the river was east of what was to become an "Iron Curtain," in the words of Winston Churchill. This geographical reality meant that the German jet engine facilities were going to be located in the *future* Soviet Occupation Zone.

1 See, for example, *Turbulent Journey*.

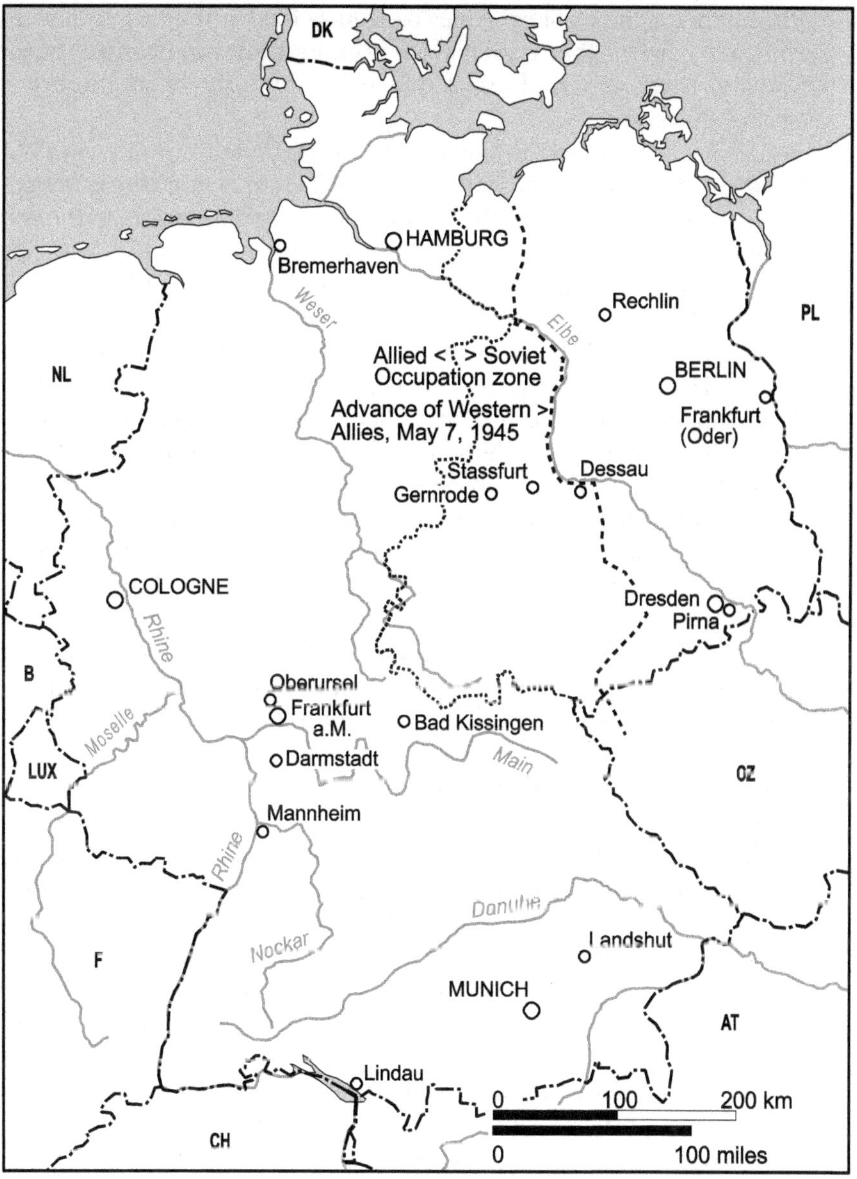

Map 2: Map of Germany showing the city locations of the jet engine facilities and points of interest in our story. The postwar state boundaries (dot-dash) together with the boundary between Soviet and Western Occupation Zones are shown (small dots). Neighboring countries are identified by one or two-letter identification codes. The US Army moved eastward as far as the Elbe River to the short-dash line. The area west of the US advance line to the small dots was the area ceded by US and British forces to the Soviet Union as their occupation zone on 1 July 1945. Map courtesy Andreas Illert.

Fortunately for the western Allies as well as the German jet engineers, significant parts of that region were initially under the control of the US Army. These geographical details will turn out to be an important aspect of this story.

Jet airplanes were in the skies over Europe by late summer in 1944. The Luftwaffe used the Messerschmitt Me 262s to engage the bombers, but it was too late to change the course of the war. The reality of the war was that Allied bombing had seriously damaged the fuel producing infrastructure, limiting Germany's ability to fill the fuel tanks of trucks, airplanes, tanks, etc. Furthermore, the available pool of specially trained pilots for the jets was shrinking in Germany during the war's last year. The war on the ground was demanding its pound of flesh.

The Allied military knew about jet-powered airplanes, not only because they encountered them over Germany but because the British and the Americans were building jets of their own. British twin-engine jet fighters (Gloster Meteors with Whittle-designed Rolls-Royce jet engines) defended the skies over England. Interestingly, they stayed within British airspace defending against V-1 flying bombs and a dwindling number of Luftwaffe bombers. There are no records of encounters between British and German jet fighter airplanes. American airplane builders also built jet fighter aircraft during the war, but these were never used in combat. They were not ready.

Winning the war with the Me 262?

Aviation played a critical role in the evolution of WWII. New technology was the key to better performing airplanes and the jet engine was quantum leap in technology. However, it takes more than technology to change the tide of war and for this war, the answer to the posed question is a definite NO! The topic is greater than just technology.

Historians have grappled with the events of WWII in Europe, sometimes asking whether this or that would have changed its course. Germany made a number of serious errors regarding aviation that, had all of them not been made, might have led to different end. The errors ranged from decisions about what airplanes to build and how to use them for strategic decisions. Technology is involved in the first set of challenges and, in that domain, errors are learning experiences. The second set is made by political leaders and there, errors are consequential.

A military airplane must serve some function and its fulfillment (like shooting down Allied bombers) led to designs that could be described as bizarre. Most of these never made it past the prototype testing stage. Even well-designed aircraft were subject to changes and delays by

Hitler and the Luftwaffe chief Göring countermanding military and engineering experts. The Me 262 falls in that category: Hitler thought it was better at use as a bomber when the designers had a fighter airplane in mind when they built it. In the following chapters we will see that the people who tackled these tasks, even the failed ones, were of interest to the Allies after the war.

At the behest of the Air Ministry (the Reichsluftfahrtministerium, or RLM), Germany built many types of airplanes some of which performed well and others that did not. Lest this paragraph devolve into a discussion of which ones might be on such a list and why, let me say that the Me 262 was probably the outstanding example in that list. The longer list includes variously practical rocket-powered and single-use interceptors, airplanes designed or modified to examine the potential of new technology and the piston-engine powered aircraft that so dominated the air war over Europe.

The even larger political aspects of war also played a role in answering the question posed above. Specifically, we note that war is carried out by two approaches: tactical and strategic. Tactical warfare might be a bold attack on defending armies using ground troops supported by air forces. German invasions like that of Poland in 1939 and Russia in 1941 are examples of such warfare. In these attacks, Hitler believed that overwhelming the enemy with terror and weapons was the goal and airplanes were counted like tanks or soldiers, the more the better. Strategic warfare involves the use of bombers to destroy the war-making ability of the enemy. That also has terror and destruction components. Success in that arena requires long-range bombers. The design and building of such aircraft were considered by Germany and a few prototypes made it to reality but never into production. One project was called the *Amerikabomber*. Insofar as aviation warfare by Germany is concerned, failure to have a strategic bomber was a fatal error on Hitler's part. His airplanes could reach London and other British cities, but as history (with Winston Churchill's help) demonstrates when the imposition of terror dominates destruction of industrial war production facilities, strategic brilliance was not in play.

This error was compounded by nearly winning the "Battle of Britain" air war (July–October 1940) and then losing it by turning away from the apparently unreachable goal of achieving air superiority over the islands. Hitler's attention was redirected to invading the Soviet Union in June 1941 to get a "win" to build on his many other wins in Europe that did not include Great Britain. Error number two. For Germany, this move made for a two-front war with a very deep country that would have required bombing capability all the way to the Ural Mountains.

The USSR did indeed move their war production faculties far to the east where German bombers would not reach them even if the German army could be held in the west. As Germany was repelled in the winter of 1943 at the Battle of Stalingrad, the Soviets breathed a little easier.

Error number three was the German declaration of war on the United States following the Japanese attack on Pearl Harbor. Germany now had a real two-front war with countries that had immense industrial capabilities that could not be reached by air. On the other hand, as long as the British held on and the Germans did not succeed with an invasion of that country (*Operation Sea Lion*), the American B-17s could base in Britain and pound Germany.

In a nutshell, that is the story of aviation in WWII. The industrial might of Britain, the United States, and the Soviet Union eventually overwhelmed Germany. Germany never planned strategically and did not build the airplanes necessary for the warfare it initiated. The long-range B-17 was the key airplane in Europe. On the other hand, the Pacific Ocean is so large that the airplanes of the day could not reach Japan from the North American continent, even from US territories. The answer was a navy with aircraft carriers and island hopping by the US Marines. Hitler's hope that Japan would so occupy American forces that they would stay out of Europe was an appalling miscalculation.

Technology was advanced in Germany as it was in Japan and in the Allied countries, driven by the war. Would you argue that technology was the key to ending WWII in Europe? In the Pacific?

The German engineers built innovative new airplanes, but their technical know-how was not up to overcoming the insane and poor decisions made by the Führer, the "Leader?" The Me 262 had virtually no impact on the outcome of the war when fuel and manpower (pilots etc.) were in very short supply in Germany. It was a limited airplane for a hopeless task. The limitation had to do with the difficulties in operating its engines to avoid functional engine failure (compressor stall and flameout) and its short service life. However, the technology was out and ready to be improved for a new war, one that was largely "cold."

How were the jets used?

By today's standards, the jet engines of 1945 were primitive with a lot of problems, but the airplanes were fast and moderately effective as weapons when they worked. By moderate I mean that the speed capability of the Me 262 was not necessarily an advantage because it shortened the time-on-target. It was not capable of slowing down once at speed, but from a bomber-crew viewpoint, it was scary because they could not easily shoot back. The Allies were, however, keen to learn if the German technology was better than theirs. How did the German engineers solve this or that?

When the war ground to a halt, Junkers had produced over 6,000 jet engines for the Messerschmitt Me 262 (of which about 1,400 were produced) and for the Arado Ar 234 bomber. The former was a capable jet fighter, provided its two engines lasted the duration of the mission. The latter was designed as a bomber but used primarily as a reconnaissance airplane. It did drop a bomb or two on the German bridge at Remagen to try to prevent the Allies from crossing the Rhine. The engines on these two aircraft types were Jumo 004Bs ('Jumo' is an acronym for Junkers Motors) that proved capable enough despite the factory's lack of access to steel alloying metals (chromium, manganese, and nickel) that might have served the engine's performance better. Among the problems of the Junkers engines was the short service life of the engine. Initial models were expected to be overhauled every 50 hours.[1] Often, the engines in service did not last even that long, especially after a pilot had demanded a high burst of power, just once.

BMW, for its part, was a little behind Junkers in its development schedule. In April 1945 BMW had delivered about 700 engines for installation in the Heinkel He 162, the Volksjäger, the people's fighter, or better, the people's hunter. A few of these airplanes managed to be put in service, but it was too late. The Americans, known by the Germans as the "Amis" (pronounced Ammies – the word "Amerikaner" is just too long!) had arrived.

Cease fire!

Fighting in the Sachsen-Anhalt area stopped in late April and most of the Allied fighting had been done by soldiers of the American First Army. The British forces swept eastward in parallel with the Americans over more northern parts of Germany.

A continuing part of the war was learning everything possible of German technology. To that end, there were cadres of technical personnel moving with the armed forces. At this time, the Allies were also preparing the details for the postwar civil administration of various parts of Germany as "occupation zones." There were to be an American Occupation Zone in Germany's south, a British one in the north, a Russian one in the east and a French one in the southwest. The

1 Consider that a modern engine today might last 20,000 to 30,000 hours between overhauls.

war was not over, yet. The end would come with VE Day on 8 May, two weeks later.

A strange quiet came over the area when the US First Army approached the Elbe River. They stopped moving and rested on the west side of this river that cut a diagonal line across eastern Germany. Why? ... Wasn't there a war to be won? ... Our colleagues, the Soviets, were moving west, fighting hard! Indeed, but the reality for the Allied commanding general D.D. Eisenhower was the fact that the region he had conquered in recent weeks was going to be part of the Soviet Occupation Zone. He did not see that going further east, wasting American lives and resources on a conquered territory to be given over to the Soviets, was in American interests.

It was apparent even then that the cooperation between the Soviets and the Western Allies was going to be difficult and tense. A second reason for halting the advance was to avoid the possibility of unintended and hostile military interaction between Soviet and American forces. Eisenhower was happy to let the Soviets finish the "Nazis" in Berlin, a point of disagreement between the US and Britain. Churchill felt that letting the Soviets take Berlin would allow Soviet influence to extend too far westward because he understood that life with the Soviets was going to be disagreeable. This was evident in February at the Yalta Conference where details of administrating Germany after its unconditional surrender were finalized. The tension that became the Cold War was baked into a world war that forged an alliance between very different economic and political systems. This reality was plainly seen by Winston Churchill, but the American attitude was that we can win Stalin over – with aid and charm! The reality was that the Soviet Union had done much to win WWII, and there is plenty of food for thought for historians on the question of whether the Western Allies could have won the war against Nazi Germany without the Soviet Army.

With the US Army in Dessau and its environs, the discovery of the jet engine facilities nearby was probably a pleasant surprise. Some would say a prize. After the region was militarily secured, the Allied technical people whose task was to harvest what was harvestable, including technically competent German people, quickly went to work. Their first step was finding the important Germans who managed the work associated with jet engine development and production. The next steps were to look over the physical infrastructure and to interview the knowledgeable people. This information was sent back to the US and decisions were made about what to capture and haul away and whom to convince to leave the area and be transported to a western occupation zone, the American Zone preferably. The Americans were the first of the Allies to contact German jet engineers where they were working. To various degrees, the Allied armies all had officers imbedded in the other Allied armies so that secrecy and mistrust among them was presumably minimized. In this case, Soviet officers were aware of the situation with the German jet engineers, but they were powerless to do much about it except to inform their superiors. The Americans were in charge here, and they had no interest in letting the Russians exercise any control of the situation.

The German engineers and their facilities were perceived to be assets and were treated as such. Part of the thinking by the military was that German know-how might be useful in shortening or ending the war in the Pacific. The Allied European theater military people understood that the war in Europe was close to a conclusion, but the war with Japan was not. The island-hopping was costly in all ways used to measure it and the conquest of the Japanese mainland was estimated to be so deadly that public support might not be sufficiently available. There was still no atomic bomb.

The first American contact with the Junkers engineers was with just the men involved, few had families in Dessau because they had largely evacuated west to the countryside, some to the small town of Gernrode in the Harz mountains after the serious bombing of Dessau in late April 1944. There, they would presumably be more safely sheltered from Allied bombing. The BMW facilities in Stassfurt were secured in a deep potash mine with most of the families living in the local villages.

Jet engines are complicated systems where the expertise of many disciplines is required for the system to be functional, operationally practical, and perform well. An important question then arises, do we, the Americans, solicit the cooperation of just the top experts or is a much larger fraction of the technical team necessary? Necessary for what? Operate a jet engine? Design a new and better one? The answer depends on your confidence to be able to take what the experts know and provide it to a capable group of Allied engineers and technicians to implement or even advance the technology. Confidence was not in short supply in American and British circles about the jet engine. After all, they were building them. The Americans and British decided to identify a small cadre of the German experts and focus attention on them. The French and the Soviets took the approach to transfer entire development and construction teams and let them play a leading role in the development a jet engine in their respective domains.

This story begins with the American approach of taking just the experts in jet engine technology. The contrasting approaches taken by the French and the Soviets are described subsequently. The outcomes for both approaches are about the same when viewed from the perspective of writing about it in the early decades of the 21st century.

This story is primarily about the wholesale use of the large groups whose work in France and in Russia was to the same ends as that sought by the Americans and the British. It should be said that a large group of specialists was taken by the US, to the US. The group was a modest portion of the V-2 rocket people who were working on the Baltic coast at Peenemünde when the Soviet army approached from the east. Several hundred individuals working in that facility decided to hurriedly go west to surrender to the Americans or to the British instead of letting themselves be at the mercy of the Russians. The rocket specialists who stayed will reappear in our Russian story. Those who went west in April proceeded to the rocket assembly facilities near Nordhausen (the location of the Dora-Mittelbau concentration camp), 65 miles southwest of Dessau, and there were taken by the US Army. This group included Wernher von Braun. He had a difficult start with the Americans due to his Nazi credentials but eventually found his place in American history. Neither his story nor that of the V-2 engineers who stayed in Peenemünde is told here except where it touches that of the jet engineers.

Chapter 2

GET WHAT YOU CAN!

The American priority for learning about German technology was, in this order: 1. nuclear weapons, 2. rockets and guided missiles, and 3. jet engines, followed by a host of narrower issues. The nuclear weapons interest centered on the question: "Was Germany close to making an atomic bomb?" Germany had the physicists competent to do the physics and perhaps the engineering, but they did not have the resources to make it happen. The necessary resources were enormous as the Manhattan Project demonstrated. The story of the German nuclear question was finalized by sequestering ten of the most important German physicists after VE Day through the summer until after VJ Day, the end of WWII in August 1945. The isolation of these physicists was in a place called Farm Hall, an English country house in Huntingdon, Cambridgeshire. Getting all the important information was an interesting process that involved just letting the captured and contained group talk among themselves and clandestinely listening-in. The German scientists largely believed that a practical bomb was possible, but such a reality lay far in the future, even out of the reach of American capabilities. The reader can well imagine the discussion among the German physicists after they learned of the atomic bombing of Japan. Many more interesting details about these events are available in documentation about the American inquiry called *Operation Epsilon* and in the book by J. Bernstein (*Hitler's Uranium Club: the Secret Recordings at Farm Hall*). The question at hand was put to rest: Germany had nowhere near the ability to build an atomic bomb. That did not keep the bomb from becoming the brandished weapon of the coming Cold War. It did, and fortunately, only as a threat.

The next priority was everything having to do with rockets, guidance systems, etc. and the jet engine. The capture of documentation, hardware and people was vigorously pursued by all members of the Allied Powers. The Americans had the advantage in that they occupied western Germany as far east as the Elbe River first and thus had first access to this treasure trove. They, and their closely-coordinating British allies, wasted no time going to the facilities and removing all that was potentially useful and shipping it back to the US and Britain. Identifying the material was done by imbedded technical people trained at Allied technical intelligence schools, one of which was located at Wright Field in Dayton, Ohio. Loading up and shipping material of this nature was easy except for some lingering sabotage and souvenir gathering by the Allied troops. An article in *Harper's Magazine* (see Bibliography) states that the "volume" of "secret" documents that landed in the US was measured in "tons." Whether the material was in fact secret, useful, or neither was probably not determined until years later. There was so much of it. Most of the material relating to jet engine technology ended up at Wright Field. The greater challenge was gathering the human capital.

In April 1945, the Americans began to identify everyone of interest to them. They had considerable, inadvertent help from the Germans in this task. It turns out that when *Operation Barbarossa,* the German invasion of the Soviet Union, was going badly (winter 1941), a ministry of the German government (the "Defense Research Association" which, spelled out in German, is a single 26-letter word!) decided that having scientifically talented individuals fighting as soldiers was a waste of their skills. A man named Werner Osenberg was tasked with putting together a list of people with advanced academic training and skill to be withdrawn from the military and put to work doing more useful things for the war-making by the Reich. Implementation of the duty transfer took place in early 1943. The Osenberg list was secret and an attempt to destroy it failed when the Allies arrived in 1945 so that a (partial?) copy ended up in British and American intelligence hands.

Industrial organization charts were also located, and the people involved were quite ready to help because resistance or obstruction was pointless. The American plan was to move the people they wanted, and who agreed to be moved, out of the reach of the Soviets. When that happened relative to VE Day on May 8th is unclear, but it did not matter. July 1st was the date the US Army was to vacate the states of Sachsen-Anhalt and Thüringen and hand over administration of the area to the Soviets who, at this time, also controlled a large section of eastern Germany. Until that time, the Amis were in charge.

The procedures for implementing transfers of German personnel to "safer," western locations were largely, but not uniformly, congenial. The interrogation teams varied in their approach to dealing with the former enemies. A more formal process would not be in place until 20 July 1945, when *Operation Overcast* ("involving about 350 chosen rare minds" in the words of official American documents) was devised by the US Joint Chiefs of Staff and signed into existence. An intelligence committee was to oversee this operation and after some administrative juggling, the name was later changed to *Operation Paperclip*. The name change had to do with a note paperclipped to the file of individuals who were cleared to work in the United States. President Truman signed a secret directive authorizing the new program in late summer of 1946 with an expansion to include 1,000 German scientists under "temporary, limited military custody." One interesting dimension of the decision regarding the number of Germans to be considered for transfer to the US was that Truman's concern that the employment opportunities for the returning US veterans might be reduced by the presence of former German enemies if the latter's numbers were large. Further, their visibility might be politically problematical so soon after the war, but we had camps for that.

The challenge

What might have been the process for identifying the "important people?" The process began with interviews to establish people's roles in the enterprises where they worked and the routes they followed to be there. Included would have been reviews of academic credentials. In many of the cases, the Germans of interest to the Americans were the individuals with established technical expertise. As it turned out, those of greatest appeal also had advanced academic degrees. For example, von Ohain, Franz, and Oestrich (among others) who will play large roles in our story had doctoral degrees from prestigious universities. Further, the next lower level of academic achievement was the Diplom Ingenieur (equivalent to a master's degree in the United States) was held by many in the next rung of technically trained personnel. It is no coincidence that most of the people who were processed by American authorities had such academic achievement status. The German professional hierarchy generally favored people who had demonstrated such abilities. This is reflected in the reality that individuals who had doctorates were addressed (and honored, of course) as Dr. so-and-so or even more prestigiously as Herr Professor Doktor ..., when that was appropriate. Everyone else was simply Herr ... (mister ...).

Engineering projects involve the melding of technical understanding from multiple disciplines into a complex object, a system with a simple or complex functionality. The engineers who put such a "thing" together must rely on others for skills they might not have. It would be fairly easy for anyone in the field to list the technology areas required to put a jet engine together, but the lay reader may find that to be a swamp. Instead, one can focus on another dimension of leadership in bringing a "thing", a jet engine here, together. That skill is managerial: the ability to work with others and bring out the best in others. An engineering project director must have some combination of technical skill and the ability to manage people and what they bring to the table.

The principals in this story had that combination. They were trusted to allow specialist knowledge to be brought forward by people who understood it and they had sufficient technical savvy, savoir-faire if you will, to recognize its importance and its place in the totality of what is being built. Leaders like Franz, Oestrich, Brandner, and Baade in our story or any chief engineer of a large project like a modern airliner, a powerplant, a chemical plant, or any other similarly complex project had that capacity.

It was rather easy for the Allied technical people to identify the project leaders building the jet engines. They had to trust the opinion of these leaders to identify the next layer of experts who were critical to various aspects of the project they led. In the jet engine projects of the 1940s, the layers of expertise were not very deep. For Dr. Anselm Franz and the development of the Jumo 004 engine, for example, the individuals acknowledged in his writings consisted of a modest handful of people. There may have been an organization chart from within Junkers, but I have not found one. I would be surprised if I discovered that it consisted of more than the people he acknowledges as having been very helpful. The organization consisted primarily of one person representing the sector of technology in which that person was an expert. Below that layer of workers might be an aide for making calculations or a draftsman to render the results into some graphical form so that a machinist can build a part. In such a scenario, the task faced by Allied technical people is relatively easy because the leader can simply describe the value of his subordinates. The company where they worked might have had records (reports, patents, etc.) that reinforce a person's importance in the organization. In my father's case, for example, he had numerous patents registered with Junkers, one of which was later applied for in the US and granted in 1954. These were the factors that got people like my father on the *Paperclip* list. However, such factors were not always sufficient for transfer to work in the US. It is challenging to speculate about the Allied thinking that might have gone into this process.

From a philosophical viewpoint, it is interesting to consider the value of the project leaders who were invited to the US. Their skill might have rested primarily in the project management arena with a reliance on others for technical input. In the absurd extreme, they might have no technical skills whatsoever, but they were the project leaders and effective as such. How would an Allied interviewer determine the value of such a person and recommend, or not, dealing further with him?

The mechanics of deciding and moving

The process started with selecting the German engineers for transfer to locations in the west. It involved interviews and asking them if they wanted to be transported there. Acceptance of that offer, when it was extended, was voluntary. The US military established a place in the American Zone (AOZ) where the German jet engineers were to be relocated. The Germans were informed that there were going to be detailed technical briefings and interviews that cleared matters associated with political and/or criminal activities during the Nazi period, the so-called denazification interviews. This aspect was important in a larger sense because criminals had to be identified and dealt with. Further, appropriate individuals who could be used to help run a civilian government under the military administration also had to be identified.

In the period between 1 May and 1 July, American offers to be transported to the west were made relatively broadly. Many German technical people accepted the offers and whatever list was made of the people initially transported (if it existed even then) was broader than the later Overcast or *Paperclip* lists. An important aspect of accepting the American transport proposal was that the Allies had put in place requirements for people to stay in the location where the end of the war caught them. That was done to control the civilian situation and stanch the refugee flood from the east. That mechanism was relatively effective even though many feared staying in the area under future Soviet control. The bloody rumors coming in from the east nourished that concern and inspired a covert, risky, and large-scale migration to the west.

My father, Siegfried Decher, was among the people interviewed. When I was a teenager in the US, I remember him pointing to the place on the sofa where I was sitting and saying that an American colonel had sat there and offered safe passage to the west. He added that a Russian officer, one of those military attaches, also sat in the very same spot and tried to convince him to stay in Dessau. He explained that the

Soviet intention was to restart the Junkers jet engine work. The plan was to do this quickly and keep the engineers and their families in Dessau, including those who came from BMW. There were promises of good treatment as far as the necessities of life were concerned, a good salary, housing, and food. Father and his colleagues informed the American interrogators that their first concern was reunification with their families that were located 60 miles to the west in Gernrode. Since whatever transport to the west was going to be leaving from Dessau where the men were, American military trucks were sent to Gernrode to retrieve the families, me included.

The question of whether to go west or stay was now in front of the German men and their wives. My father informed the American officer that the decision was necessarily an economic one because he needed work and wanted to stay in the field. The Soviets offered that much. Fortunately for our family, the political and safety considerations allowed an easy decision in favor of going with the Americans. My mother and he had heard the rumors of the brutality of the Soviet army coming in from the east. Accepting the Russian proposal to stay was pregnant with uncertainty and worry. A large part of his decision involved a desire to continue to work with Dr. Franz who, by that time cast his vote with going west to the AOZ. Finally, the decision was reached to go west, strengthened by the reality that members of our broader family were located there (in Darmstadt).

The decisions to go west were not unanimous among the engineers because opinions about the Soviets varied. The Soviet offer sounded good, and some believed the notion that the Soviets can't be as bad as it seemed to be rumored. Most of the technical people considered to be sufficiently valuable accepted American offers when extended to them. One notable exception will come up later in our story. The total number of jet engine related people who were moved west by the Americans was likely in the hundreds, including the many who later went to France. Since there were relatively few German jet engine engineers involved in the American program, some of their names are called out here and elsewhere in this narrative. The Junkers team that built the Jumo 004 engine was headed by Dr. Franz. As we will see in the next chapter, the jet engineers in this story are a relatively small part of the total number connected with many other disciplines and of interest to the United States.

The complete list of the men from Junkers, BMW, and elsewhere who were invited is not known to me, although a list, dated 2 January 1947, of approved *Operation Paperclip* people exists. It was published by the Joint Intelligence Objective Agency (JIOA). Some of the names in this story are on it. My father was among those who were cleared to proceed to the AOZ and perhaps to the US. The latter possibility was vague, but it was in the air. To confuse matters a bit, it is known that an earlier list dated 1 January 1947 also exists. Most names are the same, but there are small differences to be noted. The status of the processing must have been very fluid, even a year and a half after VE Day.

With victory in Europe, the articles of the Yalta Agreement took effect. The American military had identified Bad Kissingen (about 80 miles east of Frankfurt) as the place where the "desired" and approved Germans were to be taken to be interviewed further and put to work until further notice. Dr. Hermann Oestrich, who was chief of the BMW jet engine work, describes the methods used by the American and the British in Chapter 5.

The first of July was to be the day of the Soviet takeover of the totality of their occupation zone. For the Americans, preparations to leave included assembling trucks for the move of German technical people, their families, and a limited amount of their possessions (300 lbs. in our case). The Germans were informed to be prepared to leave Dessau on a specific day and time. Similar arrangements were made for others located elsewhere in the general area. I tell his part of the story briefly in the next two paragraphs[1] because my family and I went through it and suffered by it.

The day was 22 June 1945, a week before the last day of the American presence in the region. It was a beautiful day. Arrangements had been made to have trucks show up to pick up the German engineers and their families. A 2½-ton Dodge Army truck pulled up to our residence and, with the assistance of several soldiers, loaded our family of four and two other families for a total of six adults and four children in the back. The warm weather allowed the canvas tarp to be off so that we would travel as if in a convertible, as it were. Benches on either side served to seat us. The middle of the truck was piled with the luggage and the furnishings we were allowed to bring. The destinations were Oberursel and Bad Kissingen. Both locations were on travel papers issued by the US Army. The trip did not go well. It appears that the soldier driving our truck was caught up in the turmoil of the day with its flood of refugees moving west out of the way of the Soviet army. A woman, attractive my mother said, bribed her way into the cab of the truck brandishing a bottle of something alcoholic to hitch

1 See *Turbulent Journey* noted in the Bibliography for greater detail.

a ride. The driver did not resist temptation, consumed its content, and drove our truck off the road where it rolled over. It was a serious accident with injuries. The net consequence was a narrow escape from the Soviets and a delay in joining the other engineers in Bad Kissingen. We were still in the region to become the SOZ.

The accident injuries, specifically those to my younger brother, took time to resolve. Whether the resultant delay to my father's ability to move anywhere played a role in the American decision to abandon an interest in him is unknown. It is likely that the American interests were sufficiently satisfied by just three people associated with the Junkers jet engine effort that proceed into the remainder of this story: Dr. Anselm Franz, Hans Berkner, and Dr. Heinrich Adenstedt. These Junkers individuals constituted the core of whatever activities were going to be made possible in an American future. Of this group, Franz traveled to the US in short order, about six months. Berkner and Adenstedt followed a year or so later, all without their families who joined them, as noted in the table below, a considerable time later. The totality of the jet engine related technical people moved to the US was, as we shall see, larger.

Table 1. Dates (MM/DD/YY) of US entry for some of the German jet engineers and their families just after the war.

	Name	engineer	family
Anselm	Franz	11/16/45	5/27/47
Hans	Berkner	10/11/46	3/21/49
Heinrich	Adenstedt	1/21/47	6/1/48
Hans	von Ohain	2/25/47	na

The US entry dates are from immigration records. In general, immigration records as hard dates are fraught with some uncertainty because individual entries may have been handled by the military in which case real entry dates are recorded in military records. Official entries are sometimes affected by leaving and re-entering the US with a visa, over a Canadian border site, though many brought to and residing in the American South might have entered via Latin American countries. To identify the names above more closely, we note that Adenstedt was a metallurgist who struggled with the turbine material challenge when he worked at Junkers. He was, or certainly turned into, Franz's right-hand man. Berkner's interest is listed in *Operation Paperclip* list as "Diesel Engines" and residing at Wright Field. Hans von Ohain arrived in the US after compilation of this list. It appears that the immigration wheels of progress turn relatively slowly.

A biography of Hans von Ohain by Margaret Conner sheds additional light on this immediate postwar time. Von Ohain spent the time between war's end and his travel to the US at the Heinkel factory in Zuffenhausen (near Stuttgart, AOZ) taken over by the US Navy. A "personal service" contract was drawn up between him and the Navy, meaning that he was not employed by the Navy. His task was to help the Navy operate and maintain the He S 011 jet engines that had been designed and build at Heinkel under his supervision and he worked on improving them. The cool Navy interest in von Ohain was disappointing so that he was glad to receive an offer from the US Army Air Corps (USAAC) to work with them instead.

The USAAC offer involved transfer to the US. The travel was provided for free as was return travel, should it come to that. Free housing and medical care were provided. A salary was paid but the funds were to be transferred to dependents remaining in Germany (for the time being). Von Ohain was not married, and his parents were listed as dependents. His dependents were entitled to receive food (rations?) amounting to 2,300 calories per person per day in Germany. He drew a $6 per diem allowance for local spending money. He would be free to return to Germany after 6 months. Belongings he could take with him were limited to 175 lbs., and professional material (books, instruments, etc.) was not counted in that limit. His task was to "undertake and prosecute to the best of his ability such scientific and technical tasks as his employer may assign." Quite likely, similar activities and contracts were executed by the Junkers engineers about the Jumo 004 engine.

The American assembly of German jet engineers concluded in Bad Kissingen and a former aircraft engine plant at Oberursel near Frankfurt. The locale became the holding workplace for people, and, in some cases, the residences of people classified as "refugees" from the east. My father had family in Darmstadt where he awaited word of what next, initiated by Franz or the US Army. My father worked under Franz in Dessau and was keen on working with him again.

If the *Paperclip* list is to be believed, other folks' residences were noted. Franz's family was housed in Landshut (pronounced "Laands Hoot"), 45 miles northeast of Munich. That location was the Pinder Barracks, a major holding facility for German engineers and their families. In all likelihood, the housing was primarily for individuals connected with *Operations Overcast* and *Paperclip* evacuated from what was to become the Soviet Occupation Zone. The military barracks were convenient because little other large-scale housing was available in the West. The war's bombing had destroyed so much of it.

Conner describes how von Ohain was brought to the US by train travel to Bremerhaven, a troop transport ship (like the Liberty ships) also bringing home returning soldiers, and finally another train trip from New York to Dayton, Ohio. Von Ohain was escorted during this trip and finally put up in a barrack-like dormitory serving as Bachelor Officers Quarters at Wright Field. The accommodations were primitive but satisfactory. There were initial constraints on the men's mobility within the environs of work and residence, but these did not last long.

In 1948, von Ohain notes that the complex at Wright Field included Franz, Hans Mauch, and Helmut Schelp among a dozen or so other Germans. The latter two were cited earlier in connection with their important roles in the overall story of jet engine evolution in Nazi Germany. Eighty-six aeronautical engineers were transferred to Wright Field where the United States had amassed Luftwaffe aircraft, documents, and equipment captured under *Operation Lusty* (**Lu**ftwaffe **S**ecret **T**echnolog**y**). This operation was largely responsible for the survival of many of the German aircraft that can be viewed today in American aviation museums. The Smithsonian National Air and Space Museum in Chantilly, Virginia is a good place to view several of these artifacts. Between 1945 and 1952, the US Air Force sponsored the largest number of *Paperclip* scientists, importing 260 men, of whom 36 returned to Germany and one re-emigrated to Argentina.

The historical record (and Conner's biography) shows that von Ohain stayed in the US, married there and raised a family. He stayed in the profession as a productive principal scientist at the Air Force Research Laboratories in Dayton, Ohio until his retirement.

Franz was much more interested in building engines in an industrial setting. He identified the individuals whom he enjoyed working with and who were central members of a team he had assembled in his mind. The list of people who ultimately went to the US, though not under the auspices of *Operation Paperclip* even though their names were on the list, are given below. A man named Wilhelm Grunert was on the Franz list (no pun intended). I mention him because he will reappear in France because he did not travel to the US.

Table 2. Dates of US entry for the German jet engineers associated with Franz, most of whom ended up working with him at AVCO-Lycoming in Stratford, Connecticut.

Friedrich	Bielitz	3/24/50
Wolfgang	Stein	7/21/53
Siegfried	Decher	1/29/54
Heinz	Moellmann	2/5/56
Wilhelm	Grunert	na

Decher and Stein were principal investigators and inventors of the control system of the Jumo 004 engine and were considered essential members of the Franz "team", even if the US military did not agree with that assessment and turned down a direct trip to the US. Both men reappear in the French story to follow. The dates of their eventual arrivals in the US are noted. Bielitz was an expert in vibrations and thought to be a valuable member of any undertaking designing a new jet engine. After all, there are lots of little blades in such an engine and if one does not think carefully about resonance and vibrations, all kinds of bad things can happen. Bielitz was not a member of the Jumo team during the war. Stein and Bielitz noted Landshut on the *Operation Paperclip* list as their residences. Moellmann was a specialist in control systems and joined the group later.

During this period, my father, and probably Stein and Grunert, were informed by postcard that their services were no longer required. "Thank you for your interest." The team potentially going with Franz to the US had just shrunk to the small number indicated in the first table above.

Heinz Moellmann was on the *Operation Paperclip* list with his name spelled Hollmann but in the correct alphabetical "M" slot. It appears that the list, of which several versions existed, was somewhat sloppily assembled. In all likelihood, Moellmann also received the "dear John" postcard. To be accurate, however, there was no word on the postcard resembling "dear."

From my father's perspective, an important discussion took place between him and Franz where the latter appointed my father as his representative in Germany, pro tem. They understood that they needed each other for future work together and planned as best they could to make that happen. That appointment would be used as part of the argument against colleagues in Dessau who urged my father to return there, an invitation he had no desire to accept because of its Russian connection.

New American enterprise

To embark on the American part of this engine technology story we proceed from 1945 and follow Franz. We will return to that same year again for the other stories that center on France and the Soviet Union.

Franz was brought to Wright Field in Ohio, employed by or contracted to the USAAC and the later US Air Force. There, according to the meager writing left behind by Franz, he shared what he knew and consulted with American industrial people developing jet engines in the US. He also kept in contact with former colleagues who remained in Europe. His time in the US was well spent. It gave him opportunities to get to know the American landscape in the business of building engines. As the consulting work was winding down, Franz pursued ways to get into the business. In about 1950 he approached AVCO Corporation, a large company in the business of building reciprocating aircraft engines, and suggested they consider expanding into medium-sized gas turbine engines. The large-engine field was fully occupied by major American firms, General Electric, Pratt & Whitney, Allison, Curtiss-Wright, and Westinghouse. The smaller-engine market seemed open. AVCO agreed because the large piston-engine business was slowing down at the end of the war and the writing was on the wall that even commercial airliners were going to be powered by jet engines to the detriment of the large piston engines produced by Pratt & Whitney, Curtiss-Wright, and the firms building these engines under license. Franz was invited to head a gas turbine division. The work began in January 1951 in the Williamsport, Pennsylvania Lycoming plant, a division of AVCO. In July 1952, the Lycoming proposal for a 600 HP turboshaft engine was accepted by the US Air Force as the winning design for what became a very successful engine for helicopters, known as the Lycoming T53. This engine would become the powerplant for the Army's workhorse helicopter in the next decades, the Bell UH-1 Huey.

Production facilities were made available to Lycoming by the Air Force in Stratford Connecticut where Curtiss-Wright R-1820 (radial piston) engines were being produced and were in the process of being phased out. With former German colleagues and new American ones, the AVCO-Lycoming Gas Turbine Division came to be. The Germans on the second chart joined the program on the dates noted. A good question at this point might be: Where were Decher, Stein, and Grunert all this time? They were plying their art in France as we shall see.

The few facts available about this history are memories of the people involved, assisted by whatever the engineers left behind to be remembered. Engineers are engineers, however, and they don't fuss with details of the travails of getting through the debates and compromises that always characterize the realization of a complex product that requires the skills of many. The thoughts and facts available from Franz are those of an engineer to the bone. The book in the bibliography summarizes what Franz felt he contributed to the world. In a fashion true to form, the book is full of progress descriptions in terms of performance and dates, charts that would thrill an engineer and pictures (with model numbers spelled out) showing the airplanes and vehicles wherein the created engines were used.

I cannot fault Franz alone with this characterization. My father was not very different, and it is probably safe to say that all engineers focus on their work to the point of letting it speak for them and their skill. That is to say that engineers tend not to be process people but focused on results. I see that in myself, sometimes confirmed by others. That is reality.

This American story concludes with the company enjoying several successes that the engine community can celebrate. The company managed to be very innovative in designing and building turboshaft engines for many applications, including for other well-known helicopters. The adaptation of such an engine to become the first high bypass turbofan was a true tour de force for Lycoming and for my father. Turbofans of this basic design hang from the wings (mostly) of almost all commercial airliners today and the first article that demonstrated the concept is on display at Smithsonian National Air and Space Museum in Washington DC, as it should be.

As much as I might like to, adding the stories of others who came along that road is hard because the necessary records and writings just do not seem to exist. They may be in cardboard boxes filled by the individuals, stacked in attics of their children, and hopefully available for future historians. As an exception, Hans von Ohain's detailed biography is a valuable addition to the written history of the time.

A Boeing bonanza

The *Paperclip* list described in the next chapter reveals the name of the German aerodynamicist Adolf Busemann. More will be said about him further on but at the present point in this narrative it is appropriate to mention his important engineering breakthrough was recognized by one of the American technical teams visiting facilities where aerodynamics research was carried out in Germany during the war.

The American team was headed by Theodore von Karman, the founder of the Jet Propulsion Laboratory (JPL) in Pasadena, California. One of the members of the team who visited the Volkenröde (flight) research center was Boeing aerodynamicist George Schairer. He uncovered Busemann's (1935) idea of wing sweep and reported that finding to military authorities as well as to American industrial airplane builders, including Boeing. In the on-going postwar competition to build a jet-engine powered medium bomber, The Boeing Company adapted the wing sweep idea to its proposal to the Air Force and won the competition with the B-47. All other American industrial concerns responding to the Air Force request responded with designs that reflected a failure to appreciate what wing sweep can do for the airplane's top speed. They proposed airplanes with conventional straight wings that were 100 mph slower than the B-47! Boeing was well on the road to building fast, transonic airplanes. It also helped that Boeing had the foresight to have built a large wind tunnel which allowed the testing of airplane models at wind speeds close to the speed of sound.

Chapter 3

THE OPERATION PAPERCLIP LIST

The document dated 2 January 1947 listing the German technical people presumably cleared and perceived to be valuable to the United States consists of 97 pages and provides relatively little information about the approximately 1,600 people on it. It is published by the JIOA as noted, the agency that administered the operation. In almost all cases the names are given with the appropriate academic title such as Dipl. Ing. (Diplom Ingenieur) or Dr. Ing., or plain Dr. (Medical or Ph.D.). Titles were important in the stratified and hierarchical world that was Germany at that time.

The other notation associated with the name is the place of residence which is sometimes noted as the German place of employment during the war. The residence description is terse, almost always just the town or a facility where the person might be contacted. Curiously, in a few cases, the word "Dustbin" is used to describe a person's location with one comment reading "released from Dustbin"! In reality, "Dustbin" was one of several British (detention) operations dealing primarily with German technical and leadership personnel in 1944 and 1945. The first location was in Paris, later moved to Kransberg castle near Frankfurt (am Main). This operation paralleled the Allied *Operation Ashcan*, a code name for Central Continental Prisoner of War Enclosure No. 32 (in Luxemburg), where captured Nazi leaders, specifically military personnel, and the politically important, were interviewed. Some were arrested following the interviews. Most of the defendants at the later Nuremberg Trials were held in this facility for a time.

The important reason for being on the list is a cryptic notation of the field of expertise, summarized in one or two words. Examples are "jet engines", "aerodynamics', "parachutes", and a myriad of others that are vaguely descriptive of the person's work domain. The breadth of the fields listed is wide and includes chemistry, optics, medicine, naval weaponry, and manufacturing, among others.

Notably absent from the list are some well-known names associated with the rocket program. Wernher von Braun, for example, is not on the list of 2 January 1947. I presume that the people with that interest were already relocated to Fort Bliss, Texas or, perhaps, that fact was a guarded secret. Of the many names on the list there are 69 whose address is noted as Wright Field in Dayton, Ohio. Interestingly, Hans von Ohain (misspelled) is on the list but not yet as a resident at Wright Field where he went to work for the US Air Force in later years. Additionally, there are 93 with addresses at Fort Bliss. Generally speaking, the former are airplane and jet engine-oriented people while the latter are connected with rockets and guided missiles. The large congregations of Germans in these two facilities must have been interesting from a social viewpoint. One could probably hear German spoken and observe manifestations of German customs as these folks formed into a community of sorts.

In the later chapters, our story will cover the engineers who went to France. Some of those were on the list, notably Hermann Oestrich, the BMW jet engine chief engineer and another ten who joined Oestrich. Among those ten were my father and Wolfgang Stein.

Several individuals with very specific expertise went to smaller American military establishments such as the Army War College, Aberdeen Proving Grounds, Washington Navy Yard, Fort Hunt in Virginia, the Army Map Service, etc.

Most interesting to me are the names of individuals who either had stellar professional reputations or will make them in the postwar years. Names of aerodynamicists like Ludwig Prandtl (aerodynamics) and Adolf Busemann were among these. Busemann went on to a distinguished career at NACA (later NASA). The rocket and space experts were also there: Kraft Ehricke, Eugen Sänger, Ernst Stuhlinger, and General Walter Dornberger (of V-2 rocket fame), as were the (nuclear) physicists Otto Hahn and Werner Heisenberg. The last three rocket experts noted were on the list of 1 January but not on the later list!

Last, but certainly not of least interest, were the principals of the aircraft industry, the builders of airplanes. Willy Messerschmitt, Erich Bachem, Walter Horton, Heinrich Focke, and Rudolf Blohm whose names are associated with Luftwaffe aircraft. Other less well-known people associated with Heinkel and Hirth aircraft as engineers are also listed.

Two individuals on the list merit comment because they are part of the history. One is Hanna Reitsch, the well-known woman test pilot who circled high in Nazi government circles and the other is Helmut Schelp. His claim to fame is recognition of the jet engine's practicality for flight in the Luftwaffe administration. He and Hans Mauch successfully pushed for the wide-ranging jet engine development program in the years 1939–41, the program that ultimately led to the development of the Jumo 004 and the BMW 003 jet engines.[1] Both Mauch and Schelp are noted to have been at Wright Field in the von Ohain biography. The Wikipedia page for Schelp states that he was held (as a relatively free man) in London (for consultation) for a brief time after the war.

I don't know what happened to most of the people on the list, although being the son of one of the Junkers engineers, I met a limited number of them when I was growing up. Except for people who were tagged for travel to the US, those in the group that went to France, and the individuals who remained in the Soviet Occupation Zone, many probably settled in what would become West Germany to find work as best they could.

As a professional in the aerospace industry, I was somewhat aware of the contributions in their respective fields by the people who landed at Wright Field. The stories of those who landed elsewhere and wherever they finished their lives does not relate to this story, hence are not included. The one tangential story that is hard to overlook, however, is that of Wernher von Braun and his leadership in the Apollo moon landing program. His name, like some others, was on the 1 January list and not the later list.

The totality of the *Operation Paperclip* list is an interesting description of the technical fields of interest to the US military and its industrial backbone. It does not shed much light on the fate of the people. It would take a considerable research effort to answer even the question whether they were transported to the US, if and how long they stayed, etc. If they did land on American shores and stayed, they likely led lives like most immigrants, quiet and focused on work. They likely brought children who will have grown up having assimilated into American life much more easily than the parents. Such musings about the people on the list are, of course, pure speculation.

The British role

The British worked closely with the Americans in all affairs having to do with the execution of military moves during WWII. While they also worked with the Soviets, they anticipated the coming Cold War.

1 See Decher, *Turbulent Journey* for the interesting details.

In developing jet engine technology, the British were leaders with Frank Whittle and Rolls-Royce playing dominant roles and sharing most of that development with the Americans. If there were gaps in what was shared, it was centered on British goal of dominating the civil aviation market after the war. The so-called Brabazon Committee had been set up by Churchill to put in place the industrial machinery to manufacture a wide range of commercial aircraft for sales around the world and to service the transport needs of the British Empire. That program involved exploiting their expertise in engines, including jet engines.

The British were keen to learn what the Germans might have developed and to that end dispatched the Fedden Mission (see Chapter 5) to learn what they could. The mission was thorough in its work, examining much of what there was to learn in Germany. Insofar as jet engines are concerned, the German state of technology development caused the British to revisit previous engine designs with axial flow compressors. The radial flow compressors initially built by Whittle, Rolls-Royce and by General Electric in the US, ultimately fell out of favor with the better understanding of axial design furnished by the Germans. That, in a few words, is the extent of jet engine technology transfer to Great Britain.

The political climate in Britain did not allow the transfer of German personnel to work permanently in the UK, except perhaps for some individuals. Records available from Great Britain show however, that as the war ended and during the months after VE Day, hundreds of Germans were arrested and forcibly deported to the UK.[1] That process was rough and never seriously examined from a legal point of view. The Germans involved were important persons from a wide cross-section of industry, notably the chemical industry, (synthetic) textiles, and machinery. The men were kept under guard behind barbed wire under conditions that could be described as unpleasant. No financial compensation for the time spent was offered, although starting in October 1946, the families left behind in Germany were provided food and coal rations. The detentions lasted until the interrogation process yielded the information sought in, typically, a few months. Thereafter, most were returned to Germany. Others were put to work in private industries and government ministries until mid 1947. The British goal was to secure industrial know-how for a competitive advantage for British companies. A secondary goal was to keep that same information

1 See A. Menden, "Ins Königreich Entführt" (Deported to the Kingdom), *Südeutsche Zeitung* (Munich), 30 August 2007.

from drifting into the hands of the Soviet Union. As far as technology transfer regarding jet engines, however, the close cooperation between the Americans and the British led to the process being dominated by American initiatives in the form of its various operations.

French operations

Whereas the Americans and the British had established means to gather technical information and people from Germany, the French did not because the American government did not want the government of Charles de Gaulle to participate in this process. The English-speaking Allies did not consider France to be a full-fledged ally (yet) because the country was fully occupied by Nazi Germany during the war and was industrially behind the times. Despite tensions, de Gaulle created a Military Mission for German Affairs (Mission Militaire des Affaires Allemandes – MMAA) in late 1944 to circumvent the exclusion of transfer of technology and people to France. An established office called the Direction Générale des Etudes et Recherches within the MMAA was tasked to gather military intelligence to benefit the Allied armies. Under this cover, the work to find technical intelligence to specifically serve the French army was begun. To aid with this effort, the French air force created (in early 1945) an agency called MIST (in French: Scientific and Technical Information Mission). The French search for German people and technology was under way, whether the Americans and the British liked it or not.

Chapter 4

WAR AND ECONOMIC AFTERMATH

Our story is intimately woven into the events of WWII. The economic context associated with the war and the postwar differences between East and West are worth a few words because they are so easily forgotten and pale in intensity when thinking about or remembering the violence of war. In an American museum, I once saw a war-related display whose subtext was: the Americans marched into Germany, defeated the Nazis, and everybody lived happily ever after. Another museum's display expanded on that theme by stating that the subsequent Marshall Plan was implemented and *then,* everybody lived happily ever after. In reality, even with peace, happiness in Germany was in short supply after the war. Staying alive and striving for prosperity when starving, shivering, and economically recovering in the absence of a functional government are not as simple as the laying down of arms.

A detailed description of the Marshall Plan is beyond the scope of this book, but there are a few relevant facts. First, the "European Recovery Plan" proposed by Secretary of State George C. Marshall was not approved by Congress until 1948, three years after the fighting ended. Second, the fraction of funds distributed to Germany was small, less than half of the amount sent to Great Britain. France and Great Britain were the largest recipients of American self-interest and largesse.[1] Direct aid of various kinds flowed from the US to Europe in the days after the war to alleviate hunger and the cold of the following winters. These monies were very helpful to individual people in need

1 Of all the Plan funds disbursed between 1948 and 1952, the UK, France, and Italy together received more than one half (55%) of the total. The fourth largest recipient was West Germany with 10%.

but not sufficient to stabilize Europe. Political unrest was in the air. The goal of the Marshall Plan was to prevent another unstable period like the one between the two world wars. The Plan was necessary and multi-faceted to address unrest fueled, in part, by the Soviet Union which actively supported communist-inspired social unrest in Western Europe. In Germany, currency reform was a component of the plan because packs of American cigarettes were not practical as a substitute for money. The German Reichsmark had little value which made it useless for ordinary commerce. Students of history may recall that it was the financial reparations required by the Western Allies in the wake of WWI that gave rise to economic instability and to the rise of Hitler. The Marshall Plan was the polar opposite of a demand for reparations.

While the defeat of Nazi Germany and creation of the Marshall Plan were essential for eventual economic recovery, it took time. There was a lot of damage to everything as the war and its aftermath played out. The period of bad times in Germany began with the decline of Nazi Germany's military prowess (roughly in the winter of 1943) when, at a human level, much economic and personal misery was suffered. For the conquered countries, the misery began with the German invasions. No one can adequately describe the privations suffered by people in all of Europe even as statistics speak loudly. The brutal reality was that misery followed the war for a period almost as long as the war itself.

Economics

Wars are expensive. Throughout history many have ended when the money ran out, when the impact on the common person became intolerable, or the military was exhausted. Even countries rich in manpower and resources with a single-minded populace suffered. They went into debt. Storing wealth in bonds is a hardship. It is taxation on future citizens. That, the lives damaged and lost, together with the severe rationing imposed on the civilian population was the price the US citizens paid for war.

The war in Europe was not only expensive but destructive of everything needed to live, or to even survive. Buildings and infrastructure in the large cities of Europe were bombing targets with the intent of quelling Germany's will to fight. That approach was marginally effective because the affected people, especially the dead ones, had no influence on the government. The fanatics in Berlin saw a defeat as unheroic and unacceptable until they faced death and died, often by their own hands.

Europe in May 1945 was a shambles. Who was going to rebuild it and with what manpower? The uncounted deaths and missing soldiers and civilians were so numerous that prospects seemed grim. Manpower, or more specifically womanpower, might have been available, but it had to be fed and sheltered. There were winters ahead. Who was going to plant and harvest the fields, to raise the meat animals to feed the population without oxen or horses to pull the plow or without fuel to put into the tractor, if they even had one? Getting the process going so that more and more time and energy become available was the challenge. Growth is necessarily exponential, i.e., very slow at first and faster later, fostered by the progress made the week or the month before.

In the year 1953, eight years after the war, as a youngster I recall visiting the city of Hamburg. This was during the early days of the "economic miracle" beginning to take place in Germany when its industrial prowess came to have a meaningful and positive impact on Germans in the western portion of the country. There were still mile-long heaps of rubble along the city's wide avenues. A movable narrow gauge railroad system with little "Kipwagen" loaded by hand and pushed by hand had carried the rubble out from the narrower side streets to make them passable. Some of the buildings were spared and maintained an air of solidity but others were entirely missing. Today, Munich, for example, has two hills of rubble, tall enough to be suitable for skiing in winter.

The period when Europe was on its knees extended past the end of the war to the 1950s, plus or minus a few years depending on where the tide of war washed in. The postwar years were not immediately "happily ever after." This economic situation became the stage for the events described here.

On a personal level, survivors of the mayhem faced the challenge of surviving. The engineers and technicians of this story might have had economic security during the war, but they were now unemployed because the industrial concerns where they once worked were either in ruins or taken over by elements of the Allied forces and certainly not producing stuff for war or an impoverished economy.

The farmer knew what he must do. The engineers whose expertise the Allies might wish to harness were just mouths to feed until their value was recognized. The food rations supplied primarily by the Americans were what kept many a body and soul together. Those were very hungry days. I remember them. If one was lucky enough to have been identified as a person of interest to the Allies things improved markedly because a salary was paid.

Refugees

Compared with the rest of Europe, Germany was burdened with a special additional problem that compounded the misery. As the war ended, the Soviet army marching west was a tsunami of terror. Ahead of its troops, millions of German refugees tried to stay out of the way of a revenge-driven carnage by undisciplined troops. The refugees' goal was to reach shelter and relative safety in the regions controlled by the Western Allies. The population in the German west consequently grew by large numbers. It is hard to imagine that, in a land with a shortage of shelter and food, the easterners would be welcomed. And still they came.

After the war, Germany's borders were redrawn, and the refugee flood was compounded as Germans were driven out of parts of Poland and Czechoslovakia that once were regions of Germany. The city of Königsberg in East Prussia, bordered only by Lithuania and Poland, became a part of the Soviet Union as Kaliningrad.

The British

Even though no German soldiers' column marched on English soil, the devastation there was great, especially in London. There was a major difference however: Great Britain had a functioning government. It was steadfast in its opposition to Germany and had the confidence to think in terms of imagining a bright British future after the war. That was a firm conviction on the part of Winston Churchill after the US supported the British defense with the Lend-Lease program where Britain was materially supported by the US in its struggle with Germany. His conviction was markedly strengthened when the US finally entered the war as a combatant. Britain was also close to financial ruin in 1945.

British confidence was central to the British outlook. Like the German technology in this story, the British technology of the jet engine was also at the leading edge. Frank Whittle was an important figure in its development. He tried, with faltering steps, to show the British military establishment that the jet engine was practical and potentially useful. Even with the war raging and making heavy demands for manpower and resources, his ideas were eventually accepted for further development by British military officials. His small company called "Power Jets Ltd." was finally taken over (in 1944) by Rolls-Royce which became the driving force behind the jet engine work. Two things then happened: progress went much faster, and the technology was shared with the Americans. A discussion of the more technical aspects of British-American interaction is available in the literature.[1]

During the middle of the war (1942), when the military situation was quite dire, a committee was formed in Britain to look at aviation after the war was won. This was the Brabazon Committee cited earlier. With the potential of the jet engine on the horizon and an excellent industrial base for the construction of airplanes, the Committee set out a plan for Britain to dominate the world's air industry after the war. The details of the plan are too involved for description here, but it specified the creation of four types of commercial aircraft so that when anyone in the world wanted an airplane for a specific function, there would be a British airplane available to buy. One of these airplanes was to be a jet-engine-powered mail plane for connecting the North American continent with the British Isles. The exclusive mail function was later abandoned for passenger conveyance. The airplane became the DeHavilland Comet, the first jet-powered commercial airliner.

The history of the various airplanes to be coming out of the Brabazon Committee is interesting and involved. The Committee's goals were realized to some degree but as far as the jet airliner is concerned, serious design flaws and the entry of American competitors had a significant and difficult effect. The reason for citing the work of this committee is that the confidence engendered by its recommendations led to an attitude on the part of the British that they had the future of aviation under control and did not necessarily need a good deal of technical help from the defeated Germans. The British were confident that aviation was going to play a large role in the generation of financial income for the country. That confidence might have been a bit optimistic in that it required customers with funds. The world had just finished an expensive war and might have a need but not the cash for new airplanes.

The British need for cash after the war was severe. The Soviets, as this story will reveal, were also interested in jet engines and acquired a Rolls-Royce Nene turbojet engine. The possibility of large sales might have been attractive, but passing advanced turbojet engine technology to the Cold War adversary surely caused a few eyebrows to be the raised. Unfortunately, the British lost on two counts. They lost the technology to the Soviets and failed to make a sale. After a satisfactory evaluation, the Soviets chose not to buy but to replicate the engine. They did not have the money for purchasing jet engines and they had

---

1 See, for example, Decher, *Powering the World's Airliners*, in the Bibliography.

skilled manpower that needed to be employed. Building a copy is what an engineer calls "reverse engineering." With some industrial spycraft this effort was successful. The resulting Russian engine became the powerplant for the MiG-15 jet fighter. This is the engine and airplane that gave the USAF severe headaches during the early days of the Korean Conflict (war?) ... that is, until better engines and airplanes were built in America. The Soviet replication effort applied to jet engines is intimately related to the story about the German engineers in Russia described in the second half of this book.

The British jet engines had an important component that is a part of the postwar history of this aircraft engine. That component requires a little technical description and is physically the heart of the engine: its compressor.[1] Frank Whittle and Hans von Ohain used a compressor configuration that worked but had serious limitations in performance. Von Ohain recognized these features early and in subsequent designs adopted a different kind of compressor into the designs of later engines. The better design involved many small blades, not unlike a propeller, rotating inside a duct.[2] Such a compressor performed better, allowed for a slender engine (which is good for an airplane installation), and most important, it allowed the design of more powerful engines. This is the kind of compressor that Junkers and BMW were using successfully in the engines that are at the heart of this story. The Allies were interested in how well the Germans had mastered that technology. The reader may be interested in the mystery concerning these two compressor types: Whittle and Rolls-Royce used radial flow compressors while the axial flow compressors would rapidly be adapted, almost exclusively, by all jet engine makers after the war.

The French

French aviation history is rich. As in Germany and Great Britain, work on ideas related to the jet engine was underway in France before the war. The German invasion and occupation in 1940 brought that to an end. It is therefore natural that such work be re-established in France after its liberation. To that end, the new government did what it could

1 All heat engines require the air or fluid it processes to be at higher pressure somewhere along its path through the engine. The jet engine compressor compresses air and must do it efficiently, steadily, and reliably. A challenging task because air tends not to flow nicely toward higher pressure.

2 In reality, a rotating set of blades and a stationary set of blades is involved. When multiple sets of such blade combinations are used, 'any' desired pressure rise in the outlet air stream can be achieved. Technical details for the lay reader may be found in the well-illustrated book, Decher, *Powering the World's Airliners*.

to quickly bring French industry to a competitive level. If that required bringing German engineers to France, so be it. Our story will take us through that process. In some sense, the French did just what the Soviets did, namely use labor for war damage reparation, but they did it humanely. I know because my father was one of the German engineers who spent six pleasant and rewarding years in France working as a key member of a jet engine design team.

The Soviets

The story of the USSR's use of German engineering labor is the subject of the later chapters in this book. Described is what they built and, in detail, what the people went through in the period after the war ending in the mid to late 1950s. That description dwells on the misery experienced by the Germans abducted to the Soviet Union but is not a fair description of the environment of the Russian people. They surely suffered disproportionately during the war. Of the millions who perished during this war, the largest fraction was Russians, or at least citizens of the Soviet Union.

The Soviet economy was in poor shape compared to the West prior to the war. The difficulties associated with the war and its cost were compounded by a central planning regimen that significantly slowed the postwar recovery. The shortages described by Kurt Pflügel were also experienced by Soviet citizens. The degree to which it was felt in various parts of the country varied. Pflügel does not talk about a pay differential between the Russians and the Germans working in the same factory, but I suspect there was a modest one. Any such difference would stay under wraps because the Germans lived in a ghetto isolated from social interactions with Russians and discussing wages is generally a kind of taboo. No matter the difference, the standard of living for the two groups were likely comparable. In other words, the shortages of food, the limitations of services, and life necessities were felt by all.

In 1945 the need was for quick success to stay in the Cold War competition. Jet engine technology had to be brought to the USSR from somewhere, stolen if necessary.

The Soviet Union sought great power status in the world and needed aviation to be modern and competitive with the West. This was especially true for military aviation in the years after the war. Did they succeed? In a way, yes. Both military and later commercial airplanes were adequate but never good enough that someone in the West would buy them. They embodied innovations to be sure as there was always the push-pull associated with the Cold War competition that allowed for good ideas to be generated on all sides. That competition led to copies of important aviation milestones to be built in the Soviet Union. They were typically built faster and perhaps more carelessly than in the West. The ill-fated Tu-144 supersonic transport airplane and the Buran spacecraft that resembled the American Space Shuttle are but two examples. By the time a copy is perfected, the originators of the design usually have gone further with something even better. The Soviet Union was destined to always be a step behind.

Economics again

The last part of this book deals with an unsuccessful attempt by East Germany to build a hard-currency generating airliner with the manpower resources they had under their control, the engineers who returned to East Germany from Russia in 1954 (see Chapter 24). The resulting political and economic failure is well connected to the Cold War, the GDR's relation to the USSR, and the differences between economic systems in the Soviet sphere and the West.

An economy controlled from the political "top" and a free economy driven by needs at the "bottom" differ in fundamental ways. In a sense, the evolution of the economies in East Germany and West Germany were a very large experiment well able to illustrate the difference. The experiment was, from a scientific viewpoint, almost perfect. Similar populations starting from the same conditions, namely zero economic capability, are let loose. The end state was reached in 1989 with the fall of the Berlin Wall. This infamous wall had to be built in 1961 to keep GDR citizens isolated and served to imprison the population that knew that life was better elsewhere. In some cases, life was worth risking in order to reach that "elsewhere" and some paid dearly.

How did it go when the comparison period ended in 1989? The contrast was obvious when the Wall came down. If one looks at just the mobility sector, the difference was stark. Both economies grew from bicycles to motorcycles, to cars as would be expected. The end states, as measured by the automobiles on the market, were worlds apart. Consider, as examples, the BMW automobile of 1989 (or a Volkswagen model) and the Trabant produced by the East German state-owned factory with the slick name of VEB Sachsenring Automobilwerke Zwickau. It would be absurd to cite the differences in those two consumer products, but the mechanics of acquiring them are worth a comment.

Delivery of a BMW or a VW was usually taken the day that payment cleared. The car was usually in stock and ready for sale. On the other hand, the wait list for a Trabant might have been a year or and often much longer because payment allowed the factory to produce the car. The difference rests squarely on the question: who is taking the financial risk of buying a high-cost item? The car company in making the car available or the buyer who must provide the capital to produce it in the first place? Another question is embedded in the political system: who gets to buy the car? The person with the cash or credit or the person who is also "politically clean and correct?"

So much for economics. Is that not why there is a debate about whether economics is a science?

Chapter 5

THE FRENCH CONNECTION

We return to April 1945 and to the events in Stassfurt. The following is a translation of an undated memorandum for the record by Hermann Oestrich. The document resides in the records of the French aircraft engine firm Safran. The portion reproduced in translation here is the story of the arrival of American forces and the events that followed. The complete document continues to describe an airplane project close to Oestrich's heart. It was the design of a vertical take-off, jet-engine powered interceptor airplane with a circular (ring-shaped) wing. The design proved to be impractical as demonstrated by an unfortunate crash of the prototype. His document concludes with a listing of the people to whom he expresses gratitude for a productive and pleasant professional life in France.

Images of Dr. Oestrich are rare and the formal one (see plate section) is what one finds in typical searches. He was serious, human, and able to smile. The images were graciously provided by Pierre Mouton of Safran, the company that Oestrich had a strong hand in building.

The remainder of this chapter is written in the first person by Oestrich. I translated this writing maintaining his writing style and added comments in square brackets.

Dr.-Ing. Hermann Oestrich
(1945) Director of the development department for jet engines
BMW Works in Berlin-Spandau

My department developed the jet engine which was installed in the single-engine Volksjäger, the He 162 made by Heinkel, in the twin-engine bomber Arado Ar 234, and in the unconventional four-engine bomber Junkers Ju 287 [designed by Brunolf Baade who will appear in the Russian portion of our story]. The engine had a thrust of 1660 lbs.

which could be boosted to almost 1900 lbs. for short periods. The Volksjäger was ready for service at the end of the war. Series production had started. The other two aircraft were still being tested.

About 700 of the engines had been delivered by the end of the war. The plan was to supply 5000 engines per month, the production of which was spread over many small factories. The development of the engine and the production of the prototypes had taken place in Spandau until the end of 1944, after which the entire plant was relocated to a salt mine near Stassfurt [ca. 100 miles SW of Berlin, close to Magdeburg]. The move was completed in February 1945. [About 1,800 people were moved to the spaces created by the removed salt.] The offices, laboratories, and workshops were located 400 m [1,200 ft] underground in a series of spacious caverns 25 to 75 ft. high. Some makeshift engine test stands had to be located above ground. To our great surprise, the working conditions [in the caverns] were good. The room temperature was about 20°C [68°F] all year round without heating or cooling. Only the frequent visits of enemy aircraft were somewhat disturbing. They could easily have bombarded the two shaft towers on the site. [Fortunately for the German workers, the towers were spared. Their demolition could have stopped the underground work because the towers were the elevator access to the caves. As it was, they were sufficiently limited in capacity that the 12-hour worker shift changes took up to three hours! to execute.] We lived with the population of the surrounding villages. At the beginning of April, we were overrun by American troops and our work came to an end. The shaft was subsequently closed to German personnel.

The first [Allied, presumably American] engineering commission arrived after about two weeks. We had to prepare an engine for testing and demonstrate its operation as well as and provide a wide variety of technical information. The first visit was followed by other American technical review groups. They were very impressed by our work. When these visits were completed, the Americans turned us over to the English. English commissions replaced the American ones. Among them, I remember the names of Sir Roy Fedden[1] [who designed most of the successful piston engines at the Bristol Aeroplane Company] and Dr. Stern.[2] Shortly thereafter, the rumor spread that our region was to be turned over to the Russians. The English selected particularly valuable pieces from our laboratory equipment for transport to England. The

1 Sir Roy Fedden headed the British so-called Fedden Mission to look over all engine-related activities in Germany. They were thorough in their visitations and interviews in Germany and of people transported to Britain. Fedden was unable to convince the government to import German nationals, although about 100 did move to England in the two years following VE Day.

2 Probably William Joseph Stern, an ethnic German working for the British government. Close friend of Hugo Junkers. An expert on jet engines who was convinced in the 1920s that they would not work.

possibility of bringing some of the engineers to England was vaguely discussed and generated some hope [... that they might escape having to deal with the Russians]. In any case, they wanted to transport [only] the most important engineers to the English zone [out of the reach of the Soviets]. The problem was that the English suffered from a shortage of transport vehicles. They turned to the Americans for help. I managed to convince both parties that it was necessary to relocate a very significant part of my group of co-workers. We were transported with our families in two batches to Göttingen [British Occupation Zone]. There, we were left to await our fates in temporary quarters.

After a few days, an American officer, a Capt. Kane, came forward and offered to transport us to our main plant in Munich in the American Zone. He confided in us that this would have to be done without the knowledge of the English. We happily accepted the offer. Early the next morning, three or four buses, rented from German businesses, took us south on the Autobahn. In Munich, we were lodged in one of the few office buildings that had not been bombed out and told to stay there to await further instructions. These conditions were readily accepted, as everyone hoped that a job in the USA might come out of discussions to come. We were subsequently greeted by the new man in charge in the person of a Lt. Col. Robertson, who asked us to write numerous essays to set the stage for further conference discussions. [These essays were to probe professional relationships and political activities, specifically those involving the Nazi Party, the NSDAP.]

When we reassembled in Munich, we discovered that in order to make the [engineering staff] group complete and effective, we would need to add several missing employees. To locate them and to visit my family, whom I had moved to Westphalia after the relocation from Berlin, Capt. Kane and I decided to take a tour through the American and British sectors. Kane also took along some of the employees in our group who wanted to settle urgent personal matters. We started with his jeep and a weapons carrier.

[200 miles later] It was getting dark when we approached Bad-Kissingen. The road took us to cross the Main River near Schweinfurt. Its surface suddenly became strange, looking as if it had not been driven on for a long time. We quickly realized that we were in front of an abyss leading down to water. The bridge which we were going to cross, was blown up. We had missed the detour signs. We could not stop and proceeded down to the sand bank bracing ourselves as best we could. Our jeep crashed into the dry part of the riverbed. Behind us, the weapons carrier shared our fate. There was some shouting, but the damage to the vehicles was minor. The only injury to people was a broken forearm on Capt. Kane. To summon help, Kane fired a shot from his sidearm with his left hand. The shot went into a bedroom of a nearby building. The girl inside escaped injury but she let us know that she had a horrible fright.

Kane's arm was set in a plaster cast at the local military facility and the damage to the cars was quickly repaired. Kane lost neither his courage nor his sense of humor: "bad" Kissingen! he said in American English, and the journey continued. I was amazed to learn that one can steer a car and shift gears using only one's left hand!

The rest of the trip went according to a plan that included Kane's dream to see "the Rhine Valley". To do that, he arranged for a big detour to accommodate this wish. Unfortunately, because of the longer stay in Bad Kissingen, the time available for sightseeing was short, and we passed the Rhine Valley in the middle of the night.

On returning to Munich, Robertson continued the interrogations, this time reinforced by several US technical specialists. We continued to have to write many essays but, to the good, we received a salary for the time spent.

One evening, on a street corner, I was approached by a Frenchman who had worked a long time in our factory as a conscript. He asked me – in strict confidence – if I would like to work in France, with my group. That was an interesting question. My close colleagues agreed that the possibility was indeed interesting, but they wanted to learn more. So, our new French friends, the former conscripts Brassier, Bennett, and Yerannian, were provided orders by higher French authorities to take me to Paris, but they had no car. Dr. Denkmaier, former head of my aircraft department and a superstar in organizing, had one and offered to drive us. My colleague Kurt Donath from production was also a member of the party.

Our French escorts gave Denkmaier's BMW a fictitious military license number with the French colors, blue, white, and red, and fabricated an Ordre de Mission, according to which our French colleagues were to bring us to Paris as "détenus" [presumed war criminals]. The American posts innocently allowed us to pass the zone borders. Just ahead of Strasbourg, we reached a bridge over the Rhine. At its entrance was a large banner with the inscription "Ici commence le pays de la Liberté".

In spite of being welcomed to the land of liberty in Strasbourg we were almost quartered in a prison that night as "détenus", because it was difficult to find an innkeeper who would be willing to take us in without appropriate and presumably more official-looking papers. After a bit of looking around, the men finally found a good private accommodation. We spent the evening having fun in a pub where I was urged to play numerous German student songs on the piano. The next day we drove on to Paris where we had several meetings at the Ministry of Aviation. I presented a proposal for the construction of a French engine and the establishment of the necessary development facility. In due course, I was able to establish my wishes as acceptable and thus the conditions for the preparation of a contract were set in motion. We returned to Munich where my absence was fortunately not noticed by the American authorities.

A few weeks later, in August [1945], I was invited to make a second trip to Paris. When I arrived, I was given a draft contract which was largely in line with my wishes, and which was to make me a "directeur technique" of a development group. I accepted it as written, subject to the approval of my staff.

Oestrich drove a hard bargain, but the French Air Ministry was hardly in a position to mollify the stipulations that related to the management of the German engineering team and to the monetary reward to which Oestrich would be entitled. This latter aspect of the contract had consequences for some of the team members. The incredible details are spelled out at the end of this chapter.

On the return from this trip there was tension in Munich. Col. Robertson had sought to get in touch with me several times but had been unable to find me. The next morning, I reported to his office as requested per notes left in our quarters. The reception was icy. Where had I been? With my family. He informed me to get ready to travel on a trip of perhaps 2 to 3 days. Where to? We will see. At the airport, I was left alone in a waiting room for half a day. My American escort finally brought me back to our quarters with the stipulation that I be ready to travel again in the next few days.

The next day [25 August 1945] I was flown to Bad Kissingen, where I met Mr. Patin, the designer for aircraft control systems, who was staying in the same hotel. [He was likely Albert C. Patin, owner of the company that originated the Patin remote compass and flight control systems for the Luftwaffe during the war.] After a day or two, a small airplane took Patin and me to London and on to Wimbledon. There, a former kindergarten had been converted into a warehouse for interviewing German scientists and technical experts. The detainees were to be questioned by the English. The facility would have had a camp-like atmosphere were it not for the barbed wire around the entire complex. Every morning, we stood for roll call to make sure no one had escaped. We slept in small groups in several rooms. Everyone had to make their own bed each morning according to prescribed procedures. There were inspections (!) to check our bed-making.

The common rooms were pleasant enough. Outdoors, there was an accessible lawn, big enough to stretch our legs. The food was good to very good, certainly better than what we imagined to be normal at that time. The best thing was the stimulating company of the others also detained there. Specialists from all fields of technology and science were represented. At regular intervals, the camp inmates organized lectures followed by discussions, so that, at least for us newcomers, the time passed fairly quickly.

Shortly after our arrival in England, Dr. Wernher von Braun was also delivered here and stayed but a few days. His loan period from the Americans was apparently even shorter than ours. [The Americans, having held him in "*Operation Dustbin*" for a short time, were going to get him to the US, no matter how the interview here went.]

Most of the people held there came from the British Occupation Zone. Although they had also been asked to prepare for a trip of 2 – 3 days, most of them had been in the compound for 2 to 3 months. It was impossible to obtain information regarding how long our confinements would last. We just had to wait! Fortunately, my and Mr. Patin's stay lasted only 8 days. I was called only once for interrogation. After that review of my work, the Americans picked us up and brought us back to Germany. Apparently, we were in England on a limited-time loan. The English administration was apparently not aware of our "loaned" status and thought they would have us for much longer.

After returning to Munich [~ 5 September], I received an American offer committing them to allow me to come to the USA with a group of 10 or 11 co-workers. The offer was not bad, because I would be allowed to form and lead the group from the outset. It appeared quite generous because this opportunity was offered very few other Germans. However, the French offer was better and more binding. [By "more binding", he means that the contract with the French was of a longer duration (five years) than a presumably renewable six-month American contract.] In addition, by accepting the French proposal, I was able to include the entire team of former co-workers I had gathered. I was not limited to just a small, selected group of people to be part of my team.

I turned down the American offer. The US officers were very surprised and disappointed at the rejection of their proposal. They could not understand the reasons I put forward. They were even more surprised that my colleagues [who might have been part of the list of 10–11] didn't want to accept the offer either. They and I wanted to stay together as members of a larger team.

The Americans tried to reduce our resistance to being broken up. They took me and my closest colleague, Hans Rosskopf, to Bad Kissingen, where we were held for 8 to 10 days. From time to time, we were separately tested to see if we had changed our minds. We were eventually told that they were aware of the French offer. When we admitted that we did indeed have that offer in our hands, we were told, "You could have told us that right away. The French are our friends!" Still, they persisted and tried to make it clear that our prospects were significantly better in the USA than in France. We were not impressed. We stuck to our refusal and were released.

In November 1945, the (Communist) Air Minister, Charles Tillon, approved the creation of the jet engine working group that was to become the ATAR aeronautical workshop or, known more informally prior to that time as the Groupe "O" (for Oestrich).

We had been taken to Bad Kissingen by car, but [having made clear our refusal of the American offer] we were now on our own to get back to Munich. The railway ran infrequently and irregularly, if at all. We chose to try hitch-hiking and after a relatively short time we connected with the driver of an open bed truck going part way up the Main River loaded with coal sacks and other general cargo. He took us. The weather was glorious. We sat on the sacks and enjoyed the passing landscape. Topping that off was the exhilarating feeling of being free again after 10 days of detention. The driver could not take us all the way to Munich but with a few more vehicle changes, we reached the city that same evening.

There, our co-workers welcomed us jubilantly. They too had been under cross-examination during our 10-day absence. That is how the Americans found out that we wanted to go to France. The attempt to break up the group was successfully resisted by everyone.

The contract between Oestrich and the French government would be signed on 25 April 1946 after all the details were put in place.

We were left alone after that. We contacted our French agents to prepare for the move to the French Occupation Zone. However, this process included getting the approval of the US occupation authorities because we were in their zone. No one believed that we would receive it. It turned out however, that in the U.S. Army were units of French volunteers who were enlisted to help in various capacities. They were happy to help us get out of the AOZ and loaded us, wives, children, and some belongings, onto their American trucks and drove us across the border during a foggy night [with the loads indicated on a fake manifest as consisting of goods of some sort]. Ironically, at the zone border control, a small child started to cry. Since children were not on the manifest, the French driver gunned the engine to be very loud and the American post heard nothing [or chose to ignore what he heard].

The first wave of workers arrived in Lindau-Rickenbach (ZOF). Our offices were set up in the confiscated Dornier factory. The work could begin. The news of my contract with France had spread quickly. Interest in joining us came from many sides. For example, shortly before our departure from Munich, Prof. Heinrich Hertel, chief designer of Junkers aircraft, contacted us and wanted to know what was going on. After discussions of the new venture with him in Lindau, he got into the truck to join us and stayed as a member of our team. He was subsequently commissioned [by the French] to design the most modern fighter aircraft for the most modern jet engine.

In Lindau, the French generously gave me the opportunity to complete the group. Well-known persons who joined us were Prof. H. Triebnigg, Prof. A.-W. Quick, Mr. R. Kosin (former chief aircraft designer at Arado), and Dr. Heinrich Ebert. We also gathered several engineers from Junkers whom Dr. A. Franz had to leave behind: S. Decher, W. Stein and W. Grunert.

In Lindau, French officials in the persons of Engineer General Delbegue, Commandant Schneider and Captain Mahoudau took us under their wings and managed interactions with the air ministry. Conferring with the ministry, we quickly agreed on the technical parameters of the engine to be designed. The mechanical construction of the engine was going to be built by SNECMA [in a facility near Paris]. We were tasked to do the research, the calculations, and design work. We were able to begin rather quickly. The first French co-workers joined our group.

The name of our engine was to have the first letters of the French name for our working group: ATAR = ATelier Aeronautique de Rickenbach [Aeronautical Workshop of Rickenbach].

In June 1946 we moved to France.[1] In central France [Decize near Nevers] there was an empty barracks, which had been built before the war for the Gardes Mobiles [~National Guard] but had only served for the German occupation troops. After they left, they served as accommodations for "displaced persons" from the East and German war prisoners. The proximity between the residences and the workplace, as well as the quiet environment, were ideal for making progress in our work and we were more than compensated for France's poor economic shape at that time.

From an article by Nouzille [see Bibliography]: "Hans-Georg Münzberg [one of the principal engineers on the Groupe "O" team and a close friend of my father's] recalls: 'We had done everything to escape the Russians and we found ourselves under the thumb of a communist [air] minister and in a village whose mayor was also a communist! It scared us a bit. In addition, local youths had been arrested during the occupation and as we wore long leather coats [in June?], Gestapo

1 The move was forced by an inter-Allied decision to prohibit technical work of military utility in occupied Germany.

style, we worried the inhabitants ... It took several months for the atmosphere to ease.'"

> The cooperation with the French authorities and with the SNECMA production department was excellent. Mr. Haenel and Dr. Stieglitz did me great service by helping with the many psychological [personal or emotional?] problems.

A total of 159 names appears on a 1946 list of technical personnel who moved to Lindau. The group that moved to Decize was probably somewhat smaller because the accommodations were limited. No other data is noted with the names. Seven of these technical specialists were women. The accompanying families brought the total number of people to around 500. Over the years in Decize, about 40 French engineers joined the Groupe "O".

A note on photographs. The photo of the German specialists in the plate section is of a resolution that makes it difficult to identify individuals. I can't even find my father! Identification of people is not the point of showing it here. What makes the larger history interesting is that photos exist at all. I look at their existence as proof of the openness regarding the treatment of the Germans by the West. In addition to official photos, my family archives are full of pictures of the days in Decize. They are typically small, 2x3 inches and in black and white. They portray a happy time, especially the ones involving families and the children.

There are group pictures illustrating the text describing the time spent by other Germans in Russia (Chapters 9–14 and 16–24). They tend to be taken, not by Russian officials, but by German individuals with cameras. The group subjects are primarily of people living in the same housing unit or participating in some group activity. There are photographs of groups of German technical personnel in Russia focused on various aspects of jet engine development, the compressor group, the turbine group, etc. These might have been official Soviet photos. The illustrations used (and those available on the Haida-Clan website) were taken by a small corps of German amateur photographers with limited access to cameras and film (as well as processing). Further, their photography was clandestinely watched. There are, to my knowledge, no official Soviet photographs in the public domain or on the Internet.

Back to Oestrich.

> In the spring of 1948, the first ATAR engine was put to the test. It immediately produced the promised thrust of 3700 lbs. and we could quickly increase this level to 4400 lbs. This was a good start for our

> Group "O" because we were competing with an equally powerful engine developed by Rateau [a French competitor in the engine business]. Other development offices for competitive jet engines also existed at CEM [Compagnie Electro-Mécanique, a subsidiary of the Swiss firm Brown-Boveri Co. (BBC)] and even at the Paris offices of SNECMA. Interestingly, the latter was also responsible for the construction of our engines. Thanks to the good progress of our work, the competition between Group "O" and SNECMA was put to rest with a merger of my group into the company in May 1950. At the same time, I was entrusted with the development of SNECMA jet engines as *Directeur Technique*. The problem of merging two equally strong development groups, one predominantly German, the other exclusively French, succeeded well by balancing the mutual responsibilities and personal interests of both sides. The French employees played a decisive role in the subsequent development, so that the ATAR became a genuine joint product.
>
> A big hurdle was still to be overcome. We needed the engine to be accepted by the French air force in the face of serious competition. The French firm Hispano-Suiza [aircraft engines] had acquired a license to produce the Rolls-Royce "Nene" engine[1] that had almost the same thrust as the ATAR. The question concerning which of the two engines should be installed in the aircraft of the Armée de l'Air [French air force] was long debated but was finally decided in our favor. To help with that decision, comparison flights were made between aircraft of the same type, one equipped with the ATAR and the others with the Rolls-Royce engines. [The airplane on which this comparison was made was the Avions Marcel Dassault "Mystère" that first flew in 1951.]
>
> A similar comparison was again made a few years later with the same result. The Australians had to decide whether to build their Dassault "Mirage" airplane[2] with ATAR or Rolls-Royce "Avon" engines, the latter to be produced in Australia under license.

At the end of 1952, the quarters in Decize were abandoned and about a hundred of the engineering staff moved closer to the SNECMA production facilities in Melun-Villaroche near Paris.

> The ATAR became the engine of French military aviation. The excellent performance of the Mirage aircraft from the company Dassault equipped with our engines established a good reputation all over the world. ATAR

1 The Hispano-Suiza license was for the "Nene" as well as an enlarged version called "Tay". The Mystère prototypes flew with both of these Rolls-Royce engines. A SNECMA concern might have been that Hispano-Suiza would also acquire a license for the newer "Avon" engine that was closer in design and performance to the ATAR engine. The third prototype (Mystère IIC) flew with the ATAR engine.

2 The Mirage III, whose first flight was in 1960, was a widely-used supersonic delta wing aircraft.

engines were built under license in many countries. The engine grew in capability and found many applications in service. [Other aircraft examples were the Vautour, Mystère, and Etendard.]

In October 1960 I resigned from my post as *Directeur Technique*. My French deputy, Michel Garnier, succeeded me. We remained close friends through the later years. The transformation of the development group I founded from a German one to a mixed and now almost exclusively French one went very smoothly.

As I write this, many of my former colleagues in France reached retirement age limits. Others returned to Germany where they stepped into important positions in industry and in academic circles.

This is the end of the material translated from the document by Oestrich.

Oestrich became a French citizen in 1948 and for his work on the ATAR engines, was awarded the "Chevalier dans l'Ordre de la Légion d'Honneur" ("Knight in the Order of the Legion of Honor") in 1962. He retired from SNECMA in 1968 and died in France in 1973.

Financial aspects of the Group "O" contract

According to writings about the man,[1] a side to Hermann Oestrich shows great financial acumen and foresight. In the contract signed on 25 April 1946, he was able to include royalty payments to himself based on sales of the ATAR engines. This accomplishment is a rarity among technical people employed in industry, especially in the military industry. According to the contract, a royalty was to be paid to him in the amount of 8% of the engines' sale price for the first 100 engines in the first year. The percentage paid decreased to 6, 4, 2, 1, and 1 for the six years of the agreement that potentially involved 600 engines! In addition, he managed to tap into 2% of the salaries of his German co-workers to finance the establishment of patents arising from the Groupe "O" engine development work … patents assigned to himself! These were licensed to SNECMA without fees and with royalties shared when the rights were sold. The argument for Oestrich holding the French patents was that a French citizen had to be the "inventor of record." This was a good reason to become a French citizen.

The contract was quite a financial arrangement that left him a wealthy man, especially after the SNECMA company bought back all the patents from him. His earnings were stored in a SNECMA aircraft maintenance company in Casablanca, Morocco. There is no record

1 Personal communication from P. Mouton. See also Eckardt, *Jet Web*, and Nouzille, "La folle histoire du Dr Oestrich", in the Bibliography.

regarding where investments were made although Nouzille speculated in his magazine article in 1999 that they might have been used to help engineering efforts by other German (former) colleagues not involved with SNECMA. An important one might have been Ferdinand Brandner who will come up in the Russian part of our story. Brandner was visited briefly by Oestrich while the former was building jet engines in Egypt in the early 1960s. There are records to indicate that some of the engineers in Groupe "O" who did not stay at SNECMA later found employment in Egypt. Neither Oestrich nor Brandner wrote about any cooperative work or financial arrangements. There is no evidence that any of Oestrich's investments were sinister in nature.

A personal note

My father was the lead engineer on engine controls at Junkers and in the Groupe "O" organization. During his time at Junkers, he devised the means to make a jet engine with an axial flow compressor practical for propelling an airplane. His design innovation was for the prevention of compressor stall which results in functional engine failure. Such control had to be automatic and not a concern for the pilot of the airplane with such an engine. He filed for a patent (1942) and was granted a German patent in 1944. After the war, he was keen to file more broadly because he understood the importance of the technical idea. He filed in the UK and the US (in 1948, granted 1954) but his employment at Groupe "O" or SNECMA prevented his filing in France due to the limitations stipulated in the Oestrich designed employment contract.

This patent hijacking and the tax on his salary for the appropriation of his (and others') patents were a part of the motivation for seeking work elsewhere after his contract ran out. He (and perhaps others, like Stein) secured a new position in the United States (see Chapter 2).

In European professional circles, it was customary for a departing employee to secure a letter (a *Zeugnis* in German) written by the employer as a summary of the work and the man. Oestrich's Zeugnis for my departing father contains no hint of the matters described above and is indeed very complimentary. A reproduction of that Zeugnis is included in the book *Turbulent Journey*. Some interpersonal realities are best kept quiet.

We continue the French story in the next chapter with a few words about the mechanics of moving a large group of people and how it was done successfully. Oestrich was a key player in that successful relocation. Chapter 7 completes the postwar story in France with a description of another notable, though not very successful, endeavor utilizing German technical talent in France in the days after WWII.

Chapter 6

ACCOMMODATIONS AND LIFE IN CENTRAL FRANCE

The wholesale transfer of German technical personnel out of what became the Soviet Occupation Zone involved the necessary provision of living space for the men and their families when they arrived in the American Occupation Zone. After all, the Americans were doing most of the moving. The men and their families might have been separated for a time and separate accommodations for both were sometimes necessary. The technical people who were moved by the US Army were temporarily housed in Bad Kissingen or Oberursel and a much larger group of both technical people and families without the fathers was in Landshut in Bavaria. The facilities there were a former Wehrmacht military base taken over by the US Army and renamed Pinder Barracks. The records are not available to allow comments about the conditions in Landshut but knowing that the US Army managed the housing suggests that the utility infrastructure would have been relatively functional for the German families to have been moved there. In the United States, the technical specialists were moved there directly as a group without their families and housed in temporary wooden barracks on military installations, Fort Sill in Oklahoma and Wright Field in Ohio, for examples.

The Germans who transferred to France were initially gathered in commandeered houses near Lindau in Germany and later brought to a former Gardes Mobiles barracks in Decize in central France. A better description of these "barracks" is with the word "caserne." The casernes in Landshut and in Decize were far from simple wooden structures. They were stone masonry buildings with fittings of the late 1930s, meaning they had internal plumbing and electric wiring. These facilities were utilized during the war and survived intact. Central heating was installed when the caserne in Decize became the locale for the transplanted Germans and prior to their arrival.

These realities are worthy of note because the contrast with conditions in the Soviet Union where this story will take us, will be seen to be stark. An important contrast between conditions in France and Germany and those in Russia is, of course, the climate. The winters in the latter are longer and colder than those in Western Europe. That makes the provision of heat an important aspect of bringing people to a location if the goal is to do it successfully or even humanely.

The first accommodations for the hundred or so families in Lindau on Lake Constance were in the French Occupation Zone. The housing provided was confiscated by the French Army from local residents who were suspected to have been notable Nazis. That period turned out to be limited (January to November 1946) because the German engineers and their families were required to leave Germany and proceed to France: new Allied rules that prohibited potentially military-related work to be carried out on German soil. The more interesting dimension of housing is the quality of what was provided and available later in Decize as the quasi-permanent quarters in France and the tumult in getting there.

The bumpy transfer to France

Pierre Mouton's interest in the history of the time and that of the company where he was later employed motivated him to examine the events and the people involved. The following paragraphs are a transcription of his findings. These were primarily interviews with the Frenchman Louis Jumelle who lived through the early years of the Groupe "O" creation and later worked for SNECMA as an important member of company management.

In 1946, Jumelle was a newly-commissioned second lieutenant in the French air force having just completed his engineering studies at the prestigious French engineering school "Sup Aéro" in Toulouse, now known as the *École Nationale Supérieure de l'Aéronautique et de l'Espace*. In the interviews with Mouton, Jumelle explained how the Oestrich team was installed in France. He was responsible for organizing the move to France. Transport took place by rail in three stages. The first move was of the mostly office equipment (drawing boards, desks, etc. but no engines and little related to their construction). The second stage consisted of moving the men followed by the families in the third stage. A total 267 freight cars left Rickenbach in early April 1946. The initial destination was the Air Ministry Air Barracks at Provins (55 miles southeast of Paris). While the first stage of the move was underway and the trains were rolling though France, this destination was canceled by General Jean De Lattre de Tassigny. Finding a new destination fell to the Air Minister, Charles Tillon, who could not rapidly identify an alternative. The trains were stuck at the station in Puteaux (northwest of Paris). A few words on the French governmental organization will set the stage for the events to follow.

The SNECMA company was a government-mandated creation from a variety of smaller companies with interests and strengths in aircraft propulsion who might not have survived the postwar turmoil had they been kept private and free to fend for themselves. In creating SNECMA the government wanted to secure the know-how that was available to be saved. Among the institutions so gathered were the engine manufacturer Gnôme et Rhône (the manufacturer of the well-known rotatory engines in WWI established in 1905). That company had just undergone a punitive nationalization for acts of cooperation with the enemy: they built German engines for the Luftwaffe. The punitive aspects include loss of assets and loss of people. Another entity pulled into SNECMA was the Voisin Company, an old French airplane and automobile building company also dating back to 1905. It was pulled into SNECMA in 1945. A third part of the collection relevant to our story was a subsidiary known by its acronym GEMHL which stands for "Groupe d'Etudes Moteur à Huile Lourde" (Study Group for Heavy Oil Motors created in 1939, disbanded, and reassembled in 1945). GEMHL was involved with the study of diesel engines for aircraft propulsion. The president of the subsidiary was Raymond Marchal who did not believe in the future of jet engines, but he was also chief engineer of SNECMA at the (Boulevard) Kellerman headquarters in Paris where he wielded significant influence on technical matters. Under him was Michel Garnier, head of the turbomachinery sub-group.

While the train was waiting for a new destination, the train cars were "raided" by staff members of the GEMHL subsidiary and partially relieved of items *they* needed (drawing tables, furniture, tools, etc.). Garnier was unable to prevail in keeping the equipment in the train cars. Gas turbines were less important than diesel engines in those days, at least as far as Marchal was concerned. That was to change. As Oestrich noted, Garnier would eventually succeed Oestrich as Technical Director at SNECMA and diesel engines for aircraft eventually disappeared from the scene. This episode illustrates well the state of scarcity and disorder that prevailed in France at that time.

A decision was finally made that a caserne in Decize was to be the location of the Groupe "O" enterprise. There were sufficient residences and space that could be converted for an engineering bureau for the expected approximately 150 engineers and their families. An apparently favorable aspect of the caserne was that it was located close to but outside the small city of Decize.

The first group of trains eventually reached Decize with the remaining material and was unloaded by German prisoners of war. A press conference was held at this time to prepare the local population for the planned arrival of the Germans. In the postwar context, this prospect was difficult for the locals to accept, despite the explanations given to the press and published. Undeterred, the project was rolling toward reality in the small city.

The second group of trains consisting of about half the engineers arrived on 15 July 1946. These were housed, or rather "parked," in garages serving as a dormitory. The rest of the group followed in mid-August. The families did not arrive until November.

According to Jumelle, the barracks (known later as Cité Voisin when our family lived there) was in a deplorable state, partially unheated and full of fleas, lice, and cockroaches. He had to procure dozens of kilos of DDT to overcome these pests before the German engineers arrived (The pest attack was initially unsuccessful, but the humans prevailed as time went on.) Central heating was installed.

The confusion of the time continues, this time about agency relationships. The newly created SNECMA could have welcomed the "O" group when it arrived in France. It chose not to do so. The war memory might have been too fresh. To maintain an arms-length relation with Groupe "O", the contract signed on 25 April 1946 by Dr. "Oestrich" was with Etat (THE French state) represented by the Director of Technology and Industry of Aeronautics (DTIA) and not with SNECMA.

Nevertheless, a future integration of Groupe "O" into SNECMA was planned. In the addendum to the contract covering the transfer to France, signed on the same day, it was stated: "… that it is the intention of the French Government," on the occasion of this transfer, to prepare a close collaboration of Groupe "O" with SNECMA on the technical and industrial level, and a little further on: "However, to accentuate the links between SNECMA and Groupe 'O', it is to the company VOISIN, a subsidiary of SNECMA, that the French Government has assigned, the administrative management of Groupe 'O'."

Jumelle became first French engineer to be integrated into Groupe "O" in the "compressor" section headed by Karl Fickert (on the *Paperclip* list). A humorous aside he brought up during his interview with Mouton was a description of a time when he straddled the compressor housing of the ATAR 101V, running at full speed (picture riding a horse, but in this instance, with about 10,000 horsepower between his knees!) all while he manipulated a probe to measure the air flow angles at the outlets of the compressor's stator vanes! These were times with different safety rules!!!

Decize

The location choice of Decize on the Loire River in the central part of the country was driven by the availability of the caserne. Its buildings were built before the war, taken over by the Wehrmacht troops during the German occupation, and later abandoned by them as German forces vacated France. At the time when just the German specialists (the men mostly) moved in (in spring 1946) it was used for housing refugees, displaced persons, and former POWs. A secondary aspect of choosing that location was that it was somewhat removed from places where animosity between French and Germans was more intense, notably in the big cities. The WWII years were not a happy time for the locals even in Decize, so that the tension was also present there. Fortunately, the time of German occupation of France was short (1940–4) and its impact limited, at least in time.

Decize is located in the Département of Nièvre. From an economic viewpoint, it was a small town in the 1940s. The countryside was, and probably still is, rural, dominated by agriculture and some light industry. Among these, near the caserne, a small factory manufactured bricks, roofing tiles, etc. from locally mined clay.

The caserne was about a mile away from the center of the town with its Roman roots. The caserne residents could reach the town by walking and later by cycling. Initially, contact with the town might have been minimal but it offered goods not available in the canteen associated with the caserne. In the latter, staples, including wine, were available but life required things that mandated an increasing number of shopping trips to ordinary merchants: dry goods, hardware, pharmacy, bakery, books, bike repair, ice cream, etc. from the town shops. Since the Germans were on French government salaries, they brought well-appreciated outside money into this little out-of-the-way town and goodwill was on the rise.

An island was the location of the town's major buildings. Narrow streets, steep in places, dating back centuries lead to single purpose shops, schools, two movie theaters, churches, administrative buildings, etc. It had a wonderfully medieval feeling. Most traffic heading south on the Route Nationale was directed over one bridge spanning the relatively dry flood plain to another bridge over the active stream of the Loire by circumscribing the town. The western end of the island is the site of a park-like area with huge sycamore trees where the locals have their weekly market and "boules" players can often be seen. In summer, the river's shores were well patronized swimming areas. In all, it was a photogenic and charming town, often the subject addressed by my father's camera.

The caserne complex consisted of six buildings in a 1x2 rectangular pattern each with three entrances to six apartments on three floors for a total of over a hundred units. In addition, there were buildings for work, administration, washing (laundry and people), and the aforementioned canteen, the store for the sale of "Lebensmittel."[1] The size of the facility was about right for the Oestrich team. The Loire was the short-lived boundary between occupied and Vichy France. Someone might have worried about a future military conflict between the two Frances and built an array of defensive trenches on the hillside leading down from the caserne to the river. It never came to that. The trenches were probably dug by POWs during the German occupation and became the playground of the many pre-teen children of German families, including me.

The workplace buildings for the technical people were within the caserne and adjacent to the residences so the men walked to work and came home for lunch. The caserne complex was surrounded by a cast concrete fence that could easily be climbed over. We kids often did. The main entrance gate to the residence buildings area was never closed. There were no restrictions on Germans traveling to town or interacting with the local population.

The caserne had a two-room school for the younger children (ages 5–6) on site. The older children attended the local schools. I recall that the required study of a foreign language taught in the Ecole Communale was German! The interactions between French and German children were initially tense but as the German kids became fluent in the French language, the distinction between the children vanished as did animosities. The personal contacts trumped historical ugliness and suffering.

The apartments were generous in size. Our family of four had one with two bedrooms, a living room, an all-purpose dining room-kitchen and a small room with a toilet, a WC. Baths and showers were available in a separate facility once a week for "mass cleanings" for the two genders at different times. All other toiletries were carried out at the kitchen sink the other six days of the week. The bath facilities

1 In English, there is no good word to describe "ingredients for life," in other words, "food and …."

were also used for laundry. Tubs of hot water and washboards were available for doing laundry but no power-driven machines.

As we shall see, the issue of heat will become very important for the abductees taken to Russia. That aspect of life was markedly better in France. The kitchen stoves were wood fired, and the French government delivered an ample supply of firewood as necessary. The German men had to saw and split it, but that, as Ben Franklin is known to have said, warmed the men twice. The wood was stored in a large woodshed and retrieved from there as needed. The kitchen was always the warm spot in the apartment. The bedroom radiators were adequately supplied by central steam. At Christmas time, as a beneficial gesture, the French government acceded to a request from this German community for delivery of an appropriate number of Christmas trees, a custom that was not commonly exercised in France! A German Christmas required trees, and these were appreciated.

Our apartment was on the top floor overlooking a large grassy area between the six buildings. This central area was the venue for sports, mostly volleyball and soccer, and kids' games. For the most part, the kids preferred to play in the natural surroundings: hide and seek in the nearby woods, exploration of the river environment, the trenches, and the pits of a nearby clay mine with its narrow-gauge industrial railroad and the occasionally unattended two-axle car for hauling clay or tools. Just be home by dinner time! There was never a shortage of playmates to undertake adventures. These words may sound like the description of a ghetto, but a ghetto it was not. We children regularly interacted with French kids in the area, in town, in church, and in school.

After living and working about two years in this complex, the engineers earned and saved enough money to improve mobility beyond that offered by a bicycle. Cars and motorcycles became available as the economy improved so that my father bought a 200cc motorcycle for himself and a moped for my mother in 1949. In 1950 he traded those for an automobile, a Citroën 2CV. He was an eager tourist and travelling to visit the nearby historical sites involved the whole family. Through those years, the increasing number of Renault 4CVs, Peugeots, Panhards, etc. allowed for much enjoyed travel around a beautiful country and even trips to Germany. The travel restrictions were minimal if they existed at all. In the beginning of the stay in France, there were hardly the means to travel and later only the border crossings between France and the neighboring countries remained as boundaries to travel. In 1951 we, as a family, enjoyed a trip in the 2CV through Franco's Spain. I recall that many roads in Spain were construction sites that were not actually under construction by any workers.

The technical activities in Decize effectively ended in late 1952 when the five-year contracts between the German engineers and the French government expired. The engineers who were invited to stay with renewed, and presumably more conventional, employment contracts joined the French company SNECMA near Paris. The economy in Germany had improved substantially and, as noted by Oestrich, many of the "Decizois" returned to Germany to academic positions and industrial jobs. The company very effectively transitioned from the nearly all-German Groupe"O" to an almost all-French enterprise.

The technology transfer was complete, and it was amicable. The integration of the German engineers and their families into French schools and society was a good experience for me and all my cohorts as far as I know.

Chapter 7

TURBOMÉCA – ANOTHER FRENCH STORY

It would be unjust to portray events in France as solely those experienced by the engineers who became a part of SNECMA via Groupe "O." A significant cadre of German technical people was involved with the French company Turboméca. It was founded in 1938 by Joseph Szydlowski (1896–1988), building compressors of various kinds, including aircraft engine superchargers. The fortunes of war forced Szydlowski to flee to Switzerland when Germany occupied France. He returned to France in October 1944 to restart his factory with production orders from the Allies. In engineering circles, the news of the potential for jet engines was old by then and, given his strength in the understanding of turbomachinery, Szydlowski was very interested in following a development path for his company that included manufacture of gas turbine engines.

Turboméca and other companies like SNECMA (Oestrich mentions some of the others in his writing), went into an intensive competition for the French government interest and funds in pursuit of contracts to build French jet engines. The Direction de Technologie et Industrie (DTI) had called for expressions of industrial interest on 28 April 1945. The government was moving fast. This date precedes VE-Day! The DTI put together a military mission to visit Germany (at the end of October) and Szydlowski with his perfect knowledge of German and with two other engineers, was a member of the French team. In Friederichshafen, he met the former Daimler-Benz[1] technical director Friedrich Nallinger

1 Even though Daimler Benz did not secure a development contract for jet engines, it continued a modest effort on its own through 1943 when the advanced engine that the company was developing (the TL 109–007 ran in 1943) was recognized to require too much further work and time.

and, with Air Ministry concurrence (9 November 1945), hired him on a three-year renewable contract. This event triggered the creation of Etablissement Turboméca in the French Occupations Zones in Germany or Austria. Nallinger was to be its director. The work was to be limited to paper studies and hardware design. All manufacturing was to be carried out in France. The chosen workplace was an old shoe factory used by Dornier during the war. It was located near Bregenz on the Austrian[1] shore of Lake Constance.

The new enterprise needed more technical people. They were gathered from Daimler Benz, Junkers, Heinkel, Focke-Wulf, and former German research institutes. The company was soon forced to move to France because of the inter-Allied agreement that no work with potential military usefulness could be carried out in the occupied countries; the same agreement that forced the Groupe "O" people from Lindau to Decize.

The move came in May 1946 when 144 people moved to the region around Bordes in southwest France at the foot of the Pyrenees Mountains. As might have been anticipated, the move was problematical. Space for the necessary industrial facilities and housing for the new arrivals was in short supply. The industrial facilities were plundered by the Germans who had used them and left them in less than functional condition. By distributing the people and work into several villages and towns, the problem was mastered. There was one important difference, however, between the processes of moving the Germans into the Bordes area and moving Groupe "O" to Decize. In the move to Bordes, only the technical men (and a few women) were moved. The families were obligated to stay behind in Germany. Local residents in this relatively poor region of France consequently witnessed the shipments of food packages and portions of the men's salaries to families in Germany as such transfer was stipulated and executed by the French government. That fact led to understandable friction between the locals and the new arrivals. The local press of the day speculated that the reason for keeping the families away was the concern that intact families might chose to leave France by crossing the nearby border to fascist Spain and take the hard-learned technology with them. The lack of housing was also a factor in keeping the families in Germany, at least for a time. Through the early period with relatively heavy German involvement in the company, a total of 326 German specialists were hired.

1 For a time after WWII (1945–55), Austria, like Germany, was divided into occupation zones and the French managed the Vorarlberg and Tyrol regions.

In retrospect, it is difficult to speculate about how long the families could, realistically, be kept separated. These were interesting times in interesting places with people dealing with challenging economic and political forces.

The projects undertaken by Turboméca were ambitious and numerous. Engines to be developed varied in size (power or thrust levels) and in type: turbojets and turboprops. On the powerful end of the spectrum of the studies undertaken were designs of a 20,000 lbs. thrust jet and a 20,000 HP turboprop. These were engine size levels well beyond the state-of-the-art of the day. Next was a more practical 9,000 lbs. thrust jet engine, and a series of smaller turboshaft or turboprop engines with outputs of 200, 1,140, and 2,500 HP respectively. In short, Turboméca wanted to be active in all arenas of the new gas turbine engine industry.

In parallel, there were studies undertaken for a high-speed commercial passenger jet aircraft that would take advantage of the engines that Turboméca was going to design and build. Images of a proposed airplane (the UR-1: *le Ultra Rapide*) were the stuff of pure science fiction: A swept wing, a rather fat airplane with an air intake at the nose feeding an array of six bundled (!) jet engines at the center of the fuselage's rear end. The passenger cabins were designed to be situated around (!) the central air duct to the engines in three levels. The flight crew would sit at the front on the upper level. The passenger cabin would have been very awkward in configuration and possibly quite noisy.

Unfortunately, all that development work was not to become reality. In the summer of 1947, the times were hard, economically speaking. The Air Ministry was forced to make a re-evaluation of its on-going projects and reviewed what the various manufacturers were doing, including Turboméca and SNECMA. The conclusions were sobering for Turboméca because the following conclusions were reached:

1. The 5,000 lbs. thrust ATAR engine (built by SNECMA) was a more realistic prospect that than a 13,000 lbs. (reduced from 20,000 lbs.) thrust Turboméca engine then under study.
2. The 5,000 lbs. thrust ATAR engine had immediate military applications and the prospects for commercial jets were slim and too far in the future.
3. The reality was that SNECMA was a national(ized) company with consequently greater financial resources and political influence at its disposal than a private company.

Turboméca had to face reality with a focus on a more limited sector of the industry. By early 1948, the dissolutions of the various company projects left it with just 50 Germans. Of these, 13 finished their careers with the company. The question of separated German families became moot. Nallinger left in May 1948 and returned to Germany. The situation there had not yet become the "economic miracle" that it would later be, but matters had improved. The Marshall Plan was just getting implemented.

The Turboméca story is not as happy as the one about SNECMA. The reason is primarily an economic one: Turboméca was private and SNECMA was a "nationalized" company at the time. It was easier for the French government to protect its own and let the hardships fall on private enterprises. The German engineers from Bordes who returned to a still hurting Germany struggled to find good work.

Turboméca stayed a viable producer of smaller gas turbine engines either by itself or in partnership with other engine makers. Today, both SNECMA and Turboméca are merged into Safran with the latter known as Safran Helicopter Engines.

This description of the events experienced by people who went to France contrasts starkly with those undergone by German engineers and technicians who were abducted to Russia at gunpoint. The people who went to France and to America, went voluntarily.

Chapter 8

OPERATION OSOAVIAKHIM

At the Yalta Conference, the Allied heads of state agreed that war reparations were payable by Nazi Germany in the form of equipment, goods, and German labor. Franklin Roosevelt and Josef Stalin agreed to an amount of $20 billion, with 50% going to the Soviet Union. In terms of value equivalence in the early 21st century, this amount is about a third of a trillion US dollars. An interesting aspect of the first sentence (if that is the official language) is that the payer was going to be Nazi Germany, when in fact, that government capitulated on VE Day and ceased to exist. The Allies had seen to that. In reality there was no German government at all, and any reparations would be paid by the surviving German people who might have been part of the Nazi government, sympathized with it, or not. Some valuable reserves (art, gold, etc.) in Germany in 1945 were either stashed away by private, mostly criminal, individuals who hoped to survive the war as wealthy men. There was little else. Thus, reparations would be in the form of labor, technical know-how, and useful physical objects that could be hauled away. All three of these aspects became the currency in the reparation transaction. An interesting question arises: "How is anyone going to determine when the twenty-billion-dollar mark has been reached?", never mind the difficulties of keeping track of appropriate book-keeping in the Soviet Union by Western auditors and vice versa. In the days after WWI, such accounting was relatively easy because the victorious Allies just brought a freight train to the national treasury in Spandau, loaded the gold into it, and hauled it away. In addition to the removal of gold reserves, a list of industrial limitations on Germany were drawn up to formally put an end to the war.[1]

1 The goal of the Treaty of Versailles of 1919 was to limit future German military activities by prohibiting construction of anything that resembled military hardware. The limitations were ineffective, of course, because Hitler re-armed Germany while the WWI Allies helplessly stood by.

The Soviets were as keen as the Western Allies to take as much advantage of German technology as possible and to garner it for their exclusive use. Forced labor was specifically cited by the Soviets as a reparation for war damage. To that end, both the labor and the know-how were going to be harvested. Their emphasis was on the educated labor because the know-how resided in persons. Ordinary industrial and farm labor was of lesser value because Russia had a lot of that despite heavy wartime losses. Further, there were large numbers of German POWs in Soviet hands. The know-how they wanted resided in people and less so in documentation or artifacts. Not much of the physical manifestations of technology was left after removal by the Americans and the British. They had gotten to it first.

Soviet military chiefs were keen to learn specifically about the advances that had been made by Germany in the aviation and missile sectors. Following the war, the Soviets had reorganized various companies in Germany and their people into 'construction bureaus', formally termed as Sowjetische Aktiengesellschaften or SAGs. Because the rules of the Postdam Agreement specified that such companies could not reside in Germany, they would be moved to the USSR just as Groupe "O" had to move to France. In Russia, these reconstituted companies were later designated as Experiment and Design Bureaus called OKBs, by their Russian acronym.

On 13 May 1946, the Council of Ministers of the Soviet Union set in motion a program formally known as *Operation Osoaviakhim*. The word is said to be an abbreviation of "The Society for the Assistance of Defense, Aircraft, and Chemical Construction." The objective was to affect the "transfer of the 'construction bureaus' as well as 2,000 German specialists by the end of 1946 to the Soviet Union." On 9 July, Stalin set the date for implementing this operation to be 22 October. The following paragraph lists the technical sectors with the number of people involved from the Wikipedia website to illustrate the breadth of *Operation Osoaviakhim*. This operation was initially secret for obvious reasons. Whether US authorities knew about it is uncertain as is when they learned about it. The predecessor organization of the CIA (Central Intelligence Agency), the Office of Strategic Services (OSS) used the (mispronounced as here misspelled) term *"Operation Ossavakim"* for the first time in public on 13 January 1947.

From the Wikipedia website, the number of technical personnel (and their roles in Germany during the war) were as follows:

- 1,385 of these specialists had worked in the (German) Ministry of Aviation developing planes as well as jet engines and surface-to-air missiles,
- 515 in the Ministry of Armaments, primary concerned with development of liquid-fuel rocket engines,
- 358 in the Ministry of Telecommunications Industry (Radar and Telemetry),
- 81 in the Ministry of Chemical Industry,
- 62 in the Ministry of Shipbuilding (gyro and navigation systems),
- 27 in the Ministry of Agricultural Machinery (solid rocket engines[*?*]),
- 14 in the Ministry of Cinema and Photographic Industry,
- 3 in the Ministry of Petroleum Industry and
- 107 in establishments of the Ministry of Light Industry.

... for a total of 2,471 individuals. The reference to "light industry" refers to "optics," a strong sector in the eastern part of Germany that became the Soviet Occupation Zone. The number of Germans participating in the jet engine and airplane sector on behalf of the Soviet Union was, when it was fully implemented, significantly larger.

The aviation sector and the promises made

The Soviet authorities lost no time is pulling together the engineers who remained in their zone and were active in the aviation industry. Dessau became the site of a rebuilding of what Junkers, BMW, and others had started during the war. A joint German-Russian engine building effort was promised. Importantly, the work site was to be in Germany. It turned out to be a very false promise.

A memorial website (Haida-Clan) dealing with the aftermath of *Operation Osoaviakhim* states that the number of German Engineers was about 3,000 and provides a list of names together with the persons' birthyears (see Chapter 23 for those who were taken to Kuybyshev). The specialists had families so that the total number involved was about 6,500 (probably closer to 8,000) individuals taken to various locations in the Soviet Union. Their belongings were to be taken with them. Transportation to Russia was initially by trucks to the Dessau train station from which 92 trains consisting of passenger and freight cars traveled out of Germany at Frankfurt/Oder over a new border with Poland. From the same website, the list of institutions from which individuals were taken includes the following:

Arado Flugzeugwerke, Brandenburg-Briest: aircraft (Arado Ar-234 bomber)
Askania Werke, Berlin-Friedenau*: instrumentation
BMW, Unseburg* (near Stassfurt): jet and other engines
DVL, Berlin-Adlerhof (Deutscher Versuchsanstalt für Luftfahrt: German Flight Research Institute)
Junkers, Dessau*: jet and other engines
Heinkel Werke, Oranienburg and Rostock: aircraft
Zentralwerke Bleichenrode (Merger of Institut Rabe (missile guidance), Institut Nordhausen, Montania AG): rockets
Siebel Flugzeugwerke, Halle*: aircraft

Parts of Siemens, the builder of electrical machinery, were also included. The principal interests of the institutions on this list were centered on aviation.

People from the OKBs (or SAGs as they were called in Germany) were also collected and transferred to the Soviet Union. These were likely associated with the formal companies and noted by an * in the list above.

The Haida-Clan website, with the subtopic "Die Upra Kinder" exists, I believe, so that the history of the Russian abduction of 8,000 Germans so that almost 3,000 who served as slave laborers would be preserved and not forgotten. That is an important historical function. The images, the lists, and the commentary are intended for future historians. Painful memories will undoubtedly limit visits to this website by the people who were abducted as children and lived through the difficult years 1946–54. Most of the Upra Kinder (the children of these engineers) probably live (or lived) relatively normal lives after they returned to mostly East Germany, but they may also carry a heavy burden that could be painfully re-kindled.

Two complicated people

Two interesting people were involved in the transfer to the Soviet Union. One was Ferdinand Brandner (1903–86). He was a colonel-level Nazi official in the SS (the state security apparatus). He was employed at Junkers Motorenbau (a.k.a. Jumo, Aircraft Engines) in Dessau and involved early with the Jumo 004 jet engine construction. Before and during the war he led the development of a powerful, though not very successful, piston aircraft engine.

He was captured by the Soviets in Prague in May 1945. He agreed to collaborate with the Soviets and provided whatever information he could. He thought that cooperation would allow him to return to his native Austria, but the Soviets had other ideas. He was taken to a

Russian concentration camp where his value as an engineering manager and as a participant in the establishment of a jet propulsion industry was recognized. He was subsequently transferred to the Engine Plant No. 26 in Ufa (about 800 miles east of Moscow (see map in the Introduction) to set up production for the Russian version of the Jumo 004 (renamed the RD-10). That job well done led to his appointment as leader of the Germans involved in the engine construction effort at OKB-2 in Upra in 1948.

The Russians also abducted people who were more directly associated with and competent in airplane design and construction. That expertise was provided by Brunolf Baade (1904–69), an aeronautical design engineer at Junkers. His story is interesting in that he spent time in the US before the war (starting in 1930, during the Depression), married there, but was unable to find his place in the US aviation industry and so returned to Germany in 1936. During the time in the US his work involved aircraft licensing issues for BFW (Bayerische Flugzeugwerke, the company that later became Messerschmitt[1]). When he joined Junkers after the stay in the US, he was involved in a variety of military airplane designs, including his last German one, the Junkers Ju 287 mentioned in Oestrich's writing.

A thoroughly interesting aspect of this airplane was the absurdity of the design. It was the world's first airplane to have swept wings. A swept wing allows an airplane to fly fast, i.e., closer to the speed of sound than an airplane with straight wings can. The design advantage of wing sweep was the brainchild of Adolf Busemann (see Chapters 2 and 3). In the case of the Ju 287, the wings were swept forward which is technically fraught with difficulties so that almost all transonic aircraft built after that have rearward swept wings. If this airplane was designed to fly fast, it failed miserably because it had fixed landing gear. At high speed, the drag associated with the fixed gear could not possibly be overcome with the jet engines provided. Perhaps the designers were limited by wartime circumstances. Why this airplane was built as it was is an aeronautical engineering enigma.

Baade's capture by American forces and the interviews connected with it convinced him that the US would never again allow Germany to build any (!) aircraft. The design and building of airplanes were his passions. The negative American stance seems to have been an unfortunate turn of events because Baade spoke very good English

1 The name change for the company is reflected in the airplane Me 109 also being called the Bf 109.

and was very easy and cordial with the Americans, but they chose to be unpleasant. The interrogating officials were probably out of line with their interrogation approach. Baade consequently concluded that aligning his interests with those of the Soviet Union would suit him better. He remained in Dessau and was transferred to Russia. His location was not in the Kuybyshev (Upra) complex to be described in detail further on, but in various locations ending at the OKB-1 (Podberesja[1]) located in Dubna near (~60 miles north of) Moscow. His last work for the Soviets was design of a jet engine powered bomber, dubbed the OKB-1–150. That project was canceled after a test flight crash. For Baade, the design became the framework for its development into an airliner for the German Democratic Republic (GDR), later called the Baade 152. The story of that airliner is described in Chapter 25. It never came to be. Its stillbirth is associated with the uneasy relation between the GDR and the Soviet Union as it evolved during the time of premier Nikita Khrushchev and the time of the (East) Berlin uprising on 16 June 1953. That revolt was the first of more to come (Hungary 1956 and Czechoslovakia in 1968), all brutally ended by Russian tanks. Fortunate for world history is that the last one, again in East Germany, was not put down by Mikhail Gorbachev. The Berlin Wall fell, and the rest is history, mostly peaceful … for a time.

In the image of these two complicated people, we also have Günther Bock who was the director of the DVL (Deutsche Versuchsanstalt für Luftfahrt, German Flight Research Institute). He was among those forced to Russia under *Operation Osoaviakhim*. He returned briefly to the VEB-Pirna and spent his last years at the Technical University of Darmstadt (1954), in poor health, as were most returnees from Russia. A few details of Bock's time in Russia are noted in Chapter 20.

1 The name of this location (Подберезье In Russian) is not locatable on modern maps. The location of OKB-1 includes the then closed city of Kaliningrad (not the former East Prussian city of Königsberg), now renamed Korolyov (~15 miles northeast of Moscow city center).

Chapter 9

THE PFLÜGEL BOOK

The story of Kurt Pflügel (1903–81) is a first-hand account written in a small, self-published book consisting of two parts. The first is the story of events before and during the last phases of the war. The second part is the story of his and his family's abduction to Russia which is reproduced here in the chapters that follow. The discovery of this book precipitated a deeper look into the history and motivated the telling of what I learned. There are other first-hand accounts of the event (see 'Singer' in the Bibliography and Heinrich Singer in the list of names in Chapter 23). Each brings in details that together paint a more focused picture of the time and place. Singer's book is notable in that it includes a wide collection of photographs.

In English, the title of the Pflügel book is "Fates of the German Aviation Engineers." As such it is a little bit misleading because it describes only one person's experience working closely with the engine engineers. He did not write about the aviation aspect nor about the people he worked with. In fact, he mentions the engineers, not by their names, but by the first letter of their names. So that his story is only vaguely connected to others and to aviation. It is, however, a vivid recollection of the events that he and a large number of his colleagues endured in connection with Russia's start in the business of building jet engines. When I am able to do so, I editorially provide full names.

Kurt Pflügel was an engineer in charge of keeping the water and electric power supply systems at a Luftwaffe air base functional as the Allies bombed the base. The Rechlin air base was the site of experimental aircraft testing during the war. In his work capacity, Pflügel was intimately familiar with its engine test-stands where experimental engines were run to identify functional problems. That expertise was needed by the Russians. The air base was near the town of Rechlin in the present state of Mecklenburg-Vorpommern (Pomerania). The town and the nearby village of Vietzen where he resided with his family are about 70 miles NW of Berlin. He and his wife Lesta had four children, Christa (1932–2022), Sigrid, Dieter, and Renate (1935–68). Sigrid, the second daughter, was 12 in 1946. Dieter and Renate were twins with Renate handicapped from childbirth difficulties.

The first part of the book describes the agony of being in a place overrun by the invading Russian army. The associated mayhem is compounded to a much greater degree when the battle front moves over a location multiple times (as it did in his case) making the search for safety much more complicated. For example, Pflügel was a civilian employee at a military facility. Does that make him a combatant? He was issued a uniform, the pants of which he wore of necessity while moving around the landscape trying to avoid being killed by whatever opposing armies shoot at each other. If he was caught in the combat zone, the German army might have thought he was deserting and the Russians ... who knows? Communication with Russian soldiers with a gaping language difference could easily go badly. He states that he was issued a sidearm which he took great pains to keep out of sight and hoped he would never be caught with it on his person. As with most people, he was loathe to use it, but in war, one never knows ...

After the war and the Soviet occupation settled down, it was time to secure a job. He was offered work in an engineering collective dealing with water and electric power distribution. A second offer was an opportunity to join other people with experience in aircraft engines at Junkers in Dessau. The BMW engineers in Stassfurt had been relocated to Dessau so that all aviation technical people would be co-located (and easily rounded up later!). The work at the Junkers SAG was centered on Soviet efforts to capitalize on the knowledge and experience of the German engineers regarding aircraft engines, specifically gas turbine engines. This enterprise was well underway in early 1946. A major problem for the project was that the Americans and the British had removed much of the official technical documentation associated with the engine-building effort, together with the senior Junkers and BMW people. It may also be assumed that some people fled the area westward despite the threats by the military and occupation police that leaving the place of residence where they were registered involved serious penalties.

Kurt Pflügel states that the Americans had left most of the large equipment in working order, although there is mention of the British having removed some of it. The people who remained in Dessau were the second rung of the development teams, the first rung having been removed by the Americans by luring them to their occupation zone. For their part, the Soviets tried to bring the senior people in the West back to Dessau with attractive offers, but most would have none of it. Dr. Franz and several others were safely in the American Zone. So was my father, Siegfried Decher, and his family. That dimension focused my personal interest on this larger story. Although he was listed on the *Operation Paperclip* list for possible travel to the US, my father was not invited to travel to the United States at that time.[1] He happily avoided a return to Dessau by joining Oestrich and Groupe "O" in Lindau.

Papers in my father's files show that the Soviets also tried to seduce, better said "recapture", him with attractive promises of all that was in short supply, housing, money, and food. Others were similarly approached. My father saved the letters that were written in a collegial tone by his former colleagues. The language in the letters betrayed editorial assistance from Soviet and/or communist political individuals with words and sentences that smelled political or foreign. For example, there was mention of salary concomitant with his future contributions, in words that sounded as if they came from a political handbook. Fortunately for us, his response to these "invitations" was to reject them. He felt an allegiance to Dr. Franz and was serving as his representative remaining in Germany. At that time, Franz was committed to transfer to the US, although still in American hands in Germany. Unfortunately for my father, the possibility to rejoin Franz and other former colleagues in the US had, by then, vanished.

The Soviet-managed jet engine effort in Dessau looked interesting to Pflügel, certainly more interesting than being a staff engineer working in a collective dealing with repair and maintenance of water and electric power systems.

In Dessau, the German engineers and technicians were treated relatively well by the Russian overseers. The Russians were motivated to keep the German people sufficiently happy so that they would not be tempted to flee to potentially greener pastures. As individuals, the Germans tended to fall into one of two camps, one was happy that things were going so well (after defeat in the war) and the other was suspicious that the Russians were up to something. Technical work continued, but it was unclear what the long-term goals were. It felt like a period of marking time. On the private front, there were mysterious visits by strange people inquiring at the various residences, particularly in instances where families did not live in Dessau. Inquiries were made "Does a Mr. so-and-so still live here?" These curious visitors noted how many people were in the family, how the people were living, how much furniture they had, etc. The pessimists were suspicious.

1 Decher, *Turbulent Journey* cited in Chapter 1 describes that story in detail.

Kurt Pflügel describes an official visit in the spring of 1946 to the former Rechlin air base where he had worked during the war and to Vietzen where his family was then quartered, even as he lived in Dessau 150 miles to the south. He accompanied two high-level Germans and two Soviet officers on a tour of the facilities he knew well. The major topic of discussion was about possible ways to restart the functionality of the Rechlin air base. The advantage was that aircraft engine test cells available there and these were not available, though needed, in Dessau. The question never went any further and he was left wondering about the purpose of the trip. He speculated, as was reinforced later, that he was being looked over for his future role in whatever was being put together for building engines ... in Russia.

Higher-level Germans were invited to Moscow for conferences with air ministry officials. They ate well and enjoyed the opera and, on returning, reported that all is well and proceeding as planned. ... planned? The skeptics took this as a sign that things were not going to go well.

They were right. In the early morning of 22 October 1946, there was a loud knock on his door. A German-speaking Russian and an armed soldier standing there said that the factory in Dessau is being moved to Russia and he was going with it! Get your stuff together! A short time later, another translator accompanied an officer interrupted his packing and said: "Come with us, we are going to pick up your family in Vietzen!" What?! The whole family is going to Russia?! He was powerless to resist and found himself sitting in one of two trucks heading north. It was late morning when he was reunited with his family and, very quickly, the trucks were loaded with the family furnishings to return to the Dessau train station where a train waited. The furniture was transferred into a freight car by soldiers. The family belongings did not include much of their clothing because during the last days of the war's fighting, they vacated their house for safety and during their absence, many of the movable items, including the clothing, were stolen.

Others report that the Russians had cleverly arranged for celebrational parties to be organized for the evening of the 21st. Lots of vodka would have flowed and that, it seems, was a way of minimizing resistance that next morning.

The Russians invited the abductees to take all that they could pack in the few hours they had available. They were quite accommodating in that way. The Russian soldiers were also quite helpful in that process, while keeping an eye out for escape attempts which only a few of the single men managed. If a specialist wanted his paramour to go with him and not his wife, so be it. A Mrs. Gröttrup insisted on taking two cows to provide milk for her newborn. Whether the wish for milk during that winter was fulfilled is not known but it is reported that the cows arrived (see *Red Prometheus* by D.L. Augustine).

The Russians knew where everyone resided and rounding the specialists up was fairly easy. A Herr Waldemar Möller and his family were in the western sector of Berlin on the night of the roundup, recovering from a suicide attempt associated with fear of the Soviets and being abducted. Möller was an important catch for his expertise in gyro guidance systems. He was sent to a hospital in West Berlin and was staying there on the 22nd. Russian officials visited and pressured him as he was recovering. Americans also visited and proffered a better deal. The Russians thought they had him but were unable to talk him into turning down the American offer and joining his Askania group. He stayed in West Berlin until he thought it was safe to return to his residence in East Berlin to retrieve some valuable items. That was a bad decision. The Russians were waiting, arrested him, and subsequently got his family.

The Pflügels and other bewildered people were hustled onto a waiting train obviously ready to go somewhere. It did not move for quite some time, and they were told that the train was waiting for more people coming from elsewhere. Armed guards walking up and down the platforms made sure they stayed on the train. Generous packets of food, including cigarettes, were provided. Most did not have valid passports. They would need not them. In fact, they had no country that would issue them. They were citizens under a military occupation government.

At 3:10 PM, the whistle sounded, and the train departed. To where? and why?

The next chapters are in Kurt Pflügel's voice from the second part of the book I introduced above. My translation is suitably modified for English-language readers and hopefully true to the original intent. Russian place names are written in the English pronunciation context (largely Google maps) which differs from the German ones with slight spelling differences. Words in square brackets are mine, added to clarify the context.

The experience described by Kurt Pflügel is that of a mid-level engineer with a specific expertise. His story will merge later (Chapter 27) with a description of the same events described by the German leader of the technical specialists involved in the abduction, Ferdinand Brandner. That story is formally published (in German, see Bibliography) though not widely available. Brandner does not mention Pflügel by name but refers to the activities performed by his group. Brandner's status as a manager allowed him to provide details that were not available to the lower-level engineers so that he brings an interesting perspective. His narrative includes interactions with various higher Soviet officials and ministries. Conferences between Germans and these agencies were almost always held in the presence of the NKVD (The People's Commissariat for Internal Affairs), a predecessor of the KGB, the Soviet secret police. When comments derived from Brandner's writings help the telling of this story, the details are included, often as editorial notations so that authorship is clear.

Chapter 10

JOURNEY TO THE VOLGA

[Kurt Pflügel]
October 22nd 1946 was a black day for many inhabitants of the Ostzone.[1] A well-organized and unexpected removal of a large number of German families and their household goods affected not only most of the workers and engineers of the Junkers company in Dessau, but people working in factories everywhere in the Ostzone. After the recently finished war, people tried to do what they could to restart an economy with these factories but, instead, they faced more hardship. As much of the household goods as could be handled was loaded into the trucks provided by the Russian military. Armed and unarmed soldiers, officers and uniformed, mostly female, interpreters presented themselves at the apartments and called on those whose names were on their lists. The names had been identified as important people who were to prepare to go to the Soviet Union. No one was asked nor were we informed [about going anywhere] beforehand and resistance was futile. Even engineers who had just been expelled from the Sudetengau and recently found work at Junkers had to load up their families and their meager belongings. [The Sudetenland was a former German region designated to become part of Czechoslovakia after 1945, today part of the Czech Republic.]

During our train journey through the Ostzone, we encountered other trainfuls of distraught fellow sufferers at almost every major station. They were people from aircraft engine plants, aircraft manufacturing plants, people from the chemical and electrical industries, precision manufacturing, and optics. Large work teams and small groups were

1 Germans (at the time) referred to the Soviet Occupation Zone as the "Ostzone", literally the East Zone. That description is retained in this text where cited as such. The official country name (after 1949) is Deutsche Demokratische Republik (DDR) is referred to here as the German Democratic Republic, GDR or East Germany.

collected. Apart from the train in which we travelled, another seven trains with members of the Junkers engine works were said to be on their way to the Volga [a major river in Russia that empties into the Caspian Sea]. The people from the Junkers aircraft factories were sent to a workplace north of Moscow (OKB-1). We were joined by trainfuls of workers and engineers from BMW who had been located near the Harz Mountains [in Stassfurt] before they came to Dessau, and by a group from Askania.[1]

The removal of the people was an orchestrated blow to any future industrial activity in the Ostzone. The entire project was part of the war reparation to the Soviet Union [and to the Western Allies] brought about by robbing Germany of its intellectual [and industrial] capacity. The plan was to further impoverish the region after the dismantling of its machinery and equipment. The recommissioning of these plants immediately after the war was an opportunity for new [peace-oriented] activities for these former [some war-oriented] enterprises after the German collapse. The recommissioning made it possible to review the viability and function of the firms to provide work for the people still left after the fighting. In reality, the process served to prepare German workers for new jobs [in the Soviet Union].

Immediately after the war a few German scientists had voluntarily committed themselves to work in Russia, probably with employment contracts. Just such a proposal was made to me on my visit to Rechlin in 1946. I was promised a job in Moscow, with the prospect of a life better than seemed possible in Germany after the war and the German collapse. I turned it down at the time.

The removal of the technical people on 22 October 1946 was obviously an act of violence and a deprivation of liberty. On the other hand, the work in the German factories under Russian management had been in a comparatively humane atmosphere. The promise of exceptional treatment regarding food and lodging compounded by the hopelessness of finding work and livelihood elsewhere in the Ostzone, softened the coerced move, at least initially. The move may have inspired some with hope and curiosity about the [worker's] paradise that is [supposed to be] the Soviet Union. For us, it meant a reunion of the family, because my work and the family housing had been in widely separated locations. The departure was from the spoiled remnants of a

1 A firm specializing in time pieces, instrumentation, and control systems for numerous military applications. Askania was a complicated enterprise in that several of its principals were executed for the July 20th attempt on Hitler's life and others were convicted to prison sentences by Allied military tribunals after the war.

lost time. We were joining a collection of strangers and were destined to become a new community.

The reality of our situation, our helplessness, and our complete lack of freedom became starkly apparent later. For many, it brought despondency and despair. It seems, in retrospect, that the origanization of people into small work groups or employing them individually caused them and their families to fare better than as a group of engineers in a large work collective like the one we were about to experience. In managing these large collectives, the Russians were overwhelmed by the details of living, housing, and care. In large groups, the behavior of the individuals was not easy to oversee, [hence a strict regimentation of life was imposed. By necessity] we resorted to using our limited means to solve a myriad of issues. The resulting tension between Russian oversight and our initiatives was always a source of mistrust on both sides. When we returned to Germany, years later, it was possible to compare our "Russian" experiences with those of others and I concluded that lives like ours in the large collective in Kuybyshev[1] on the Volga must have been particularly tense and stressful when compared to those of the many other, especially smaller, groups of specialists.

In the Yalta agreement of 1945, it was stipulated by the Allies that the Germans would have to make reparations for the war damage after their defeat by providing physical and intellectual laborers. Looking back, I can readily say the Soviet Union, of all the Allies, has certainly carried out the largest measure of that part of the agreement and derived most of the payback from German labor. The construction of the Russian space rockets, for example, was built on the achievements of the V-2 engineers. Similarly high-speed aircraft and the construction of gas turbines and jet engines for their propulsion, advances in electrical engineering, precision mechanics, optics, and the associated technologies were the achievement of the abducted German workers and engineers. These men also were the teachers for many young Russians who were indeed eager to learn. That last aspect was a reparation that could not have been paid with money.

We were told that we were "invited" to get to know the life and working methods of Soviet socialist society. We were told of the privilege [!] of knowing the Soviet way of life. Thanks, we said but, no thanks. We were to encounter many misunderstandings between us as

---

1 Sometimes written as Kuibyshev. Outside the years 1935 to 1991, the city was and is now named Samara, a large city 550 miles southeast of Moscow.

people, based on the different ways of life, the difference in economic ground rules, and political ideology.

The course of our journey – 23 to 31 October 1946 – and the days until November 11 are well described in a diary I kept at that time. I start with the 23rd, when in mid-afternoon, the departure whistle sounded in Dessau.

On our way ...

[The journey will take Kurt Pflügel and his family on a long railroad trek to the East, over about 1,900 miles (3,000km) to today's city of Samara located southeast of Moscow. Before entering Russia, the train would cross a small part of Germany, much of Poland, and then today's Belarus. Belarus was part of the Soviet Union in 1946. When the war ended, the Allied powers redrew Germany's as well as other borders. The western part of Poland was a part of Germany before 1945.

The provision of food to the abducted Germans varied substantially. To provide a contrast to the Pflügel experience, we note from Helmut Breuninger departing with other Askania people from Berlin that they got very generous food packages for the journey. This from a letter to his family in the West, sent from Upra: "We (family of 3) obtained six heavy food packets (two per head). Therein, among other stuff, was ca. 2 kg Speck (bacon), 2 kg stewed plums, 8 cans of condensed milk, 68 small packages of crisp bread (125 grams each), 2 large sausages, 5 kg of preserved meat, over 1300 cigarettes, tea, coffee, more than 2 kg sugar, macaroni, pastries, rice, flour, and whole wheat. In addition, two meals per day were provided and generous amounts of bread." It is interesting to speculate about the length of time for which this generous supply was meant to last. These provisions were meant to keep the abductees in good spirits.]

The Kurt Pflügel travel diary

On the train from Dessau-Rosslau

Oct. 23.
Wittenberg [Martin Luther's city] evening meal: meat broth with mashed potatoes. At night: heating system broken, our train coach is very cold. With many stops, we move on.

Oct. 24.
In Cottbus [East Germany] we wake up. While getting up, we write letters and smuggle them [to a German mailbox] with the help of

German railway staff. Meal: meat broth with noodles. At 3 PM in Frankfurt/Oder, border crossing, the first Polish soldiers. The land behind the river Oder is deserted [the Germans had been driven out], barren, and uncultivated. In Schneidemühl [Polish authorities had not yet changed the names of the towns from German to Polish] dinner: millet and beans. That evening until around 10 PM we entertained ourselves by candlelight, waiting for the promised coffee. It never came. Two eggs [for a family of 6] and bread are distributed. We try new sleeping arrangements. I sleep relatively well. Mutti [a diminutive word for Mutter (mother), a common German way of referring to his wife, the mother of his children] and Dieter sleep very tightly confined. (NB. The mail did arrive in Munich). About 150 Germans with children of all ages are on the train. It seems that many trains left at the same time and all of Junkers seems to be on their way to a new elsewhere. Every family has an [assigned] freight car containing their furniture.

Oct. 25.
Get up at 7 AM. Wash, tried a new sleeping arrangement, clean up. The heavy wooden boxes served as fill between the two seating benches of our compartment to make a bed. Breakfast plentiful. No one is hungry anymore. Weather is becoming wintry. Sky cloudy, the landscape, Polish. Small, isolated houses, a few cattle, few people. In Kutno [a city 80 miles west of Warsaw] a catered meal. Real coffee. We meet a second trainful of Dessauers. Renate, who was overtired and stressed out [over the unsettling events] to this point, becomes herself again. In our environs are few other children. In the neighboring compartment are two, in the rest of the wagon only married couples and a 17-year-old boy. The doctor makes rounds. He speaks good German. It's 3 PM and it's already getting dusky. The stays at the stations are getting longer and longer. In the evening we ride past the lights of Warsaw over the Vistula River bridge. Later bread and biscuits, group singing with the people in the neighboring compartment.

Oct. 26.
In the morning we are close to Brest [in Poland on the Belarus border] but don't go any further. Stay for hours at the border crossing. Polish women and children trade butter, white bread, bacon, sausage. We had no local money. For trading 1 pack of cigarettes, I get 5 white bread rolls. For 5 packs, 1 pound of butter. The border guards try to prevent trading. More mail smuggling with German-speaking railway workers. Will these last letters from Brest get to home? (NB: No, they never got there) At 4 PM over the Bug River. Clock is set to 6 PM. The last 20km

at a snail's pace to Brest. Arrival at 8 PM. Across the platform is our new Russian train with sleeping car, 3rd class. We have more space. Then to the station building for dinner: noodle soup, roasted meat, mashed potatoes, tea. Restaurant spacious and clean though dirty in the corners. Large paintings, a bit barbaric. At midnight a company of soldiers shows up and starts reloading to the Russian train.[1] They sing and laugh a lot. They are very careful when transloading. At 2 AM our car is ready. Watching the transfer, Mutti notices that many things which she thought were left behind in Vietzen have indeed come with us. At 2:30 the train leaves. We sleep in two bunkbed layers. It is very hot. Someone has an accordion in the car.

Oct. 27.
Late getting up. We slept badly because of the heat. We fold the bunks away and settle in relatively comfortably. Sigrid darns and draws. Outside very foggy. At 2 PM it clears up and a wide endless plain is evident. The houses are getting smaller and smaller. The people in the stations are poor, just like our former Eastern workers. They want to sell a few eggs, some milk. We have no rubles [Russian currency], and the prices are very high. 3 PM in Baranovich, nice weather. Large marshalling yard. Continue through slightly undulating land, a variety of larger and smaller wooden houses. Snow. In the evening, a train station with a large wooden warehouse. The farmers come with small wagons and offer potatoes, cabbage, grain. Open freight wagons [gondolas] are evidently used to transport people. In the dark, dinner at about 8 PM, actually lunch, since it was forgotten earlier. For dinner we wait until 2 AM in the restaurant of Baranovich station. Small and cramped. At 3 AM we finally get to sleep.

Oct. 28.
8 AM we wake up. Clear weather, about 2 degrees C (35 degrees F). We are south of Minsk [capital of Belarus]. Long queues at the washroom, breakfast: 2 eggs and tea, beds straightened. Mutti succumbs to being overstressed. In Mogilev about 11 AM. Flat land, wide valley, narrow ravines. Many small wooden houses with white church mixed in. Factories. The area becomes lonelier, always flat. Only wooden houses, forest, little cultivated land. Cold east wind. It becomes cloudy, as far as we can see only forest, heath, and groups of the small wooden houses. Traces of war are limited to destroyed bridges and burnt-out

---

1 European trains cannot operate on track of the Russian gauge hence a transfer is required. Legend has it that the Russian rail gauge is wider (by 3½in) than the European standard to thwart any European invasion of the Russian Empire.

factory buildings. The rumor mill says we are going to Kuybyshev on the Volga. At 4 PM a station built of wood. Sigrid draws. Mutti is feeling a little better. Some music. The doctor arrives. Sergeyev[1] makes a tour stop. In the evening arrive in Roslav. Dinner is cancelled. Mutti worse in the evening: diarrhea, vomiting. The Russian doctor was very concerned about us. In the evening he played German folk songs on his accordion.

Oct. 29.
Get up at 8 AM. Mutti has to stay down. Sigrid also vomited, also stays in bed. Dad does room service. We travel towards Tula, south of Moscow. Few settlements, wide forests, broad heights, steppe, monotonous plain, all poor. Weather cloudy. Past Kaluga. Russian churches, rivers. Mutti sleeps a lot. Better towards evening. Dinner of dried milk, sugar, and dry bread with preserved plums. The stations are not indicated in our small map. In the evening toward Tula with a promised stop. 11:30 PM Tula, at last. Dinner with Dieter and Christa in the station restaurant. Small, with carved square wooden columns. Molded rubber tree models [decorations] on the tables. Service girls with white bonnets and dirty blouses. All primitive and eastern. 1 AM in bed.

Oct. 30.
Get up at 8 AM. Mutti is still staying down but feels better. Sigrid gets up, darns stockings. I do bed service. Hot water from the locomotive. Some poor Russian peasant women with chickens, miserably preserved cucumbers, all in small quantities. Chicken for 20 R [rubles]. Land stretches with rich, dark soil. Every now and then larger cultivated areas. Some larger towns. 3:30 PM Ryazhsky, wide, spread-out "city". Houses dirty, old. Two-story wooden houses with carved beams and posts. No forest, black earth.

Oct. 31.
3:30 PM we cross the Volga. At 6 PM we are supposed to be in Kuybyshev. Is that where we are headed? About 8 PM we arrive Kuybyshev station. Our bedding is collected but Sergeyev is not revealing any plans. We continue into mountainous and wooded terrain. [German] prisoners of war work in quarries as we pass slowly and wave to us. The access paper slips for our quarters are distributed. One for the woman, one for the man. On deciphering them, we had our

1 Probably a Russian in charge of communicating with the Germans

first of many disappointments. Our note reads: "Family House no. 35, Apartment 14, Room 1." We don't want to believe that they arranged for 1 room of 25 square meters [270 sq. ft.] to be occupied by 6 persons. Everybody compares their documents. The interpreter translates but there is nothing better. At 4 PM we stop at our station of Krasnaya Glinka. Several military officers are waiting for us, the women and children are picked up in buses. The men wait for the unloading carts. There are too few [carts] and it takes a long time till we have one. It is dark and cold. At 10 PM our furniture is loaded onto 3 carts. Off we go! I can already see lights and two-story houses. We stop in front of a large four-story [brick] house (Steinhaus). Staircase with central heating, everything seems modern. Mutti is waiting in the apartment. The children are settled on the floor. The furniture is unloaded in front of the house. Some of it comes up into the apartment. Then the helping staff disappears. It starts to snow. All our furniture is still outside. I work with Mutti. We drag it in. It is exhausting. Beds upstairs. Cover the furniture outside. Later on, Mr. K.[1] and I help each other. At 3 AM, two helpers appear! We now bring all the furniture upstairs or at least into the hallway. At 5 AM I go to sleep with Mutti and the children in our bedroom. There is one large room with a tiny radiator for heat. The whole apartment has 3 rooms, small kitchen, bathroom without tub. In our room we have only beds, no space for cupboards or table.

[Kurt's daughter, Sigrid, was kind enough to sketch the floorplan of the apartment (see plates section). It was originally planned to serve one family but, in this case, two were squeezed into it. The descriptive words in German are Bett (bed), Tür (door), Clo (toilet), Durchgang (passage), Tisch (table), Wasser (water: sink), and Herd (oven-cook surface), and Flur (hallway), to cite the most relevant ones. The second family shared the kitchen and the toilet. The bedroom held five beds so that its approximate size is about 12x15 feet. It was tight with small night tables fitting in as shown. Sigrid notes that her sister Christa slept on the couch. Mutti had a Singer sewing machine under the lamp ("Lampe") where she would make clothing of all sorts, often far into the night. Note the long path between the kitchen and the dining table. There are small discrepancies between the words in the text and this sketch.

To stay on the subject of space for living, Sigrid notes that occasional "whole body bathing" was made possible behind a curtain across the kitchen corner near the sink. Personal hygiene and the securing of privacy were significant challenges. She writes further that there were bathing

---

1 Pflügel identifies an individual by a single last name beginning letter so that their identity remains private.

facilities she calls a "Russian sauna" available at times in a nearby building. In it was a large room with stone seats and spigots with running hot and cold water together with buckets and ladles with which to dowse oneself, but no bathtubs or showers. Unavoidably, she says, the group bathing was an introduction to the role that aging plays out on the human body!

In addition to the running water, there was a very hot and steamy conventional sauna heated by wood burners. The adjacent washroom was all that was available for keeping bodies clean at times. The Germans avoided this dirty facility when possible, however, because of the ever-present infestation by lice and other bugs in the changing rooms and lockers. At various other times, the facilities were used by the inmates of the nearby prison camps.]

Where are we?

[The specialists (engineers and technicians) and their families were brought to a place called Uprawlentscheskij Gorodok (modern spelling: Upravlencheskiy), a settlement where an aircraft engine building plant was to be expanded. The location is 20km upstream from Kuybyshev on the Volga and 6km from the railroad station at Krasnaya Glinka. The word "expanded" means that there was a plant there before 1946 and yet, as we shall see, the Soviets regard 1946 as the start year for the engine plant in the commemorations described later in our story.]

First day of settling in – lots of things to do:

1. Sergeyev arrives in the morning. We complain bitterly that the apartment is too small for 6 people. He advises us to take the living room as ours, stipulating also that no one should know that he made that suggestion. We move in. That makes things somewhat better. A bedroom for 6 people and large living room subdivided by wardrobes.
2. Cash withdrawal 5000 R [rubles] and food stamps with special allocation: 1 kg butter, 1 kg sugar or chocolate, food stuffs, coffee beans. After an hour of queuing, it's all in our hands. More stuff is arriving.
3. Short trip to the sanatorium [the word is used here to describe a combination resort/recreational facility and a facility to provide short-term rest and medical services]. Wonderful view of the Volga with mountains and forests. The market is attractive and interesting, but the prices are steep. We feel rich and think we get 5000 rubles every month.

4. The first neighbors arrive. Ing. R. family of four. According to documents, they are assigned to live in what is our bedroom (no.2). We refer them to room no. 3. They also have a lot of furniture and don't know where to put it. Two children. On the good side, they are Rhinelanders and Mutti enjoys hearing familiar, native voices. The next few days pass quickly with cleaning, shopping. The weather is dry and frosty. When it thaws everything turns into mud. At the market I buy a primitive electric hotplate. This has somewhat helped with the shortage of wood and the difficulty of using it in the central brick oven.
5. Asked Sergeyev where the scheduled 3rd family should stay. He has only excuses and is no help. He implies vague threats if I persist in discussing the matter further. We expect difficulties.
6. Wednesday morning, the third family arrives. Ing. K. The colonel [Sergeyev's supervisor] comes in person with the quartering documents and decides that R. must go to his assigned room no. 2 and K. in room no. 3. We are horrified. I explore other possibilities without finding anything better. A man referred to as a house "commander" gives me the tip that there are still apartments available in the next house. We go to the top story. Inconclusive! Mutti comes along. We do not give way. Finally, Ivanov (?) and this house Kommandant arrive and tell us they managed to get another apartment for K. We are finally secure to set up [in their apartment with the extra room].
7. 4 holiday days. All transport material has arrived. 1,500–2,000 Germans in the compound. In the shop and in the market, large crowds. In the Magazin (store) soon no more goods. The goods are not resupplied. On the free market, prices are rising. 1 kg butter 150 R, Honey 100 g. 130 R., Pork 60 R., Milk 15 R.
8. Assembly is convened in the Clubhouse [in German "Klub," a community building]. Colonel Olechnovich [the military manager of the Junkers factory in Dessau until moved here] says that we have been "invited" to Russia. The work begins today. First, pass[1] photos and registration. Winter clothing cannot be provided. The situation seems grim. We are very pessimistic and depressed. In my first letter to Munich [to his mother] I write "we lost all hope."

[Before November 1946

Regarding the houses into which the German specialists moved, there exists an article with the title "Memories of my time as a POW in

1 Here, a pass is an ID document. Passports were not issued.

Uprawlentscheskij" translated from German. Sigrid Karkavelas had a copy and shared the following from it.

The author, Kurt Genske (1920–2011), was a soldier in the Wehrmacht who had surrendered to the US Army who then turned him over to the Soviets. He was put into POW camp 7234/4, one of several in Uprawlentscheskij.[1] There he worked as a locksmith and mechanic starting with work in the Sanatorium building. It was soon rumored that a contingent of specialists from the German air industry were going to be settled here. "We had to build the Finn houses and a large group of us had to get the heating and waste-water systems of the stone houses 35 and 45 in working order. My specific task was to install and repair radiators in numbers appropriate for the sizes of the apartments." The comments made by Kurt Pflügel about the heating system in particular bears witness to the degree that Genske's tasks were accomplished. Undoubtedly, the resources available to for repair were limited.

Genske continues "I had no contact with the German specialists during my work on these houses. At the time the stone (brick) houses were occupied by Russian families who had to vacate the buildings and relocate just before the specialists arrived." He stayed in one of several local POW camps until 1948 when he was allowed to return to Germany. Neither he nor his fellow prisoners ever encountered the specialists, except perhaps accidentally.

German POWs in America

The reader may wonder about the treatment of German POWs in American hands. They were brought to the US by the thousands and typically spent the last two years of the war and a year or two after VE Day in servitude to American enterprises that needed labor. Most of that labor was demanded by the agricultural sector of the American economy where the depletion of men by the military services was profound. The POWs were safe from war. They were fed, housed, and their health needs were largely met. How well can be argued. They provided labor. The totality of POW experiences in America is beyond description in a short paragraph or two and yet the topic deserves mention.

One example is described in the book by Koop detailing the experience of POWs dispatched to cut pulp wood in the forests of the

---

1 The number 7234 refers to the Kuybyshev region. According to former POW Wilhelm Klein (see Bibliography), there were 15 POW prison camps in the area and Klein spent time in 4 of them, including Genske's no. 4.

US state of New Hampshire. The work was hard and stressful. What is difficult to appreciate and well described in the book is the complexity of interactions between the Germans who were either pro- or anti-Nazi or neither, the guards, the military camp management that presumably enforced or overlooked rules prohibiting fraternization with Americans nearby, the community in which the camp was located, the contractor receiving the wood and last, but not least, the federal government and the public political opinion that shaped its actions. The prisoners and the locals were human beings with much cultural commonality. Interactions between them were inevitable and human. These tended to improve with time and contact. However, the forced viewing of films of concentration camp atrocities, once they were discovered, sent the feelings between American keepers and German POWs into turmoil. Bitterness, anger, vengeance was heaped on the former German soldiers who were largely conscripted. They likely had no part in and little (if any) knowledge of the inhuman Nazi horrors. After VE Day, the US government sought to quickly return the POWs to Germany but the US military government in Germany was not ready to have them there and their labor was still needed on American farms. After all, for Americans, the war did not end in May 1945. Some who had lost everything wanted to stay which was impossible, of course. Deportation from the US was jumbled over the first postwar years and was not necessarily repatriation to any part of Germany but to Britain and other places in Europe to provide work for the immense and necessary repair of almost everything.

In terms of the American experiences contrasted to the Russian ones, both sets of prisoners were freed from fighting, both labored for reparations and returned to Germany. Those from America generally were treated more humanely, ate better, and were repatriated sooner. During the war, the feeding of German POWs in American hands was relatively generous because there were American POWs in German hands, and the hope was for treatment reciprocity. After the war, however, the rations for Germans working on US soil were reduced or tied to the meeting of sometimes harsh work output goals.

In later years, some of the POWs exposed to life in North America found their way back to the US or Canada via the immigration process when that possibility became available.

In Russia, few people ate well, least of all the POWs. The Russian treatment of these individuals undoubtedly led to significant numbers of deaths.]

Chapter 11

UPRA (OR UPRAWLENTSCHESKIJ GORODOK)

[Of the total number of abductees to Russia, the number taken to Upra was about 645 specialists. The number of Germans in that location was 2,200 of which 900 were children. Over the years, about 60 children were born to this group.[1]

The following word description of the Upra complex by Pflügel takes the reader into the area. Helmut Breuninger put together the sketch which I reproduced to better orient the reader. In the sketch, made from memory in the mid 1960s, north is roughly at the top of the image. No scale is indicated. It displays the relative positions of buildings and their function. The detailed notation is in the original German with specific places of interest as follows:

The Zavod buildings are grouped around [10], the wooden houses [18], the stone houses [43], and the Finn houses [51]. Section [43] is the location of schools, clinics, etc. Specific locales of interest are road to Kuybyshev [1], road to Krasnaya Glinka [2], road to the ravine [3], bread foundry [22], Club house [17], Sanatorium [58], cemetery [54], bath house [42], river dock [59], among others noted. The bathing facilities cited by Sigrid are [42].

In the remainder of this and the following chapter, a number bounded by [square brackets] is a location reference on the site map.

We continue in the voice of Kurt Pflügel.]

1 Personal communication from Karl Breuninger

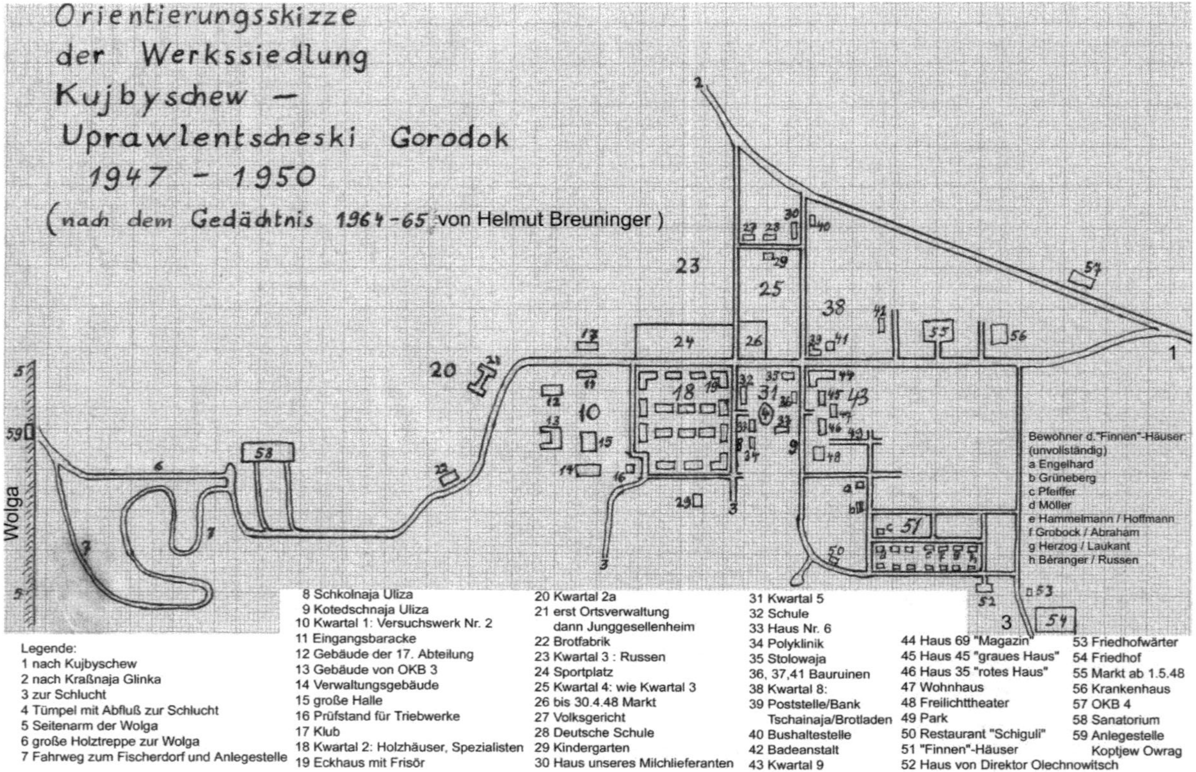

A sketch map of the Upra complex made by Helmut Breuninger. The references are in German. The word “Kwartal” means “quarter.” Stolovaya (35, dining room), Volksgericht (27, courthouse), Friedhof (54, cemetery), etc. Note that the gyro expert Möller resided in the Finn house area. (Courtesy Karl Breuninger).

Are we to spend the coming years here, where we unloaded??

The next morning when we woke up in our new quarters, we took in the larger world outside our windows. We had an unobstructed view of a mountain ridge wooded with deciduous trees and of a stream ravine running out of it. To the southwest, wandering into the distance, was the shore area of the otherworldly Volga landscape. In the foreground, a paved road ran in front of our house. There were crumbling house foundations, the construction of which had probably begun some time ago and was subsequently abandoned. Behind them the ground fell off a bit and further on were groups of two-story houses, partly stucco, partly log cabins. Another large four-story building, made of yellowish and red bricks, stood out. It was the Russian school building. From the larger of our rooms, the window offered a view into a now leafless forest. In the foreground was a white and blue painted windowless building covered with wooden board siding. It turned out to be the summer cinema and theater. A footpath meandered toward the forest. To its left, obviously part of the summer theater, stood a kind of pavilion, decorated with ornaments, and further to the left, was a brick residence building where it appears that work was halted during the construction of the second floor.

I couldn't stay in the apartment. I had to explore the surrounding area. The road on which we had arrived yesterday, ran in front of the house from the south on the left to north. Proceeding on it and looking to the right there was a little side road with another four-story, somewhat older-looking building on our side of the road. Furniture was still heaped in front of it. More Germans were apparently moving in. It was a house with 45 apartments [46]. I came to an intersection with another paved road running east-west. At my corner was yet another four-story brick building [44] with the official state shop, called the "Magazin," on the ground floor. Russian officers and engineers with whom we will be working lived on the upper floors. On the other side of the street from this long stone house was a wooden structure. It had the post office on the ground floor. In front of it, there was a bus stop [40?] frequented by old, rumbling, boxy buses taking people from here to the city of Kuybyshev. In the direction of that city, one could see the road climbing up a gentle, wooded hill. The street on which I had come extended beyond the intersection and was lined on both sides by two-story wooden houses spaced at intervals. Further on, the road became more primitive. These houses seemed to have no water supply and no toilets. The drinking water was provided by wells at the edge of the road. Between pairs of buildings were outhouses and wooden sheds.

These places became a haven for vermin and source of much stench during the months of summer.

The road also led to Krasnaya Glinka station, where we arrived a day ago. The buses also went there. If one followed the crossing east-west road to the left, a two-story white building with cornices and columns stood out. It faced our residential buildings and was the factory kitchen and canteen, the "Stolovaya," [35] meaning "dining hall" but was, in actuality, a basic, utilitarian cafeteria. The workers and engineers could have lunch and dinner there if they choose not to eat at home. Further on, next to the road, a narrow, asphalted footpath was for our daily commute to work. Here, in the morning, at noon, and in the evening, the workers and engineers hurried in tight groups to and from work. Finally, a short distance further, after passing some more wooden houses, we reached the factory's boundary fence. It was unpainted, wooden, 2.5 to 3 m high, topped with barbed wire. The site boundary was dominated by watchtowers along the fence. The timbered main entrance and the gate house with heavy double wooden doors gave access to the factory [10] through an entrance building [11]].

On the opposite of the road was an outdoor market with three rows of wobbly and dilapidated stalls where the peasants and the locals sold their goods to the workers from the factory, usually when the workday was finished. Next to it was the two-story House of Representation, the "Clubhouse" [or the "Klub"] [17] of the plant [a community-oriented building external to the factory], built of wood with gable decorations and columns around its entrance. The walls were hung with large colorfully painted posters calling out appeals to be better and do better. Red flags everywhere as were images of Lenin and Stalin. The Club was the cultural center of the village. In it was a large hall with a stage for concerts and assemblies, a library, and smaller rooms for dancing, music, and for playing chess.

[The Clubhouse was also a movie theater where German and American movies sub-titled in German and Russian and dating from the 1930s were available and shown at intervals. The collection had been "liberated" by the Red Army from the UFA film studios in Babelsberg near Berlin. (Singer)]

The road ran further on over a sparsely built-up landscape with individual wooden houses. A large turn to the South took it to a steep cliff above the edge of the Volga revealing the brightly lit and decorated building of the sanatorium. Several German families were temporarily housed there because not all the residences had been readied in time for their arrival. It was a place for rest and relaxation for workers of the nearby air industry factory.

In front of and to the right of this building on a hillside was a one-story stone building with a very large metal chimney: the state bakery [22]. We quickly designated this building as the "bread foundry" because the black Russian bread contained so much water that it could not be baked in loaves. Instead, the dough was poured into bread pan forms. The finished bread was gummy and turned out to be very useful for sealing cold air leaks in the windows during the winter.

All the houses [18] along the road were identical and laid out with generous spaces between them. They were attractive with nice proportions. Overall, one got the impression of a generously laid out town of farmhouses. It did not take long, however, to appreciate the primitive state of the construction and the neglected interiors. Loudspeakers that broadcast all programs of the Moscow radio station, morning, noon, and night, were mounted on the high posts of the streetlights.

As I came to an intersection which seemed to be the center of this town [31], I saw soldiers in blue uniforms with gray fur caps. My knowledge of Russian was sufficient to ask one for the name of the town where we were. He gave me a long word that could not be understood by German ears. He recognized my problem and tried to say, again more precisely and slowly, the word "Uprawlentscheskij Gorodok" [spelled Upravlencheskiy on Google Maps]. The words mean "administration city". The older name was apparently Krasnaya Glinka or "Red Clay." It became apparent that we were not in an older settlement but somewhere with a recently changed official designation describing its function. [The station retained the old name. Modern maps show Upra and the Kuznetsov factory to be in Krasnya Glinka.]

Before the war, Upravlencheskiy Gorodok was to be the location of a large hydroelectric facility named for the nearby town of Kuybyschev. The present buildings were planned to serve the engineering and development community associated with the power plant. The abandoned foundations suggested that the employees for the construction of the power plant, and later for running it, were planned to be housed here. I learned that all this infrastructure was not needed when it was decided that the dam and power station should be located further upstream on the Volga. This semi-finished facility was our new home.

To ease the pronunciation of the town, the German community reduced the long name to "Upra" and the residents became Upra-people.

The town was about 100 meters above the river. From our window we could see a ravine with a smaller stream that emptied into the river. At this confluence, there was a floating dock for boats [59]. During the summer months ferries connected Upra with the more important nearby city of Kuybyshev. Besides this rather romantic water travel, buses served the same purpose. In winter, the river was generally frozen over and the streets deeply covered by snow so that the bus remained as the only option for travel to the city.

The first few days after our arrival were bitterly cold. The ground was frozen hard with only a small dusting of snow here and there.

The residences

The German families were accommodated in three groups of houses. These groups were widely separated and different in architectural design. We called them the "brick houses" (Steinhaus), the "wood houses," and the "Finn houses." In the early years of our stay, these housing groups were quite separate from the residences for Russians who were then housed in distant corners of the complex. Social contact between Russians and Germans was virtually non-existent at that time.

Brick houses

The two four-story brick buildings were most city-like. They stood, not far apart, on one side of the main road and were designated as House 35 and House 45. The numbers indicated how many apartments were supposedly in them. The various apartments had 2 and 3 rooms with kitchen and a toilet room [a WC in the parlance of the day]. House 35 had several relatively large rooms. We were lucky in that we obtained accommodation in that house with two rooms of about 270 and 160 square feet for our family of six. This was just what we needed to be able to use the furniture that came with us. The kitchen furniture stayed back in Germany.

From the outside, the house made a reasonably good impression. The disappointment came when we saw the uncared for and sloppy state of its interior. During our early years, the electric system and the central heating barely functioned. Many a winter evening was spent sitting and shivering in rooms with temperatures between 50 and 55F with candlelight casting weak shadows on the walls. When a winter storm struck, no amount of sealing windows, doors, etc., kept the cold wind out. The annual routine was to seal every possible cold air path in October allowing just one little openable window to supply "fresh" air from interior spaces in the building.

The large brick and tile kitchen oven [for house heat] with its cooking surface was very poorly built. It leaned to one side and its working surface was quite a bit off horizontal. The wood burning in it did not draft properly and often filled the room with smoke. The women in our community used it as infrequently as possible, preferring an electric hot plate or a petrol burner [with its risk of carbon monoxide poisoning] for the preparation of meals. The 90 sq. ft. floor area was dominated by the tiled brick oven. The kitchen space became a refuge for us and for the neighboring couple when the winter evenings were very cold. It was the warmest place available where the four adults and six children could review the happenings of the day in relative warmth. Heat from the wood-fired stove sometimes had to be augmented with heat from the hot plate(s), rewired to produce more heat. Engineers know how to do this! Relief from the daily stress was sometimes created by singing Rhineland songs. Their words portrayed an idyllic life in the German countryside and for us were a source of gallows humor.

As the years went by, these houses decayed steadily. It seems that care and maintenance were not a part of any plan. Broken windows in the stairways were replaced by plywood because glass was not available. The stucco fell off. The pipes rusted through. The frost-damaged radiators could not be replaced. The situation became barely manageable, and, by the end of our stay, the doors just hung loosely by their hinges.

In the years 1950 and 1951, some of the German families returned home[1] [as we shall see in Chapter 19] and vacated their apartments. Those of us who had to remain hoped for more room but, alas, there was the prospect of Russian families ready to move in. They had also been living in very tight quarters, but since they did not want to [or were not allowed to] live among Germans, the rooms were indeed freed up and each departure led to moves from one apartment to another, a kind of game of musical apartments. The space available was, in fact, never better or greater and we continued to struggle with delipidated dwellings.

Wood houses

The wooden two-story houses were closer to the factory. Most of these buildings had two rooms with a kitchen and several entrances. The houses assigned to Germans had running water and a WC. Heat was provided by a large wood-burning brick oven. The buildings were Russian in style and appeared to be comfortable.

1 The early tranches of returnees were from the lower labor levels.

In one of the wood houses, a single room within a shared apartment was the assigned living quarters for the German chief engineer Brandner.

Finn houses

The Finn houses were built between the brick houses and the nearby forest that ended at the ravine whose creek waters went into the Volga. It appeared that these single-story wooden houses were prefabricated in Finland and were used by the American advisors present during the war. As a consequence, they ware termed the *Amihäuser* [American houses] by some. They were typically located in pairs with the kitchens adjacent to one another. The trees near them were part of the still uncleared forest. When we arrived, there were German POWs assembling these buildings. The new arrivals who expected to move in were temporarily housed in the sanatorium. These Finn houses appeared to us to be little more than an aggregation of typical weekend garden houses common in Germany. Next to each house was a very primitive outhouse [or, as a German might say, a Plumpsklo!]. In Germany, a heart shaped opening would have been carved into the door. Water had to be dragged in from one of the several wells [probably outdoor water faucets subject to freezing in winter] distributed throughout the group of buildings. A little garden area was laid out adjacent to the houses, but the residents had to clear the land. When they did, they were happy to find beautiful, rich black soil. These plots provided an appreciated advantage of being able to grow potatoes and vegetables for the betterment of their diets. Some of the more ambitious people were even able to raise goats. The Finn houses had agricultural advantages but in winter with deep snow, life was hard, particularly for the "soft" city dwellers who were assigned to live there.

The assignment to one of the three groups of houses was not a matter of equality, but a reflection of the person's place in the work organization. The brick houses were assigned primarily to department heads and people with advanced academic degrees. For example, about 75 families lived in House 35 [75 families in 35 apartments!] where some had enough stature to occupy generous square footage. People with specific technical skills were housed in the wooden houses, whereas ordinary workers were assigned to the Finn houses. The pay-scale for the various individuals paralleled this hierarchy. The size of the family was not a factor in determining the size of the apartment or the number of rooms. Organization status mattered. The adjustment to a fairer, more "German", arrangement where family size in relation to living space mattered took time. The monthly rent was 57 R which was cheap when compared to the cost of food and other consumer goods. There was a Russian rental cost normalizing system where the maximum area per person was 80 square feet, and a luxury fee was imposed for families who occupied a larger per person space. If a family of three had been accommodated in our unit, they would have paid about twice as much as we did. I was left with the reality that, as far as the Russians were concerned, our unit was just right for our family of 6 not to be paying the luxury premium!

One universal feature of the apartments was that they shared one common key for all doors. We called it the "Volga key." There were no doorbells and door knocking [with agreed-to knocking codes[1]] became de rigueur. The other common feature was the presence of cockroaches. They were the worst in the Finn houses and the least problematic in the brick buildings, although present in every crack of wherever wood was part of the buildings' structure. These creatures appeared instantaneously in newly constructed buildings. It was a hopeless fight to eliminate them until a large shipment of DDT arrived from (East) Germany. Chemical warfare was needed to win against the pests.

The long trip from Dessau to the Volga allowed for lively discussions about our fates. The optimists were the loudest in their pronouncements. Wasn't life under the Russians in Dessau a good thing? they asked. The disappointments were, however, deep and frequent. The first were the accommodations. Closely behind that was the desperately poor provision of daily necessities by an economic system that did not function well.

The soldiers who packed our furnishings grabbed and loaded everything from our houses in Germany. Many families had so much they could not place what they had into the apartments provided. These people were the fortunate ones having been able to save their possessions from the ravages of war. Others who arrived with almost nothing were far less fortunate. They were the people bombed out of their homes or driven out of them by the tides of war. They came to Dessau for work and found it there but quickly found themselves whisked off to Russia, still with very little. All abducted families were pushed into very small quarters, regardless of the number of people in the family and the amount of stuff that had arrived with them. Out of necessity, a kind of market arose among the Germans where excess materiel was sold to those in need.

1 To properly prepare for inspections by Russian officials (hiding hotplates, for example), the electric power use assessor, in particular.

The economic conditions

[Pflügel advises the reader to interpret the value of the ruble in effect in 1946 (at the time of the writing around 1974) by dividing the given values by ten.[1] That is probably of little help to the modern reader.]

With rents set so low, it was no surprise to find that everything else is very expensive. When we arrived, we were given 5000 rubles. The amount varied with the status[2] of the recipient. We rejoiced at this amount thinking it was to be our monthly salary and went shopping. We were lucky to be among the early arrivals because the state store (the Magazin) had plenty of butter, sugar, chocolate, even coffee beans. In a very short time, however, the store was empty, and the later arrivals had to contemplate empty shelves. The coupons in their hands entitling them to certain goods brought nothing. Often, even with cash and coupons, only a fraction, or perhaps none of a shopper's needs could be satisfied. There was never enough. When the Magazin got new supplies, there were always long lines of people waiting to get what they could. The question in our minds was always whether planners had miscalculated, the supplies simply did not exist, or had somebody diverted part of what there was to the "free market?" We soon noticed that a few days after new supplies were delivered, the same items would be available to buy from private free market dealers at many times the price.

The Soviet Union had two economic systems. One was through the state stores with show windows to display what's new and supposedly available but often wasn't. These were open night and day and staffed by state workers. The prices were fixed by the bureaucracy. The other one was a free market running next to the official market. This market existed for peasant farmers to sell what they could produce "on the side." Officially, the prices were to be set lower than the official ones for the same item. They weren't. These "free" markets or "bazaars" were officially sanctioned to exist and held in formal covered booths at appropriate locations. Most transactions were carried by individuals sitting on the ground amidst their wares and making deals with passers-by.

[In an economy with shortages, people are desperate and resort to thievery to survive. The writing of the POW Wilhelm Klein provides

1 Meaning that the ruble had increased in value in that time.

2 Status in a country where social strata supposedly did not exist! According to Breuninger, the Germans were paid about twice the salaries of their Russian counterparts and within the Germans, the salaries varied from 7,000 rubles at the top, to 1,250 at the bottom of the pay scale. The median salary was about 2,200 rubles.

examples of his observations when he was assigned to work for a time in a flour mill. Employed there were three groups of workers: the POWs who did the heavy work, the ordinary Russian workers, and the security people watching the workers to make sure that nothing improper took place. The Russian workers diverted or stole flour on small and large scales. The large-scale bounty found its way onto the resale black market. Klein could not say how but it surely involved miscounting or misplacing sacks and likely involved cooperation of the people watchers. On the small scale, the process was delicate because getting caught by the watchers and by the gate guards on leaving the mill was serious for the Russians and very serious for the POWs. He describes two methods used by the Russians. One involved cutting a sack, mixing the flour with water in the sidelined sack, and making a batch of dough, clandestinely of course. During the workday, small chunks of the dough would be wrapped (or not) and thrown over the boundary wall, hopefully unobserved, just as the Russian workers ended their shift and were subjected to exit searches. The dough balls would be retrieved once the workers were on the other side of the wall. Another method involved making a sheet of dough, somewhat like a pizza bottom and pasting that to the naked back of a worker, covering it with his shirt, and exiting the mill ... with fingers crossed.]

The state-provided goods were never offered in sufficient quantities. In Upra, for example, during all our years, there were never fresh vegetables, eggs, milk, or fresh meat. Items like these were available only in the free market. The amounts of butter or cooking oils were meager. Flour was available only on special holidays.[1] Prices went according to the law of supply and demand. When the state prices fell, so did the free market prices. The price differential, however, was always substantial. Butter might be price at 66 R a kilo [2.2 lbs.] in the Magazin or 150–200 on the market. Typical market prices were 15 R for a liter of milk, 80–120 R for a kilo of pork, and 17 R for a kilo of potatoes. The arrival of the Germans late in the season and their sheer numbers made for tight supplies of all commodities and that brought higher prices. Compounding the economic problem was that the Germans were relatively well paid by the state so that market prices rose for the Germans arrivals by a factor of 3–5 from what had been the norm in prior times. Bread, butter, and other groceries were sold in the Magazin when they were available. The ration coupons were generous and seemed to us to be better than those rumored to apply in West

1 It seems that noodles were more available, and these were ground to make "Ersatz-flour" to make a cake or to thicken a thin soup.

Germany. We had no way of knowing the reality, however. The worst aspect was a lack of access to potatoes, vegetables, and foods with vitamins and minerals. We consequently paid a severe health price for the seven years we spent in Russia.

[The purchasing procedure at the Magazin was as follows: one approaches the cash register, orders what is wanted and pays for it with cash or coupons or both. The cashier provides a slip that is handed to a person behind the counter in exchange for the goods (Singer).]

The ration coupons were discontinued when currency reform took hold on 1 January 1948. We hoped for better times, but it was just the beginning of more calamity. Nothing really changed. The span of time between the Magazin running out and the arrival of new supplies did not shorten, not in all seven years we were there. Life improved a bit but never to a point we considered normal.

Assembly

February 11, 1947. A note posted on the wooden entry column of the clubhouse entry called for a general assembly of all the technical specialists, only the men. We were to be herded together for a meeting of our small town, if one can call it that. We were to be handed over, for better or worse, to the "Zavod" [the factory, officially known as Experimental Factory No. 2, or OKB-2 for short] and its director, Col. Olechnovich. In the Dessau days after May 1945, he was the director there and was seen as an accommodating man. He was now showing another side of himself in his Russian language address to the group. We listened carefully to the awkward translation and tried to discern the double meanings of the words spoken by the translator. We hoped to better understand what was in store for us. The clues were vague, but he said: "We have invited you to the Soviet Union to learn to appreciate the accomplishments of socialism." Really?! I couldn't believe my ears! "Invited" – at gunpoint to this desolate place with our wives, our children, and all our belongings?

Olechnovich proceeded to tell us that the monies we have been given so far were "transition monies" to cover expenses of the move. We were advised to be frugal from then on because, beginning soon, the salaries would be substantially smaller. That was a heavy blow because our large family's cash reserves were already close to gone. That first "new" monthly paycheck was for 1,800 R at a time when a kilo of potatoes costs 8 R! What could we do? Sell stuff of course, our porcelain pieces, the little clothing that was of no use to us, furniture… Fortunately, I am a non-smoker so that the cigarettes in the provision packets could be sold.

Late in 1947, my salary grew to 3,000 R but prices were rising faster. On many occasions our 15-year-old Christa went to the market in Kuybyshev to find bargains and sell the stuff we did not need. We needed the money not just for food, but for warm clothing because all such clothing was plundered from our home in Vietzen during the time we were hiding elsewhere from the fighting. The lowest temperature here in Upra was -40F. We had no overcoats, no fur caps, no insulated boots, no gloves to traipse through deep snow on Sundays to find wood for the kitchen stove. That wood was supposed to be delivered but it never appeared. That first winter we lived in constant cold at home with very little relief when we worked in the offices.

Other ways to stay alive

In the spring of 1947, we were offered a piece of a meadow for use as a garden plot. The plot was an hour's walk from the apartment. The plot size was reasonable for our family, about 70 x 100 feet, but it required a lot of shovel work to make it productive because a major part of it was thickly covered in native grass. That summer, we lived on saltbush and nettles for greens while we waited to harvest our garden. Every father, even the most inexperienced city dwellers back in Germany, became a gardener that year. The entire family spent every bit of free time in the garden tilling, weeding, tending, and harvesting. The harvest was meant to augment the meager supplies for that winter and the following year until the next harvest. Our crop that summer was 600 kilos of potatoes, 300 of carrots, together with substantial amounts of cabbages and beans. We felt like real farmers. Fortunately, the weather was good that year. It was also good that an unspoken law of the land was not to steal from another's garden.

My wife took on a job as a sport and gymnastics coach to help out financially, even as she was fully occupied with household chores, assisted by only our children. Our income grew about 20–30% in 1948 but the toll was high. She was overcome with stress and overwork and finally had to give it up. Our lives returned to shortages and close encounters with poverty. Our clothing fell apart and a lot of time was spent by the women in the family repairing it as best they could. New articles were seldom affordable. Everyone in our ghetto shared the same misery and, in a way, that made life under these trying conditions more bearable. Our Russian colleagues did not fare much better, regardless of whether they were managers in the factory or party officials.

The lower ranks of workers, especially those with children, were in even greater misery. Every year and all summer long they gathered wood from distant places, sweating as they climbed the steep ravine walls of the nearby creeks and the bluffs along the river. This wood gathering led to a slow disappearance of the forest behind the summer theater. Officially this "destruction" of the forest was prohibited but the occasional watch patrol by Russian guards was quite ineffective at stopping it.

Many of the resourceful people increased their monetary incomes with crafts of all kinds. The reality was that the established handicraft collectives could not be counted on for supplying many needed items or services. So, we became part-time seamstresses, washwomen, cleaners, carpenters, shoe repairers, haircutters, etc. There was even a service for making eyeglasses. One young man used his skills as a stone mason to carve headstones for our dead. A nearby quarry was handy for the necessary rocks. For the many single men cooking was difficult. They consequently became temporary members of larger families to share midday meals. Such arrangements were made by subscription.

A particularly important and profitable service for enterprising women was "purchasing." The idea was to put together a list of what was needed within such an entrepreneur's circle of friends and go to the local markets or the stores in Kuybyshev to get it. Typically, a 10% surcharge was applied to the items delivered. The women who did this got to know their sources and developed good relations with these suppliers. It was a great service particularly for those who shied away from going into the city. Enterprises like these became small businesses providing community needs running in parallel with the official collectives.

From the very beginning, the German specialists had the option of sending funds to the Soviet Occupation Zone and later to East Germany. The sum was limited to half the monthly salary and the exchange rate was 2 Ostmarks[1] per ruble. At the beginning, the conditions here were so bad that few managed to send anything to relatives in Germany. As matters grew better, the high earning Germans, particularly those without families or children, deposited more and more into East German banks, hoping to be building a nest egg for an eventual return. As these dreams came closer to reality, the money transfer turned into a flood. Some sold their furniture to Russians who could afford it. The plan was to start anew in the Ostzone that was increasingly referred to as the GDR or, better said, the DDR by German speakers.

1 The Ostmark was the GDR currency after reform. The coinage was made of aluminum which symbolically emphasized the reality that the Ostmark was not a "hard" currency.

Some of our community would later testify that, in the last years, times were not really all that bad. They felt reasonably good about having accumulated some savings in Ostzone banks. Most, however, just scraped by. These individuals filled their hearts with bitterness and anger toward those who moved them to Russia against their wills and forced them to work under relentless pressure that served to diminish their self-worth and humanity.

Chapter 12

KUYBYSHEV – THE CITY

[Kurt Pflügel]

A visit to Kuybyshev by bus or boat was possible only with permission from the headquarters of the Russian residence administration. We were strictly forbidden to leave the small area around "our" houses. People wishing to make the trip to the city had to apply for a permit the day before a planned trip and pick it up that evening. The permit had to be surrendered upon returning so that the authorities could make certain that everyone had returned to the compound.

Kuybyshev was founded about 400 years ago. It had the eastern-sounding name of Samara before 1935 [and became Samara again in 1991]. The boat ride from our living complex to the city took about an hour. A trip would start at a dock located near the inflow of a creek issuing from a ravine on the left side of the Volga and took the traveler downstream to the city. A limestone cliff bounded the eastern side of the Volga and both sides of the ravine. Traveling by boat to the city, the river widened, and the higher ground revealed old romantic-style villas overlooking the waters where rich merchants lived in the "old days." Scattered huts of wood and mud were more recent additions to the shoreline and the land above the beaches. The right [western] bank of the river was, by contrast, rather flat and monotonous with hills in the distance.

The boat trip ended at the foot of the city where the station was a stop for ship and barge traffic between Moscow and the Caspian Sea. Over the years, large, white, modern, steam- and diesel ships were seen making calls. Smaller, new as well as old-fashioned, boats for trafficking to nearby places were abound. The station buildings were wooden and floated on the river to accommodate water level changes associated with the seasons. The foot-traffic of people going here and there was purposeful and resembled a beehive.

As one ventured into the city, a cobblestone covered street took the visitor uphill away from the water. Old, well used trams stumbled along the wide streets in the center of the old city. In its newer parts, the buildings, including an opera house, were of concrete in the heavy architectural style of the 1920s. Further out, the houses were almost all wooden with carved or sawn patterns decorating the siding boards and with fancier wooden sculpturing on the door and window frames. Where paint was called for, it was blue. We were reminded of toy houses.

The most frequently visited place in Kuybyshev was the big bazaar located further out from the city, in a flat area close to a large church with bell towers and golden domes. The general area was well trodden by people: hard and dusty in summer, frozen and covered by snow in winter, and muddy when it rains. Groups of people gathered in tight bunches where there was something to buy or haggle over. Buyers and sellers were everywhere trying to find one another, just like in any free market. It was, however, a black market with very high prices where rusty nails, barely functioning sewing machines, unpackaged single light bulbs, head coverings, and clothing of all sorts could be had. Even old American military radios! The German women quickly learned the art of haggling. They had to.

The people were an ethnic mixture, often dressed in colorful native clothing. In addition to the Russians, there were dark-skinned Tartars, black-haired gypsies, Cossacks, and descendants of the Volga-Germans. Further, driven here by evacuations from the West during the war were Jews, Poles, White Russians [Belarusians], and other members of the Soviet family of nations. Among all these, were uncountable numbers of beggars and the feared pickpockets who hung around the edges of the bazaar. The latter were a constant and inglorious aspect of Kuybyshev.

Most of the humanity at the market wore bleached jackets that were once blue and pants of quilted material all year, summer and winter. The footwear consisted of pressed goat hair boots [known as Walenkis] that reached up to the knees. Men's heads sported fur hats [Ushankas] or ex-military visor caps while the women typically wore wool cloths over their heads. The dress extremes include the fully down and out as well as well-dressed folks. The latter of these were usually curiosity seekers visiting the mayhem of the market, open to possibilities. For us, the market was always an attraction.

The Volga Germans

As we spent time in this area of Russia, it became clear on thoughtful reflection and certain experiences that we were living at the edge of the region settled by the Volga Germans. For example, on a visit to the city, the former Lutheran church of that community was pointed out to us. It was not a large building but unmistakably German in its style. A staircase leading upward to a portal topped by a square tower and finished with a peaked roof, the circular headings over windows, all without decorations, were typical of a Protestant church design. Several of the nearby houses were apparently owned by German merchants. Occasionally, we encountered descendants of these shy and retiring settlers who kept to themselves. [This population, though encouraged to settle in the area in the 18th century did not fare well under Stalin's purges. Many, if not most, were killed because they were not Russian enough and those who fled back to Germany during the war were not German enough!]

To our surprise, we discovered that the children's arithmetic books were in German! These books originated in Engels, the former capital of the Volga German Republic that was created after the Russian Revolution. We found many of the exercises were wrapped up with assumptions about the validity of the socialistic economic system's ground rules and consequently turned out to be very tricky to solve. Helping the children with their schoolwork involved extreme forms of frustration on the part of the fathers trying to be helpful. The exercises did not make sense to us!

One of the Russian history classes for our students from Dessau was covering the reign of Catherine II. The teacher did not want to believe the Tsarina was once a German princess in the house of Anhalt-Zerbst before she ascended the Russian throne. Zerbst was part of the area around Dessau and the Dessau children were very proud to be able to relate to the Tsarina in this way. In 1763, this powerful monarch launched a campaign to bring settlers to the region between Samara and the Caspian Sea. Farmers and skilled workers were especially welcomed to raise the productivity of a desolate land. Many people, especially Protestants, went by road and waterways to the area around the city of Engels. Unfortunately, starting in 1845, drought brought the colony to its knees. The purges during World War II and deportations [to cleanse Russia of non-Slavs] reduced their numbers to very few. It is said that the descendants of the blue-eyed survivors can be found in Kazakhstan.

Chapter 13

OUR ASSIGNED TASK

From the August 1955 issue of the [West German] magazine "Flugwelt," [Flight World] we learned after our return, a number of interesting facts about the Kuybyshev region. Kuybyshev is a city of half a million people at the confluence of the Volga and the Samara rivers. It lies 400 miles north of Stalingrad [called Volgograd after 1961] and was one of the 30 largest cities in the Soviet Union. The region was industrialized in connection with the 1937 5-year plan and was further developed in the years since then. During the Second World War, the area became Russia's aviation center, overshadowing Moscow's position. The military aviation construction group "Volga" was located there during the war, producing about 60% of Russia's military airplanes. The area is also the center for development and production of aircraft engines. That was not news to us. Kuybyshev was the only aircraft industrial center where Russians worked with Americans and later with Germans. The American help was focused on the industrial organization and the production of airplanes [and engines during the war] and the German effort was directed toward acquiring jet engine technology [after the war]. The significance of the center was expected to grow substantially when a new nearby (1,900 megawatt) hydroelectric dam was expected to be completed in 1957. A giant water retention reservoir will be created north of the city. [Today in 2023, it reaches northward to Kazan.] The region is rich with oil and gas production resources. So much for what we learned from the "Flugwelt" article.

We had no idea of the significance of the Kuybyshev region when we arrived. As time went on, we learned that on the road between Kuybyshev and Upra, there was a large aircraft engine plant, and its Russian engineers were going to be working with us. It is therefore quite understandable that this location was chosen for relocating the Germans from Dessau and Stassfurt. The American engineers worked who here during the war [technical help from the US for building military airplanes] left the wood frame housing behind as a reminder of that time. These facilities are now used by the German "specialists" left behind [in the Ostzone by the Americans] and brought here by the trainload together with all the materials necessary to set up shop. Everything that could possibly be useful was carefully packed, labeled, and identified when it left Germany. The setup of machine tools, drawing boards, desks, instruments, etc. in the new surroundings was quick and efficient. At the early stages of the unpacking, people charged with planning and construction required only desks and drawing boards and thus were able to start work immediately. The men who were to use workshops with its metal-working machinery had to wait a little longer.

In Dessau, I was part of a planning group for engine test stands so that I was included in a group of 17 engineers with a similar purpose. [Kurt Pflügel's spring 1946 trip to Rechlin established his role in this aspect of the work. At that time, the trip acquainted Russian officials with the nature of jet engine testing and his expertise. He helped determine what parts of the installation could be moved to Russia.] I was the mentor of a young Russian engineer and his assistant. The engineer spoke excellent German. The daughter of one of the German engineers was installed as the secretary and two Russian draftsmen completed the organization. Our department was important because it had to cover the immediate need for the designs of wind tunnels and test stands to be built as soon as practical. These would be required to evaluate the performance of the turboprop and jet engines produced later. To put up these facilities, new buildings were required. We were tasked with designing them using wood as the construction material. To us, this seemed completely crazy, partially because they were to be built in the middle of winter!

[There were other consequences associated with the wood construction of not only the wind tunnels and test stand but of the space where the instrumentation to measure engine performance was located. In part, this instrumentation consisted of banks of open mercury manometer tubes to measure pressures in test compressors. When stall was encountered during the testing, the mercury was often blown out of the tubes, sprayed around the room, to disappear among the wooden planks of the measurement room. The building and the test stands were later rebuilt in concrete when several of the technicians came down with mercury poisoning.[1]]

1 From the book by Ferdinand Brandner cited in the Bibliography.

Anselm Franz (left) and Hans von Ohain in the 1970s.

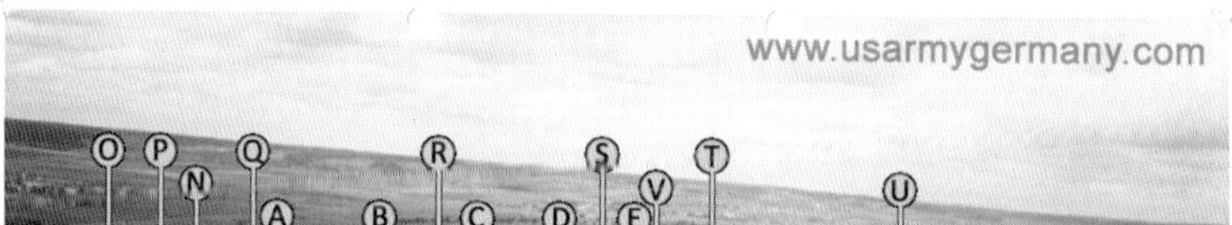

The Pinder Barracks in Landshut where the German dependents as well as *Paperclip* engineers transported from the East were housed. The image is from the website noted with an index (not included here) identifying the various buildings. Note the buildings indicated as "German barracks." The complex was originally built for the Wehrmacht and no longer exists. (Courtesy of www.usarmygermany.com)

The Lycoming engineers from Junkers. From left to right: Adenstedt, Mōllmann, Franz, Stein, Bielitz, and Siegfried Decher. This picture was taken in 1976 at the Lycoming plant with the Jumo 004 engine on loan from the US Air Force Museum to celebrate the 25th anniversary of the Lycoming plant in Stratford, Conn. The picture also shows the axial flow compressor blading at left and two of the burners, sectioned for display purposes. The single stage turbine is under Decher's arm. (Lycoming image C7506005-7)

The 104 German scientists and engineers at Fort Bliss, Texas in 1946. Most arrived in two shipments arriving 16 November 1945 and 3 February 1946. Werner von Braun is pictured seventh from right in the front row. (NASA)

Herman Oestrich. Formal and informal images, ca. late 1940s. (Espace Patrimoine Safran)

Brunolf Baade (left) and Heinrich Hertel in 1942 enjoying a light moment. At the time, both men were employed at Junkers.

An aerial view of Decize with the Cité Voisin caserne building array in the top center of the image. Note the temporary bridge adjacent to abutments of an earlier one, probably destroyed during the war.

Decize looking to the bridge over the dry (north) arm of the old Loire. (Courtesy of S. Decher)

The German technical people in Decize, ca. 1947. Photo taken in front of one of the work buildings, Bât. L.

General view of the Cité Voisin residence buildings. (Courtesy of Karsten Eggers)

Wood delivery from the French government to the men before the arrival of families, winter 1947. Two of the six residence buildings are shown with the woodshed between them. Both this and the previous photo were taken from about the same location. (Courtesy of Karsten Eggers)

A modern image of the platform sign from which Kurt Pflügel and his family started their forced journey to Russia.

Kurt Pflügel. The two images were taken about 1972, after he returned to West Germany where he wrote the book whose translation constitute some of the pages of this book. (Courtesy of Christa Pflügel)

Sigrid (Karkavelas) Pflügel during her time in Russia. (Courtesy of Christa Pflügel)

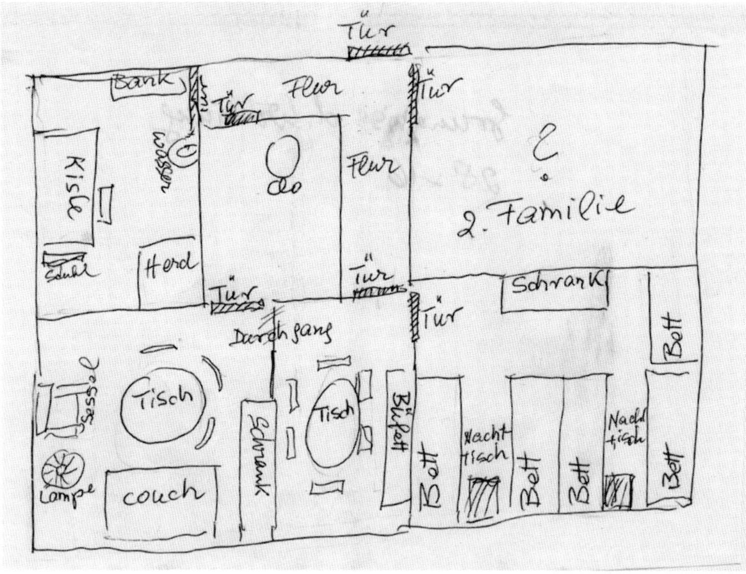

Sigrid's floorplan sketch of the apartment in Upra, residences no. 28 and 16. The space assigned to the Pflügel family is the lower half of this image and measured about 480 square feet. The top right room is occupied by another family. The shared kitchen and WC are at top left and center.

The sanatorium on the hill and the fishing village near the shore of the Volga. The sanatorium building is now gone, the site having been used to build a residence for a wealthy Russian (according to visitors to the area in the early 2000s). (Courtesy of Karl Breuninger)

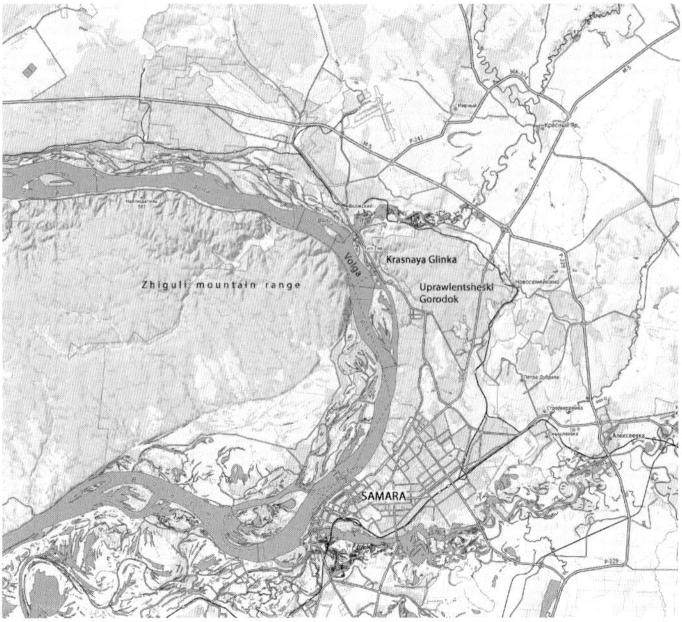

Map showing the location of Kuybyshev (today Samara) on a modern map of the elbow turn of the Volga. Upra is located 20km north of the city and Krasnaya Glinka is 6km further north. The river entering the Volga from the east is the Samara. (Map data from https://opentopomap.org, CC-BY-SA OpenStreetMap contributors)

The Volga River valley, view from near the sanatorium. (From the Haida-Clan website with permission)

Two images of Houses 35 and 45. These houses were built in the late 1930s and reconditioned (in early 1946) by German POWs after Russian families were forced out. The image dates are about 1949. (From the Haida-Clan website with permission and Karl Breuninger)

The wooden houses. (Courtesy of Karl Breuninger)

A Finn house in summer with its outhouse. (Courtesy of Karl Breuninger)

(Unidentified) residents of Haus no. 13. (Courtesy of Karl Breuninger)

Brandner (fourth from left) with unidentified members of one of his technical staff sections. (Courtesy of Karl Breuninger)

Ferdinand Brandner as depicted in a Russian book entitled "German Flight Specialists in the City of Kuybyshev in the First Postwar Years (1946-1953)," Samara 2010. The caption in the book reads "First Deputy Technical Leader of OKB-1 for motor development, former chief of the construction department of OKB-1, Dipl. Ing. Ferdinand Brandner, end of the 1940s, photographer unknown".

Nikolai Dmitrievich Kuznetsov (1911–95).

Two views of the Kuznetsov NK-12 engine on a static display of a Soviet Tu-95 bomber. (From the website http://culturaaeronautica.blogspot.com/2011/10/kuznetsov-nk-12-o-mais-poderoso-motor.htm)

The East German Baade 152 airliner prototype. Note the bombardier nose window present only on the prototype.

Conference between F. Brandner (l), B. Baade (c), and G. Bock (r). This photo was taken in Savelovo in March 1954. Photo Archive Holger Lorenz. (Photographer unknown)

The German cemetery with boundary stones and crosses (Photo: Karl Breuninger). The right-hand image was taken in 2007 and shows the addition of Russian gravesites surrounded by traditional fencing. (From the Haida-Clan website with permission)

The cross for the German POWs who died in (probably) prison camp no. 5. The photograph may have been taken by Christa Pflügel. A similar one taken by her is pictured in the book by former POW Wilhelm Klein. (From the Haida-Clan website with permission)

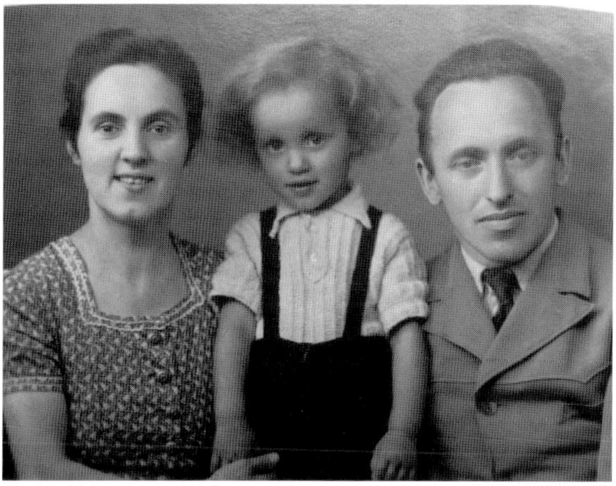

The Breuninger family (Mathilde, Karl, Dr. Helmut) in Upra in 1947.

The East German-built houses for small families. Note the 9 ft. high perimeter fence in the background.

The Clubhouse in Tushino, not unlike the one in Upra.

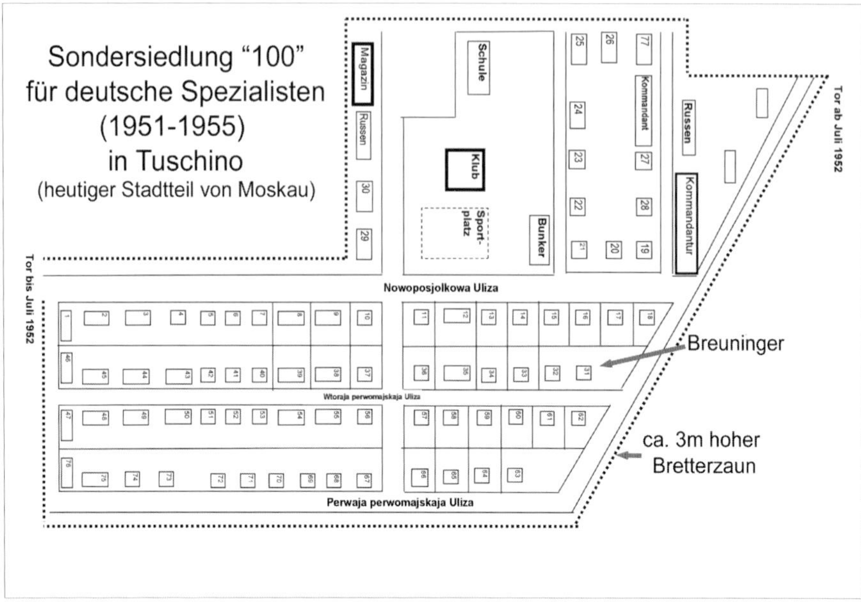

Sketch of the “Special Compound 100” in Tushino; the clubhouse (referred to as the “Klub”) and the Magazin were still standing in 2006. Noted is the Breuninger residence, location of the gate after 1952, and the 9 ft. high wooden perimeter fence.

Views of the stone and wooden houses as they appeared in the 2000s. (From the Haida-Clan website with permission, Kurt Breuninger.)

The normal work week consisted of six eight-hour days. Our work began immediately and with pressure. Overtime and Sunday hours became the norm as schedules could not possibly be met otherwise. Incentives and additional payments were promised although these were never delivered.

The task in front of us was immense. We had to develop not only turboprops, but jet engines that would be much more powerful than those we built in Germany. Our test stands had to be able to accommodate over 5,000 HP and 12,000 HP engines or jet engines with thrust levels that corresponded to such power. Starters for such engines had to be built. [Recall that his expertise was in electrical machinery.]

For the testing of these engines under realistic airflow conditions, wind tunnels were built. The layout plan was to build them with horizontal air entry and vertical outflow. In our first attempts we used wood which proved inadequate so that they were redone later with reinforced concrete. The test cross-sections of the tunnels were huge: 6x6 meters and 10x10 meters, controlled and monitored by staff in a nearby dedicated building [the one that had the mercury problem]. We designed water brakes to absorb all this power. We did all the calculations and designed the hardware that was built elsewhere. My first assignment was to design a high-altitude test chamber for gas turbine engines so that the engines could be tested in flight conditions as high as 60,000 feet altitude. This chamber had to be supplied with large amounts of fresh air and the exhaust had to be dealt with. For me, the technical challenges were very appealing. This work was a throwback to the time when I spent 10 years in Rechlin [air base]. The facilities there were smaller, and we enjoyed working with experts from Brown Boveri Co. (BBC) in Mannheim. BBC supplied the necessary [electrical] equipment to the Luftwaffe. In 1935 I worked at BBC and was transferred to the Rechlin base. [Pflügel returned to BBC (now ASEA Brown Boveri, ABB) upon his return to West Germany.] At that time and until 1940 [more likely 1941 when *Operation Barbarossa,* the German invasion of the Soviet Union took place], the USSR was also buying equipment from BBC and the Russian engineers involved were thoroughly trained in Dessau to use this equipment. The Russians were delighted to be able to move it from Dessau to Kuybyshev. It was all here, carefully packed in many boxes and turned over to us, the Junkers engineers in this new location. Plans were made for rebuilding all this equipment, but it quickly became evident that it was too small to be useful for testing the bigger engines to come. It stayed in the boxes and rotted there.

In Munich, the first large high altitude test chamber had just begun operation in 1945 when the war ended. It was admired by the British and the Americans who immediately dismantled it for a move to Great Britain. Similar facilities in Rechlin were ruined by the bombing. Still other facilities ended up in West Germany where the engineers associated with them readily accepted American offers to move there. We, on the other hand, stayed in the Soviet Occupation Zone from which we were forcefully transplanted to the Soviet Union. At the time I was an engineer working for BBC, responsible for electric power and water distribution. That part of my work was firmly in the past as I am now on a new professional path.

I was pleased one day when one of Russian engineers gave me the latest copies of the in-house magazine from BBC in Baden, Switzerland. The continuing access to the magazine gave me at least a literary contact with my old firm regarding electro-mechanical systems and thermodynamics. The Mannheim Division had also not forgotten me. Every year I received a letter report about former colleagues and their activities. My work here was more theoretical because the kind of systems I would have helped build in Germany were not going to be built here in Upra. I did, however, stay in the field for a time and was consulted by engineers from Moscow, people I had met in Dessau before the war. I also took care of special questions regarding the test stands and their construction. In effect, I became a facilities-engineer under Russian supervision. The instrumentation part of the project was handled by the staff of precision instrument company Askania that was also transported here from Berlin. [Today, Askania makes high-end mechanical watches.]

Chapter 14

THE BUILDUP TO START WORK

11 November 1946. We march into our work facilities for the first time. The halls and offices are empty. The countless wooden packing boxes that followed us from Dessau and Stassfurt lie about inside and outside the buildings. Drawing boards, desks, tables, chairs, laboratory equipment, machine tools, testing machines, the electric equipment (lights, fans, etc.) for the building and even the toilets were being set up. According to the paperwork involved, the plan had been to reconstruct these facilities in Russia in the summer of 1946. Inadvertently, it revealed that the relocation was a long time in planning. It also became evident that the Dessauers who continued working there after the war were the bait to draw in as many of the former employees as possible, especially those who had relocated to the West.

The Russian leadership was under Col. Olechnovich. Under him were several Russian officers we had gotten to know in Dessau and who performed similar functions there. The central administration was augmented by several, younger, intelligent, and competently German-speaking Russian engineers who were not in uniforms. They were assigned to work with the more senior members of our teams. The totality of the Germans, a group that could be called a "collective," came from the firms Junkers, BMW, and Askania. Their functions were identical to what they had practiced in Germany after the war. The Junkers and BMW people were to build engines while the Askania people were to deal with control and instrumentation issues. The engine people were grouped together in a large room while the Askania people worked in a separate building. Those concerned with performance calculations and manufacturing were housed separately from the other two groups and were, in effect, checkers of our work. Both engine groups provided the information required for the construction of the test facilities.

[The initial engine building task put to the engineers was completion of a turbojet engine design that once was designated as the Jumo 012. This engine was a more powerful development of the Jumo 004 built during the war.]

Col. Olechnovich was a demanding boss. We quickly learned that people who did not pull their weight were hit with salary reductions. Those who made errors were monetarily fined. Who, among us, did not make occasional calculation errors or even errors of other kinds? If you were late to work, you would be called to explain. Violations of the transit permit rules for going to Kuybyshev might lead to detention in the factory cell.

Is it possible to never make an operational or mechanical error? [apparently not: "To err is human!" – Alexander Pope] An example: on 20 April [1949?] a small mistake was made in the testing of an engine. The Russians quickly jumped to the conclusion that sabotage was in play because the date was Hitler's birthday! German workers and engineers were interrogated by very suspicious and nasty state police people. It all blew over but could have been bad for someone. The tension between the Germans and the Russians was ever-present and did not ease until the very end of our confinement.

During the setup of the workplace that winter, we were assisted by groups of grey-clad women prisoners. They did the heavy work of moving things, opening boxes with crow bars, etc. They were no strangers to hard labor. The German men felt sorry for them and occasionally discovered individuals in a corner resting or warming themselves. Outside, at the same time, one could see columns of similarly grey men accompanied in front and back by armed soldiers handling mean-looking dogs. This sorry, tattered column was headed in mute resignation to a large sawmill. They worked the logs that floated down the Volga. These men lived in a compound of barracks near the road to Kuybyshev surrounded by barbed wire and manned watchtowers. At night, we could hear the bell signals of the watchmen who kept awake by banging on iron bars in sequence around the compound. This compound later emptied out as the workers were moved to new quarters for the construction of new roads and the dam further upriver on the Volga. The bright flood and search lights along the river were always a reminder that people were imprisoned there.

The setup work ended in mid 1947. Life took on a monotonous regularity. We got to know our German and Russian colleagues although friendships were singularities. We accepted our fates but were certainly not reconciled to the implied future.

The organizational arrangement under Olechnovich made for a difficult and tense time. Fortunately, it came to an end in the Winter of 1947 when a new man from Junkers joined our group. He was the engineer Mr. B. [Ferdinand Brandner] we knew well and who led one of the Junkers Divisions in Czechoslovakia. He was captured there by the Russians, held in a prison in Moscow, and later, was transferred to Upra. We greeted him warmly and were glad to have him with us. He quickly became the leader of the engine groups and reorganized the various groups into a more streamlined administrative structure. Life became significantly easier.

His later Russian counterpart was to be Col. Nikolai Kuznetsov. [The Kuybyshev Engine Design Bureau eventually became the Kuznetsov Design Bureau, OKB-276.] Fortunately for us, the new director Kuznetsov was more collegiate and a better engineer than Col. Olechnovich. He avoided punishment, threats, setting very short-term and unrealistic goals, and was less strict when it came to meeting deadlines. He was also quite skilled at getting good work out of us.

[How was it going from a Russian viewpoint?

The written record includes an "Upra Inspection Report" to the 'Secretary of the All-Union Central Council of Trade Union Federations' on the "Review of the supervision of German Specialists at the Experimental Plant No. 2 of the Ministry of Aviation Industry in Kuybyshev." The report is dated May 1948.

The report was marked "top secret" (Streng Geheim, in the version translated from Russian into German). It consists of six pages of single-spaced typing that cannot remotely be characterized as a literary masterpiece or as an effective business communication. In fact, no part of the report is quotable. The report is, nevertheless, the essence of how the auditor/writer saw the management of the German OKB at Upra progressing.

An overarching sense in the writing is that the Russians expected the Germans to work happily on the task assigned to them with management direction provided by Col. Olechnovich. At the time of the auditor's visit, Brandner had been part of the German team for over a year. His role is unclear because there is only a brief, parenthetical mention of his name in the report. A major management issue for the Russians was that the Germans outnumbered the Russians in the various departments dealing with technical issues which meant that "control" (of what is said and thought) by the Germans was difficult.

Most of the jet engine people in Kuybyshev were from Junkers. There had been an organizational structure at Junkers before the war and at the SAG (the Sowjetische Aktiengesellschaft) brought together at Junkers by the Soviets after the war's end. While many senior principals at Junkers and BMW were whisked off by American officials to the western occupation zones, there was still a large contingent of the older organization(s) left and these were the ones transported against their will to the USSR. A significant fraction of these engineers were leaders in their fields and were naturally able to organize themselves in a way that gets the job done. These leaders also had been (or had chosen to be) members of the Nazi Party, the NSDAP, whether their hearts were in it or not. The Russians knew who the members of the party were, and when they joined. These men were consequently described in this report as "Nazis" and assumed to be a threat when it came to contact with others. The leaders of the various OKB's together with Kurt Pflügel and Heinrich Singer were identified by name as members of the Nazi group.

Among these engineers were also men who held political views more closely aligned with socialism and / or communism. People of that persuasion typically joined the new party created by the communist East Germans working with the Soviets in their occupation zone. This new party came out of existing parties, the SPD (Sozialistische Partei Deutschland) and the KPD (Kommunistische ...) and was called the Social Unity Party (or SED in German). To the Russians, adherents of the SED were the good guys, and the "Nazis" were not.

One important dimension of Soviet communism was that meetings of more than a few people to discuss just about anything, be it some social life concern or a technical matter, had to be under the control of Soviet officials so that the discussion could not drift into undesired directions. Specifically, the Russians wanted to prevent political contamination of the SED people by the "Nazis." This was an important aspect of the less-than-perfect management of the Germans.

The technical meetings required to do the work were almost always dominated by the men labelled as "Nazis." In the audit report, these leaders were always described with that label, both individually and as a group. While Russians were referred to as "Comrade X," the Germans were "Nazi X."

In the first year and a half in Upra, the management of the Germans by the Russians was a turbulent affair with Col. Olechnovich in the middle. His Russian supervisors tried to keep the "Nazis" out of leadership positions. With little success, he tried to elevate the SED faction over the Nazi faction. In reality, no management scheme satisfactory to the Russians could be devised. The Russian imposition of rules forbidding this or that was a manifestation of the Russian attempts at managing the Germans, specifically two senior individuals who felt and repeatedly expressed anti-Soviet sentiments regarding the treatment of the Germans and work protocols. This tumult led to a situation where work was not getting done. Further, there were talented people who were under-utilized and salary distributions that were out of step with the productivity and capability of certain individuals. In the report, there is a reference to the reality that some of the senior Germans simply occupied their time with activities they, and not the Soviets, thought important. In short, there were Germans who did not contribute much and productive others who were miserably underpaid. Cited as a component of the mayhem were communications via a kind of underground news medium within the German community. It (supposedly) spread false, inflammatory, and potentially mutinous rumors. The existence of this channel was thoroughly unacceptable to Soviet authorities and the report suggested that someone "do something" about it. Finally, the matter of the Möller suicide attempt was interpreted as a Soviet management failure.

Parenthetically we note that Möller and Dr. Peter Lertes, the leader of the OKB focused on guidance and control of aircraft, were the important people in the Soviet development of this aspect of aircraft technology. Their contribution to Soviet capability enabled the successful shoot-down of Francis Gary Powers in his American U-2 reconnaissance flight over the Soviet Union in 1960. At the time of his release (1958), Karl Breuninger remembered the time when U.S. officials visited his father, a member of the OKB headed by Möller.[1] The Americans wanted a status briefing on Soviet capabilities.

Ultimately, Olechnovich capitulated and decided that getting the work done was more important than promoting individuals with the "right" political outlook. He appointed Brandner as the German director, a man with strong Nazi credentials. This appointment as well as the replacement of Olechnovich, perhaps precipitated by the Brandner promotion decision, allowed for a better and smoother work environment.

One might wonder why a document reporting the difficulties to the higher authorities in Moscow were so secret. Reading between the lines of the report, it is apparent that this enterprise was not going as well as expected and must therefore be kept quiet lest confidence in Soviet

1 After he turned down an offer to work in the DDR, Möller together with 32 other (Askania) specialists and their families, was returned to the FRG in February 1958 (see Chapter 26). He continued his work in the West German air industry and retired in 1974.

authority be damaged. The other dimension is that the document lists many names of individuals, Russians and Germans, who were not performing well. That information was kept in the record because it might become valuable for a later persecution of an individual. It is best kept under wraps. Finally, the document was not a blueprint for future activity. That would have been a normal reason to keep a report secret.]

Chapter 15

LEADERSHIP PERSONALITIES

This chapter interrupts Kurt Pflügel's words to shed light onto the major actors in this history. It is written in my voice. The changing leadership from Col. Olechnovich to that of Kuznetsov requires a bit of a side trip to describe the roles played by these two men in the execution of the changing tasks assigned to the German specialists.

To begin, we note that Ferdinand Brandner, the most experienced of the German engine engineers, was a prized capture by the Soviets. He had worked for Junkers in the mid 1930s and was responsible for the development of a Junkers version what was then a very high-power class of aircraft engines for a planned medium bomber. Junkers' significant competitors in the business were BMW and Daimler Benz. Brandner enjoyed considerable success in this work until wartime priorities ultimately led to cancellation of the project late in the war. For the reader interested in this engine, the following facts about the 2,500 HP Jumo 222 are interesting. It was liquid-cooled with a configuration resembling three V-8 piston engines wrapped around a single power output shaft, for a total of 24 cylinders. The engine was scheduled for production in Prague (Czechoslovakia) in 1942 which is where the Soviets apprehended Brandner at the end of the war. Parenthetically, we note that design work on the 222 was carried out at the Junkers Otto Mader facilities in Dessau, where the Jumo 004 jet engine was developed at the same time. These facilities were badly damaged during a heavy bombing raid on 28 April 1944.[1] Subsequently the 222 engine project was moved to Oberursel, which later became an important reassembly location in the AOZ for German engine experts by US forces. Building piston engines like the 222 was the challenge of

1 This raid prompted the author's father and many of the other engineers to move their families to a safer location in the rural Harz Mountains.

the day by all engine builders and the success enjoyed by Brandner at Junkers was recognized and well appreciated by the Russians.

Kuznetsov worked in the Ufa engine plant beginning in 1942. After the war, he met Brandner when the latter was assigned to manage the production of the Klimov RD-10 engine, a copy of the Jumo 004. Brandner was alone as a German in that factory and directed his work to Russian engineers through translators. Kuznetsov recognized that if Brandner worked with a German staff, he would be more effective and productive. Brandner was consequently transferred to Kuybyshev in January 1947.

The design of the Jumo 012 engine, extending what was available from the experience of building the Jumo 004, proceeded at Upra, albeit with serious challenges. The reality was that difficulties with the manufacturing capability available in Russia and the limited Russian personnel resources forced an abandonment of this jet engine project. The thinking was that a new powerful turboprop engine would better suit the needs of the Soviet military. The redirected focus became the Jumo 022 turboprop engine which, like the Jumo 012 jet engine, was just a design on paper at war's end. The 022 engine was designed to provide about 6,000 HP[1] to a propeller. Because of his Junkers experience in directing engine building undertakings, Ferdinand Brandner became its project director.

Brandner was pleased by the transfer. He struggled to keep the Russian state and the Russian people as separate realities. He loved the beauty of the land near Ufa where he was initially held, and he liked the people for their humanity. He harbored no love for the state, for it held him prisoner. Compounding these feelings toward the state was that he learned in late 1946, a year and a half after his capture, that his wife and children were alive and living in Austria. The only choice given him by the Soviets was to invite his family to join him in Russia. His circumstances, while perhaps acceptable from a professional viewpoint, were unacceptable from every other viewpoint. He wrote to his wife that "on the basis of promises made by Russian officials you should never leave Austria to join me here." He did this not knowing how much longer they might be separated. When he left the Ufa factory to join the other Germans in Kuybyshev, he drew some comfort from the anticipated companionship of the fellow Germans who were already there.

---

1 WE note that the most power a piston engine could produce in practice even after the war was about 4,000 HP. An example is the Pratt & Whitney R-4360 that first ran in 1944.

Brandner worked for a time under Olechnovich when he arrived in Kuybyshev. He considered him a competent engineering manager well able to deal with matters even where he might not have understood all the technical details. As a human being, however, Brandner thought Olechnovich was rough and crude. The German team, including Brandner, was happy to see him be relieved of duties and replaced by Kuznetsov.

Brandner's book provides a postscript on the disliked Col. Olechnovich's fortunes. It appears that they declined when he killed a child while driving his car in an inebriated state.

The design goals for the 022 engine (with the Russian designation Kuznetsov TV-022) were achieved in 1950 and production was turned over to another facility. On the military application side, the plan was to use an interconnected pair of these engines to power the contra-rotating propellers of the Tu-95 bomber prototype. This bomber, when it was put in service, was code-named "Bear" by NATO. This use of the engine pair was unsuccessful for mechanical reasons and further work was stopped.

The next logical goal was to build a single turboprop engine of twice (!) the power output to avoid the mechanical interference issues in the gearing necessary for the two smaller coupled engines. This large and successful engine became the NK-12, named with the initials of the Russian lead manager. It was ultimately perfected to produce 15,000 HP, a record in the annals of aircraft engine building. It first ran in 1954 and was used in a variety of Russian aircraft, including the Tu-114 airliner that was probably the noisiest large airliner ever built. In Chapter 19 we will see that Kuznetsov's taking on the task of this enormous engine played a role in an unhappy extension of the time served by the German specialists in Russia.

For readers interested in the technical and historical aspects of the NK-12 development, the book by A. L. Kay (see Bibliography) is an excellent resource.

Chapter 16

THE WORKDAY

[Kurt Pflügel does this topic justice!]

7:40 AM. The head of our neighboring family sharing our apartment left for work. The kids are on their way to school. On closing the door, I met another of my neighbors from across the way. He lives in an apartment with three other families. You can hear doors closing all around and see men hurrying to work from all doors of the complex. To the "Zavod"! as the Russians call their workplace. People who customarily walk to work together have found each other and the talk was almost always the same:

"Mail from Germany ...",

"BBC radio news from England ..."

"I still think they will let us go home, someday."

Somebody might respond with

"Never! – You know what the Volga German woman said: What the Russian has, he never lets it go!"

"Yes, but they released most of the POWs."Yes, for them the war is over, we are forced labor, modern slaves! Do you think the government in the Ostzone [GDR] cares about us? One of the ministers even said that we don't exist!"

"Did you hear about the punishment of one of the German workers? The Russian underling messed up on the lathe and the German must pay for the damages?"

As we walk, more and more people come together to form a black worm of humanity moving along the narrow path to the factory. Russians blend in with the Germans and the conversations are dampened. The Russians understand German, and they don't need to know all about our feelings. Even among the Germans, not everyone can be trusted.

We reach the wooden fence surrounding the factory. Two narrow entrances to a barrack-like building slows the process to a crawl. While we wait, we have a chance to "admire" the primitive posters showing the achievement of the plan to finish the big dam and a graphic showing the growing coal production numbers in the Soviet Union. Directly over the entrance to the factory is a red sign with white Cyrillic lettering "For the Fight and the Victory of Communism!" These signs are brightly lit for special occasions and the scene reminds me of an entrance to a circus.

I finally push through to a narrow passageway to reach a window opening with a small lockable opening through which stuff could be passed. The space above it was enclosed by wire mesh. Behind the window sits a woman from the security organization, always with scarf-covered heads. In winter (September-May) they wear brown soldiers' uniforms and in summer they change to olive drab ones. I lean down to the opening in the window and call out my ID card number in Russian. She, in turn, fumbles through a file and passes to me a badge with my picture on it. Three steps further on, another woman checks to see if the picture is of me and lets me pass. She also checks to be sure that no briefcase or other closed containers are brought in. The concern is that drawings, documents, or paper could be smuggled *out* of the building at the end of the day. Now that we are inside, we cannot leave without special permission until lunch break.

Just like in prisons or detention camps, there is a second barbed wire fence inside the shabby wooden one surrounding the factory complex. The sandy space between the two fences is about 2 meters wide and kept clean and raked to reveal possible footprints. About every 100 meters, watchtowers break up the fence line. The towers resemble a hunter's watch in a German forest, made crudely with wooden posts and boards. They are staffed day and night by men and women with guns. During the nights, searchlights sweep the area around the towers. The crude wooden outer fence is rotten here, leaning here, and the boards, some long, some short. It is enough to drive a German crazy! His sense of order and beauty is so blatantly violated! "Ordnung!" [orderliness!]

The road to our office was muddy and potholed when we arrived and, over the years, was occasionally improved with patches of asphalt. The door to the factory building had another large political poster display calling for progress or some such. It was changed twice a year during the country's big festive days, 1 May, and 7 November.[1] On these occasions we also had to participate in the spring and fall

1 A review of the Soviet calendar reveals 1 May as "International Worker's Day" and 7 November is the (Gregorian) "Day of the Proletarian Revolution," a day that falls in October on the Julian calendar.

cleaning that consisted of removal of the accumulated trash and junk that piled up over the previous months.

We enter the main building, the spiritual and nerve center of the factory. Unauthorized people cannot enter without special permission. A watchman at the door controls who enters. The ID pass we used to get this far must now be deposited into a rack so that it can easily be determined who is present and who is not. Russian and German engineers use separate racks.

Nearby, a bulletin board shows an exhibit of photographs and the latest copy of the factory newspaper. The pictures are under glass and show faces of German and Russian engineers in two side-by-side sections. The whole setup is rather crude and unattractive in spite of the sign on the top stating: "The Best." The pictures are changed about twice a year, and the norm is that two or three people from each department would always be on display. For one's picture to be displayed requires not just good technical performance, but acceptable social behavior and proper political attitude. The newspaper is the critique sheet from the Factory Functionary Committee on the attitude of the work force. It might show, for example, a picture of a worker sleeping at his desk or a group of younger engineers in a lively discussion of private matters during work hours. The paper is meant to be a caricature but is, in reality, a pillory, a public shaming.

At exactly 8:00 AM, the bell rings. Everybody must be sitting at their desk. The ID passes are counted by the security people, and everyone present is accounted for. The doors to the cabinet with the ID passes are locked. The names of latecomers are put on a black bulletin board also used for new orders of the day. Repeat offenders are listed there together with notations as to whether monetary fines or salary reductions were imposed by Mr. Kuznetsov. Accounting errors are also noted here for all to see.

The end of the work period is noted by a bell and a reopening of the ID pass cabinet. A 1½ hour break for the midday meal is now in effect. A small buffet is set up in the building where butter or sausage might be had today. That would be nice since these products have disappeared from the Magazin store shelves and were delivered exclusively to the "Zavod." I line up to see what is available. Today is also the important semi-monthly payday. The money is given out at the end of the workday and only in the building where people are assigned to work. Another long lineup to get one's signature on a long list. The paymaster arrives with a suitcase full of bank notes. He stands behind a barrier does a lot of counting before handing over a wad of bills to an individual. The store does a good business on these celebratory days, especially selling vodka.

Typically, we return to work at 2 PM bearing neither joy nor enthusiasm and the bell rings again at 6 PM. The Germans are done working, but the Russians stay on. Their workday is not over because today is socio-political education day. Somebody is tasked with reporting on the latest news [of "appropriate" material tailored to the people] from Moscow authorities. They are in for a long night of discussion! Two days later, after an evening's respite, they will be spending yet another night at the office, this time for technical education. Each week someone is assigned to give a lesson on some technical subject related to his work. This is how the technical education is augmented in practice. "Learn, learn, learn" is an order attributed to Lenin and posted in schools and much more widely in places where people gather. Participation in these evening sessions is, of course, voluntary but everyone knows that an attendance list is kept, and it is not to one's advantage to go home early.

We leave the factory and find, to our chagrin, that this evening is random body search night. That means that after we return our ID passes, two heavily bearded guards go through our pockets thinking, perhaps, that we are smuggling nails, pencils, writing paper, or other valuable items that are seldom available in stores.

[Other sources (Singer among them) note that a functioning engineering office requires writing instruments, paper, etc. to be effective and these were rather primitive or unavailable in this environment. Pencils had to be nursed to very short lengths, ball point pens were unknown, and most writing was done with pens, the kind that requires dipping into ink wells. The poor quality of the paper made writing with a steel point pen tricky at best. The ink tended to run, and the paper tended to tear. The ink had to be made up with dye pills dissolved in water. Calculations were made with slide rules or mechanical machines, some of which did additions, others, multiplications, and still others did divisions. These noisy machines were staffed by young men (and perhaps women), called "rechenknechts," (a calculation aide) who were old enough to do it but were not "specialists."]

Unwinding with colleagues on the way home, an important question arises: would it be worth my while to stand in line at the Magazin store to buy some sugar? Or, more urgently, do you think we will have electricity tonight? This is the beginning of winter. The poorly functioning hot water heater system might have to be supplemented by using the electric hot plates.

Speaking of electric power ... There is no such thing as power metering. The fuse panels had no fuses, just big jump wires across the terminals. The network was often overloaded and when it went down, the only remedy to a blackout was to turn off lights and hot plates and wait until power returns, usually very late at night. Tonight, we turn the corner and, happily, the lights are on! We can look forward to a nice evening! What a joy to be granted this one small thing when so much is out of reach and missed.

[Singer adds to the power picture with the following observations. Electric power was charged by periodic counts of the number of lightbulbs and hot plates and their wattage. The energy was not free. The various parts of the stone houses were furnished with either one or the other of the phases of the 3-phase supply. Power cuts, mostly on cold days, usually involved cut of one of the phases so that about half of the residences in houses 35 and 45 would have power and the other half was dark. Normally power was available for a few hours during the day and after 10 PM. Occasionally all power was cut but never to the house with the Magazin on the ground level and with Russians living in the upper stories. The Germans called it the "Bonzenhaus," the fat cat house!

Friedemann Singer, the author of the referenced memoir, left the Soviet Union on the first train home in 1950. His father Heinrich did not. He was convicted of being a counter-revolutionary for which he was executed. The collapse of the Soviet Union allowed access to the relevant files where Friedmann found that his father was one of 927 Germans from all over Russia to have been executed. Their ashes are located at the Donskoye cemetery in Moscow where they are memorialized ... together with countless others.]

Chapter 17

OTHER ASPECTS OF LIFE … AND DEATH

Remuneration

[This section of Pflügels's writing is focused on the systemic difficulties in determining salaries for engineers doing development work. I summarize it briefly. In general, the Soviet reward system was based on achieving and surpassing set goals. The meeting of production goals, like kilos of potatoes harvested (good ones or just any potatoes?) or tons of steel produced, are relatively easy to establish. For engineering projects, however, deadlines and output are hard to set because the work is technically risky and achieved on uncertain time scales. With these realities in mind, the Russians simply paid engineers according to academic degrees, passing of exams, and a person's administrative level. Specific achievements were recognized by one-time premium awards that supposedly increased productivity and happiness.

Again, in Kurt Pflügel's voice.]

In 1950, we successfully completed our first large project, the 6,000 HP test stand for [turboprop] engines with propellers. A monetary premium came from Moscow where everyone in our organization received a cash bonus. Mine was about a third of my monthly salary. The entire sum sent by Moscow was distributed but not all to individual workers. Some of it was used for asphalting roads, planting flower beds, and improving the working conditions.

The management of productivity in my and other departments responsible for construction of facilities was in the hands of special accountants who sat down with people at various levels. They worked out achievements to be reached and schedules for meeting them. In our department, we set the goals so that we would be able to (over) achieve them to 110–115% and claim success. In reality, all this "planning" was just theater. The accounting and reward system prescribed by Moscow was not applicable, but the bureaucracy had to be satisfied.

Bonds

A particularly irritating aspect of the salary picture, especially in the early years, was the mandatory participation in the purchase of government bonds. Beginning in 1948, there was an annual drive scheduled to be completed inside a week's time. Participation was voluntary, of course, but not so in reality. Russians were expected to buy 100–120% of a month's wages to be withdrawn every month in 10 installments. It was a tax of sorts. The factory and its departments were entered into competitions to measure their enthusiasm for the country and the way of communist life. Failure to win or achieve a high score usually reflected badly on the party officials involved, thus a lot of pressure. The Germans were expected to participate and whoever didn't sign up would be cross-examined by the functionaries in charge. "Why aren't you an eager supporter…?" Threats were never far behind the spoken words.

During one signup period I happened to be on vacation [just what constituted a "vacation" and whether it was taken with family is unclear] when I heard that I should report to the factory to sign up to purchase the bonds, I avoided the issue, successfully that time. My apartment neighbor, who happened to be sick in bed at the time, did not. He was visited in his home and threatened. In the end, the commission people left without his agreement to sign up. In a way, that established that we, the fathers with large families, could not and would not participate in an involuntary reduction of our meager salaries. Very few of the German community signed up for anything near the demanded 100%. We used our tepid participation as a way of protestation against the groundless salary reductions. Their counterargument was "Whoever does not sign up is against the Russian state and for the war!" … the war? What war? The last one? The scenes were awful. Some of us did not shy away from serious confrontations, others signed up just to get them off their backs. There was, however, no winning these arguments and the next time, they would make abstention harder.

Volunteering

Another dimension of work in the Soviet Union was the so-called (universal) Voluntary Work Service where work, for which no workers were available, would be done by everyone else. The work involved building footpaths, digging ditches, planting trees and flowers, etc. It quickly came to German refusals to participate because it boiled down to a reduction of our humanity in the eyes of the Russian authorities and especially the Russians who were unwilling to do their part.

Training

Everyone, not just the Russians, must be continually educated after work hours. For the Germans that meant we were to be exposed to the history of the Communist Party in the Soviet Union. We knew nothing about this and when the announcement was made, we were curious. The basis for the "course" was an official book. The Russian leader urged us to read the various assigned chapters so that we could discuss the subject with him. He must have been very unhappy because the Germans simply refused to believe or agree with what was written. The book was a kind of dogmatic Bible replacement that the Soviet citizenry could adopt to guide their lives and feel good about being miserable. The discussions were aggravating and pointless. We did not champion Hitlerian views but were thoroughly offended as German citizens. We had to listen to official party views about the justified war [WWII] and the concept of a peace-loving democratic populace, the common logo "fight for peace" notwithstanding! They even tried to convince us that a reunification of Germany was a real possibility [presumably on different terms than those realized in 1989]. They also stated that the return of East Prussia [now Poland] to a new Germany was also a good possibility. [How that might have been brought about would certainly have been entertaining, though not to the Polish people now living there.] The Russians correctly concluded that these discussions with us Germans were not fertile soil and the "re-education seminars" stopped being held. Instead, the order came down that everybody was to learn the Russian language. It was evident that linguistic difficulties were present although many of the Russians who mattered spoke good German. Presented with the threat of salary reduction, we gave in to the demand. It was not easy to master the intricacies of the language, but we recognized that better communication would result in all kinds of transactions. I had taken some Russian language courses during the war and took more private instruction here in Upra. I politely declined to take more. The children had an easier time of it and adapted quickly. An unhappy aspect of my difficulties with the language was the inability to form personal relationships with the increasing numbers of Russian engineers who worked with us. [The easiest way to learn a language is by immersion in it. Children do it easily, but the process is more difficult as people age. The prohibition of social interactions made immersion difficult and made Upra, in fact, a ghetto.]

Interactions

The young Russian engineers came primarily from the technical training schools. Their education varied and was very specialized. They were intelligent and many came from Jewish backgrounds. Their parents were workers or farmers without much education. The young men were competent in the theoretical aspects of technology but lacked the practical training and the common sense required for the execution of their assignments. They preferred to dig into the books and ignore practical considerations. That led to long and fruitless discussions with these eager-to-learn, though often shallow, young men. They were strong and blind believers in what the party wanted them to believe and do. They were convinced that a bright future lay ahead by marching to the tune to the Communist Party. There was always talk of the old days and the belief in better days ahead.

We wondered whether there was any plan to have Germans and Russians living together in a communal setting. There was not. All such interactions were thwarted when there was even a drift in that direction. Keeping the required distant, but collegial, relations with the Russians was difficult. Spats of anger arose at times and the enforced formality did not help to comfort either side. Interaction between the Russians and Germans within our residences was forbidden. When we encountered a Russian person we knew from work on the street, we became transparent: no eye contact, no greeting, and no human acknowledgement. Their ice-cold behavior was drilled into them as the appropriate way to interact with us. Exceptions were the braver farm women who came to our houses to sell eggs, butter, etc. They smiled. The enforcer of these rules of engagement, the residence "Kommandant", graciously overlooked their transgression.

On the street, the situation could be described as "tolerated equality". We were foreigners and treated as such. At work, the necessary interaction brought us a kind of pleasure when showing the Russians, how a complicated task could be accomplished. The implied subtext naturally was – we knew better! It allowed us to retain a sense of pride.

We were often reminded of the reality of our situation. The coercive power and lack of freedom was everywhere around us. The limits on us were their tool to render us defenseless and powerless. We were never allowed to forget that we were forced to be here. We watched anxiously as the world changed. The situation in Berlin [the blockade of the city from June 1948 to May 1949], the war in Korea [starting in 1950] were events we could just observe from the perspective of the Moscow-controlled media here. What is to be our lot if the world burns once more? Are they holding us, with wives and children, as hostages to work and stay silent? The demands of our work were a bit of a firewall against the darkest of our thoughts.

In 1949–50 we were offered work contracts. Was that to legitimize our presence here? Probably. We recognized that a contract was just another trick to keep us here longer. United in our resolve, we turned down the opportunity to sign up.

We knew that not only our work was scrutinized, but so were our private lives, monitored by Germans among us. The state police knew how to pressure and threaten one or two of our comrades to watch us and deliver reports about us. Nobody knew who, of course, so that we lived in a world of constant insecurity and caution. The incessant pressure on some of our colleagues eventually overcame them and they had to be treated at the psychological clinic. Others attempted suicide, some successfully.

For example, on a very cold winter night one of our ablest engineers was found in the snow, unconscious, and with his hands frozen. [The person was Waldemar Möller and this was his second attempt at suicide, the first one in Berlin and referenced earlier.] He was attempting to freeze to death. His life was spared but his hands were beyond repair. [His wife was not among the abducted but rather, was subsequently called to Russia to help care for him.] On another occasion, a German woman hung herself. The news that followed to explain her suicide was that she feared being "denounced," because, according to rumors, she had sold a Christian bible to someone.

In 1952, many had given up hope that they would ever return home. One morning, one of our co-workers jumped down a deep stairwell just as the workday was to begin. Not one of us missed his funeral. A long, dark column trailed the hearse, silent, and dogged. The Russians on the sidelines whispered "demonstrators!". They understood what we meant to show, and they were quite uncomfortable. [There were other means[1] employed to escape the abduction. A specialist named Herbert Lederman managed to associate himself with one of the groups of POWs hoping to be released when their turn came. He made it just to the German border, was captured there, and convicted to 25 years in prison. He was ultimately pardoned, married a Russian woman, and stayed in the country.]

1 Personal communication Karl Breuninger.

Social welfare (abridged)

During our first months in Russia, the German workers were completely separated from the Russians. No social welfare structure was in place. To remedy this vacuum and provide a mechanism to help each other, a working group of Germans decided to form an agency for taking care of people out on sick days. Since workers were not paid when absent from work, the idea was to collect monies from everyone and dole it out to those in financial need. The group held meetings and elected a council. To their dismay, they ran into the ever-present [Soviet Communist] Party bureaucracy: meetings were forbidden and candidates for election could only be those approved by the Party. In short, the official union for the factory will take over and the Germans would be allowed one representative [to the union council]. We were reminded that in the Soviet Union, the union members own the factory so that there is no need for a confrontational relationship between the workers and factory management. The state will take care of everything! The problem of dealing with the welfare of the German workers was finally "solved" [from the Russian perspective] by holding meetings with only those people from whom agreement with resolution of the issues on the council agenda would be assured. That was the end of our attempts to take care of our own.

Medical care

Medical care, hospital stays, and medications were free. Very near our quarters in Upra was a barrack-like building that served as a local [urgent care] hospital [56]. A more extensive polyclinic [34] was in a house on the road to Kuybyshev. The polyclinic was the main place for ambulatory care and where childbirth and dental services were provided. Lots of young women doctors staffed this establishment. They were state employees and did not practice on their own. When home care was required, these women went to the sick in their homes. The clinic had no waiting rooms. The incoming patients simply sat and waited on the floor in the hallways.

We avoided going to the clinic whenever possible because we had no positive regard for the staff's abilities. Not only were the Russian women doctors predisposed to not caring about the Germans as patients, but they were also not very competent. They often misdiagnosed symptoms and their medical prescriptions bordered on voodoo. The gap between our experiences in Germany and what was available here in Upra was wide. The mistrust on all sides rarely benefitted the patient. The German nurses in our group ended up doing most of the first aid and assisting the sick on a volunteer basis.

There was one surprising exception: an old Russian woman doctor actually preferred to deal with the German patients. She was Jewish, spoke German, and had studied in Heidelberg. She understood our situation and did for us what she could. She came dressed in old clothes and thankful when we gave her a glass of milk and a piece of white bread in addition to the fee she charged and collected, under the table, of course.

The facilities in the hospital and the care were primitive. Modern technical instruments were either not at hand or not functional. X-rays are used for broken bones only after they healed improperly. Almost everyone who suffered a broken bone dealt with healing issues later. When it was needed, the X-ray machine was typically broken or located somewhere far away. One of our younger people died of appendicitis because the surgeon was unable to operate. He had been called in from his garden and his cold hands were not sufficiently nimble.

The dental facilities were from an age long passed. The drill had to be operated by a foot pedal, a matter we fixed with a small Askania motor. Crowns and cavities could often not be addressed properly because the materials for a crown or a filling were not available. In an accident I required repair of my two front teeth.[1] I now have shiny steel crowns. The dental clinic was often overrun with patients. Fortunately, the working men [only!] could access the factory's on-site dentist, although only during work hours. Those who had the good fortune (!) to be sick enough to require services that the local hospital could not provide were transported to the one in Kuybyshev. There, the facilities were modern and up to date. Best of all, the staff included a German-trained doctor who understood our medical needs. He went to great and well-appreciated lengths to be of service to the members of our community. [Politics sometimes found its way into the arena of medical care. The German community was not of uniform political bents and included hardline Nazis, socialists, even communists. Breuninger reports on an incident where a Nazi-leaning family was confronted with a medical issue that would require a blood transfusion for their child. This blood would have to come from a Russian, a Slav, considered to be less than human by a believing Nazi. The transfusion was refused, and the child died.]

Russians were extremely frightened of epidemic diseases. There were strict requirements for vaccinations and isolation of sickened people. Every April, an army of vaccinating women went everywhere to

1 This accident was a fall induced by losing consciousness in the Russian sauna, precipitated by the combustion gases in the chamber.

immunize the children. At the slightest suspicion, people were coerced into an isolation ward where they sometimes got really sick. In Russia we were exposed to and suffered the consequences of a wide variety of health threats: yellow fever, malaria, infections of many kinds, as well rheumatism and heart issues. At the core of the health issues was the shortage of vitamins in winter. No fresh fruit or vegetables and little sunshine to provide vitamin D. When we returned home to Germany years later, our whole family had to undergo extensive dental restoration care. [Even the most important (and reasonably well treated) of the engineers came home with health conditions that measurably shortened their lives. The general health impact would not be apparent until the Germans reached their older years and, as we shall see, the principals in this story did not enjoy long lives.]

The cemetery

The path out of the hospital sometimes led to the cemetery. Taking care of the dead was the responsibility of the living kin. The Germans had constructed a cemetery of sorts in the woods where, by the end of our time, a substantial number [54, of which five were by suicide] of our people were buried there. The plots, initially mounded, were sometimes decorated and often well-cared for. A wooden cross or stone with the person's name stood at the head end. The plots were perpendicular to a straight path, with even spacing between them. The grave was dug by relatives and friends. In winter this arduous task required a crowbar and pickaxe when the ground is deeply frozen. Burials involved singing, a speech or two, prayers, and when available, flowers. During the summer months fresh flowers would be maintained on the graves.

From the German cemetery site, we could look over to the Russian "place" which is all we could call it. The plots were randomly oriented wherever it was convenient to dig a hole. No paths to guide the visitor. Most had a cross of the Orthodox Church at the head and the plots some of the important deceased men and women were overlaid with wooden pyramids, painted red, with the Soviet star on the top. A few of the plots were surround by a 3-foot-high fence, sometimes wooden, sometimes of welded of steel giving the impression of a child's crib when the snow covered it. The weeds were everywhere. Nature always did its best to reclaim the leaning, rotting wooden crosses.

What does the difference between the Russian approach of letting nature take over after a person is dead and the German pedantic orderliness say about us, about humanity? A Russian teacher once told me that "Ordnung" [orderliness] is a sign of a bourgeois, a man elevated above the masses. [The concept of social stratification is an anathema for communist ideology and yet it is everywhere. It seems to be a natural state of humans, despite egalitarian aspirations.]

The road past House 35 took Russian funeral processions to their gravesite area. We always learned about the parades from Upra to the burial grounds from the sounds of a marching brass band blaring slow and dark tunes. If the dead was an important individual and earned medals, the carrier of a placard decorated with them led the parade. The band followed. A group carrying the lid of the casket led the wagon with the open casket. Women in head shawls sitting on either side of the casket wailed and whined. A train of walking mourners trailed along, its length a measure of the dead person's importance. Only a few would be dressed in the black garb of sorrow.

One day we discovered the mounds of about 200 graves on the nearby hillside above the Russian burial ground. These were overgrown with weeds and grass. We learned that it was the burial site of German POWs and found the remains of the structures and fences that housed and contained them when they were held there. A friend and I erected a large birchwood cross to bring a little brightness to the spot. Over the years, first the leaders, and later the younger took to cleaning up the grave site area and rendering it German. When we were done on a special day in that year's spring and had the place in flowers, we held a ceremony with singing and much reflection about lost lives. When I visited the place one last time in 1953, few flowers remained, the weeds had regained supremacy, but the cross still shined.

The school

From the dead we go to the young. We had the full spectrum of ages ranging from the young born here to older students going to high school [grades 9–12], even some ready for higher education. It took until 9 January 1947 before we cleared matters related to the schooling for the children. On that date, the German Specialist School no. 88 was opened. The building had been a diplomatic quarter for the time when the Soviet government moved from Moscow to a safer Kuybyshev during WWII. [The modern Google map of Samara identifies the location of a bunker building where Stalin was sheltered, presumably now open to visitors.] The rooms were suitably large, and instruction took place in shifts during the morning and afternoon. The number of students was about 270. The total count of the young under the age of twenty was about 600.

The director was Russian as was his female assistant, both of Jewish "origin [!]." They were good educators and more approachable than the people with whom we worked. Even so, they were cool and distant when we encountered them in public. The assistant was well read and was the only Russian woman who visited the Germans in their homes [except for the Russian doctors]. We wondered whether she was gathering intelligence on our behavior and the state of our mental health. Russian teachers taught the language, Darwinism, Russian history, and the Soviet constitution. Teachers for all other subjects came from the ranks of our community. The extra earnings involved were a godsend for those who participated as teachers and helpers. There were ten grades in the school. The schooling was rigorous, and the curriculum paralleled that for Russian students. A concern was that the children had missed two years of school during and after the war. Parents often spent evenings tutoring their own children to help them to catch up. Always present was the relentless pressure to perform because grades [marks in the courses] were publicly displayed on bulletin boards. Not until the Germans shared classes with the Russians in the higher levels, did they learn to ignore the pressure [of having one's capabilities in public view] and adopt the characteristic Russian "whatever ...!" attitude.

Grades 4 and up ended the year with brutal exams to "graduate" to the next grade. The written and oral examinations took 2–3 weeks. These exams were festively administered by a commission sitting behind a table with a red [of course] tablecloth. Invariably, the discourse wandered into propaganda for the Soviet Union and the "Fight for Peace". The parents hoped that by merely shrugging their shoulders, the students would be made aware that the dispensed words were mostly nonsense. The first of May was always a festive 'holy' day for communism. The school's classes marched in parades with black/red/yellow flags [postwar German colors] and slogan posters behind the teachers and the director. It was always unwise for the adults to be absent from the jubilant crowd because attendance keepers with papers and a pencil were always about.

In 1952, the director rewarded the uppermost classes with a field trip of 15 hours up the Volga on a boat to a town named Ulyanovsk. The trip was said to have been lovely and climaxed as a pilgrimage to the town where Lenin grew up. His birthplace was a museum. [Apparently still is, according to Wikipedia.] For the students, the trip was their first outside the boundaries of the confinement compound.

In those last years (1951–3), the graduates from School no. 88 and from other similar schools in Kuybyshev competed for places in higher education with exams commonly administered to both Russians and

Germans. That year, all ten of the German students who took the entrance exams passed them; a good reflection on the [German and Russian] teachers for a job well done.

The degree of acceptance for these students who were to go on to further studies in Russian institutions to pursue their specific interests varied considerably. Students in medicine and education were readily accepted. They studied and lived with their Russian counterparts. Technical studies like engineering and science were generally not accessible to German students, especially when quotas for such studies were [or said to be] filled. These students were advised to proceed with studies in other directions.

The programs in education in which our daughter Christa participated included a wide and extensive list of courses, including optional foreign languages like English. The schooling years at the Russian higher-level institutions were miserable for the German students. Life was regimented and the feeling was that older Russian students were always keeping a watchful eye on them. There was little commonality between the Russian and German students to allow them to become friends. The reality was even worse: one had to watch what one said because reports of bad words about political officials were potential roads to prison.

The Volga and the forest, in summer and in winter

[Germans generally love the forest and nature and the abductees in Upra were no exception. Despite much misery around meeting the needs of day-to-day life, there were moments for looking up and seeing the larger and beautiful natural world. Pflügel waxed elegantly about what there is to see, what is green and natural. The remainder of this chapter takes us off the main course of the book but serves to remind us that nature's beauty is there for us to see to lift the human spirit.]

In the part of Russia where we were, the Volga flows from north to south, starting southward near the city of Kazan. In this region the river landscape is peculiar. The right bank on the west side is hilly and forested while that to the river's east is meadows. To the north of Kuybyshev, the river encounters the Zhiguli mountain range that forces the flow eastward in a sharp left turn. The Zhigulis reach to an altitude of about 1,000 feet and extends across the river to the east. The river cuts through the range after a 90 degree turn to the right to reach the town of Krasnaya Glinka [the present-day site of a ski area]. The high plateau area east of the river is the location of Upra. [The natural barrier of the land on either side of the river was the planned location for a hydroelectric dam during the 1930s. The dam was built in 1957, further north.] The cliffs above the river near Upra are about 300–350 feet above the river.

The views of the landscape from local high points to the south were magnificent. On a clear day one can easily see Kuybyshev. The view to the north shows the river emerging from behind the Zhigulis and turn south in a tight, majestic turn. The path of the river was made evident by the slow motion of white steam plumes from the river boats and, in summer, by the wind-driven clouds. Where we stood, we could see the river coming toward us and pass through a large natural gate. Here, the west bank is steep, and on the opposite side are sand banks that change their shape every spring when it floods. The view down from the sanatorium to the water includes a large island thickly covered with large trees. Below us, the narrow stream of the river forced several small fishing-village houses to be built close to a narrow beach. Boats were pulled up the embankment. From the sanatorium a rather unstable wooden staircase with rest platforms or a winding road led down to the water. At the bottom, a floating dock served as a stop for boat traffic along the river. Several hundred meters downstream we could spot the [Koptev?] ravine emptying eastward into the river.

Here, near the sanatorium, the narrow river raises its water level by some 30 feet in spring to accommodate the water from melting snow. Downstream of the river's narrow section, the river widens to about two kilometers with numerous islands. The various streams around these islands reunite with the main river flow further south. In summer, the water surface served as storage for rafts of logs to be processed by a sawmill nearer Kuybyshev. From our high viewpoint, the east bank falls gently along the river to reach Kuybyshev where the Volga meets with the Samara River from the east. After passing the city, this side of the river opens to more wide low-lying meadows and the river turns once again, this time to the west. The view of this wide landscape always struck us as majestic and fascinating.

Around the higher hills near Upra, the land is hilly with leafy forests. Lakes empty into small streams feeding the Volga. Interruptions by cultivation were uncommon. The composition and structure of these forests were new to us. It was largely untouched by the hand of man and consisted primarily of linden trees, oaks, birches, and aspens. Evergreen trees could be found at the higher elevations of the Zhigulis. Open meadows within the forest had boundaries of a thick understory and bushes against the forest edge. The soil was chalky with sink holes indicating a karstification of this land underlain by limestone. These holes filled up with snow in winter and retained it long into the spring when the lowlands were filled with beautiful wildflowers.

It struck us that the beech trees that are so characteristic of the German forests were entirely missing here. We were at roughly the same latitude as Mecklenburg, so that we often pondered the climatic differences and their impact on the vegetation. The seasons here were more extreme in temperature with winters colder and longer and the summers hotter and drier. The transitions to the next season were more abrupt than we were used to in Germany. Toward the end of March through the middle of April, a warm south wind would begin to blow, promising spring. A nice warm spring day was not necessarily a harbinger of summer. Invariably, there was a last attack by winter in June. Similarly, the late summer warmth could easily be upended by snow flurries. These were not always the beginning of winter.

The winter could bring temperatures down to -40F. The icy winds swept over the Volga. They pummeled our houses and local streets with blowing snow that came to rest in drifts everywhere. We were always cold in our poorly heated rooms. Outside, it was hard to breathe and the beginnings of frostbite on ears and noses were hard to avoid. Even enthusiastic skiers gave up being outside when the winds blew. It did not always blow, however. There were days of brilliant sunshine and wonderfully clear air. We could easily imagine ourselves to be at an alpine resort! The loveliest of winter's days were in spring when the air was warmer and the snow still deep and beautiful, especially when dusk added its reddish glow and charm with shadows of pink and blue. The blue and green of the buildings' window frames added even more to the kaleidoscope offered by the sun. At times, it was magic.

In spring, the linden buds grew a reddish brown and the golden catkins of the aspen appeared on the branches of the grey-green tree trunks. The snow and the birches provided brilliant whites under an infinite blue sky. Toward evening, it seems the day did not want to yield to night: the light shined longer from the snow and forest with its sky turning more blue/green with every passing minute. And still, evening arrives. The cold air is pierced by steam and smoke rising from chimneys.

Some days, the world would be covered in frost, ice crystals coating tree branches and man-made structures. With a few rays of sun, they quickly disappeared. The migrating birds could be seen as they flew north. Everything is warmed a bit and nature comes alive. Heaps of snow shrink, and rivulets of water are everywhere. It was a time to stick to using the paved roads, for all else is mud. The birds sing and as soon as the first ground surface is liberated from snow, the first blades of grass appear ... and the leaves come out. Next, the brightly colored anemones and the bright green birch leaves take over coloring of the forest. New greens here and there and the white flowers of cherry trees are followed by the pink and fragrant apple blossoms. In the forest, we found flowers we considered rare: wild yellow tulips, larkspur, corydalis, and dozens more. Our favorites were the larkspur.

We welcomed the spring here, as we did in Germany, and we were impressed with the manifold breadth of nature here. The colors were brighter and, it seems, more greatly varied. Is it the rich dark soil and the climate with its drier summer air? ... the air that looks and feels like what we knew back home, high in the mountains on a nice autumn day?

Chapter 18

THE GERMAN COMMUNITY

[Life in the German community is also outside the tale midstream, but it is hard not to take time to glimpse at the resilience of the souls as their circumstances are described by Kurt Pflügel. The history line continues in the next chapter. After 1950, return to Germany begins to become a possibility but let's step back to 1946.

In Kurt Pflügel's voice.]

Life in the German community prior to the summer of 1950

For our family, a new period of our lives began when we boarded the train for an unknown destination. Friends from Vietzen and Rechlin were scattered to the winds, and we were face-to-face with strangers. On the trip, I met a few people I got to know in the half year of work in Dessau. Our train was one of the first to arrive in Upra. In the still almost unoccupied House 35, I found the leader of the Junkers group to which I belonged. Outside my work, my social circle was relatively small so that when this friendly face greeted me, it was as if I had met a friend on the street or while shopping. I was eager to learn who else would show up. The first social contact, especially for my wife and children, came a little later when the fellow residents in our apartment pulled in. These new friends came with two small boys and, like us, had to deal with the shock of seeing the room that was to serve as their quarters. They realized that it was far too small to accommodate the furniture they had brought. During introductions, it came out that this new family, like my wife, were from the same part of Germany along the Rhine. That reality bridged the gap with warmth and friendliness.

More and more involuntary travelers arrived and as the discussions with them revealed, they came not only from Junkers, but also from the BMW facilities in Stassfurt and the Askania factory in Berlin. It was obvious that people largely unknown to each other were pooled to a common destiny. And yet, one day, to my great amazement, I met an old acquaintance from Rechlin. He was associated with Askania and, in 1936, had moved into a nearby house when we moved into our home there. Later, in Upra, he played a record for me that was recorded during a Christmas festivity before the war. Many of the voices on the recording were familiar. Where are they today?

The Junkers people were quick to reunite because they had worked together for many years and built working relations at the company. Within the BMW group were many young engineers who had come to Stassfurt as military engineers. The men from both organizations were organized rather quickly under the command of Col. Olechnovich. It took longer for the wives and the families to bind into a kind of German community. Small social circles grew with the passage of time. The bond was the common difficulties facing us all.

It was a matter of luck whether the families, with or without children, forcibly squeezed into close proximity, were indeed compatible. We had the good fortune to have had intimate neighbors within our apartment with whom we got along well and with whom we spent many dark hours as well as happy ones. Our wives were fundamentally convinced that it was bad form to spoil lives by being disagreeable with each other when there was an overarching misery to share.

On 9 December 1946, we received permission to write letters. There was no mention of censorship or other formalities. I had sent a letter to my mother in Munich on 23 October via the last mail posting in Germany and we could now, after 7 weeks, finally inform her that we arrived in Russia, somewhere on the Volga.

Mail out of Russia was censored. Many wrote with letters numbered sequentially and kept track (via the return mail) which letters made it past the censors, and which did not. It became obvious that mail with comments that were less than glowing about the experience in Russia was stopped. Writing in code to describe reality was tried with varying degrees of success. In time we learned that letter recipients in the West were confused about the welfare of their correspondents in Russia.

Our first Christmas was sparse. I constructed a kind of Christmas tree with wooden sticks and pine branches. The children decorated it with colored papers. The presents were homemade dolls. The cardboard boxes that once held foodstuffs during the trip became doll houses. On this special night, the first feelings of a community came about when a family of four came into our stairwell by candlelight to sing carols.[1] The missing physical aspects of the season were overcome with emotional ones. There were tears aplenty.

The winter days were cold, -4 to -40F outside and it was also cold inside, 50 to 55F. Our family did not have sufficient cold weather clothing so that my wife and the children sought shelter in bed for many of the day's hours. Whoever had to leave the house was outfitted with all we had.

After the currency reform [1948] and the lifting of ration coupons, the standing in line for food and necessities got worse, but there were glimmers of light. Our clothing situation, for example, was partially improved, even as it could still be described as primitive. Stores never had enough to supply all we needed. They were merely places for distributing what little there was.

Daily life became ever more regular and rigid as it evolved but time was also made for activities beyond those that were absolutely necessary. We looked everywhere for activities to provide a change of pace and to find relief from our all-too-real circumstances. It was wonderful to find that talent of all sorts was awakened and to see that even people generally predisposed to passive conversation became surprisingly inventive in making things.

The players of Skat [a card game] were the first to find each other. People with musical instruments found each other. A youth orchestra was pulled together for evenings of music and dancing in the club house.

Early on, we met a nice family living in an apartment off our stairwell who later moved to one of the Finn houses where we often visited them. The parents had four cute and gifted children. In 1945 they were driven out of the Sudetenland to the Ostzone with just backpacks and the clothes they were wearing. He was an engineer and had just found work [at Junkers] and consequently shared our destiny by being "invited" to the USSR. They had only two boxes and a couple of bedsteads. The parents were unbreakable in their positive attitudes and inner spirits. They lived lives as "free wanderers," a youth movement we remember from the 1920s. They worked hard in the garden, built their own furniture, and even kept goats. Through all their travels, they always kept their guitar and their music handy. As soon as they were settled, they gathered a choir around them to sing old folk songs and were ever ready to learn new ones. On one occasion, I was able to give them a well appreciated song book I requested from Munich. This choir group was always present for any event that called

1 Singer states in his book that his family was one of the caroling groups.

for singing. Our warm relation to these fine people was strengthened further when I agreed to write two pieces for their puppet theater. My wife carved the puppet heads from potatoes. The performances in their home made for joyful times.

We also developed a tight friendship with a young couple from Stassfurt who originally came from Berlin. In December 1946, they brought the first German child into the world in Upra. She was a graphic artist and when she learned of our daughter Sigrid's interest in drawing and painting, she became her teacher. That was a very successful move. Sigrid also had talent in that area, and they created a painting community centered on depictions of the Volga River as a motif. In 1950, enough drawing and painting had been done to have a real art exhibition.

Crafts and hobbies are always something that piques the interest of engineers. Many had brought tools with them. One major project for engineers with electrical leanings was focused on building a radio. The project was critical because we had no way to satisfy our hunger and curiosity regarding news from the outside world. We needed a radio with good reception from broadcasts far away. On the free market in Kuybychev, we gathered radio parts and old American military radios. It was a real challenge to build one with the parts that were available, and in a small way, I helped. Happily, we succeeded in this endeavor. Lively discussions were brought on by the incoming news we were able to receive. For example, the station in Leipzig sent greetings to the engineering specialists in Russia on the 1948 anniversary of our abduction. This was particularly meaningful for us then, and every year thereafter, because the world was reminded that we, in our special circumstances, existed! Indeed, when some of our people had just moved to a new location in December 1953, one of our friends tuned in to the BBC [British Broadcasting Company] and learned that a portion of our group had been moved from Kuybychev to Kimry near Moscow. That was fast!

In its way, the city of Kuybychev was helpful in providing some entertainment. The city orchestra, playing well-performed classical music came to the clubhouse several times. We were very appreciative. I also remember an evening with folk music when blue-uniformed Cossacks came to dance, sing, whistle, and throw their swords about with sparks flying in all directions. Compared to another group of talented Cossacks from the Don region who often also performed for us, this was very original entertainment. Added to that was the occasional visit of the gypsies who came around and performed in the summer theater.

The living conditions had improved markedly by 1949–50, in part because we had lowered our expectations as we went through the first years. Thereafter there were real improvements, and every betterment of our condition was appreciated for what it was. Specifically, by the second winter, every member of our family had a heavy winter coat and a pair of lined boots. That Christmas, the children got ice skates and the shoes to go with them. An ice rink near the clubhouse was the scene of hours of fun. The three oldest also had their own skis by then.

In summer, we wore canvas shoes. [It appears that leather for shoes was hard to come by.]

My wife expanded her sewing skills to a great extent and made dresses for the girls out of various tablecloths and seat cushion covers. From nettles she made cloth and turned that into bedding and a wonderful, heavy jacket for me.

There were always small celebrations among the families, especially birthdays. Our daughter Sigrid's birthday coincides with Fasching [Mardi Gras] and that year we celebrated her 15th by moving the main room furniture into the bedroom and left the emptied space to be enjoyed by the young. Even the adults celebrated the occasion with friends. Everybody wore homemade traditional masks. The adult session was louder and ran until dawn.

The days of Christmas were workdays, but they were celebrated festively. Small handmade gifts were passed out to everyone and greetings from the Heimat were received by mail. [The English word for Heimat is "homeland" but the German one is nostalgic, stronger, and warmer.] In the Soviet Union's communism, Christmas was just another day. The new and important celebration day is New Year's Day. There were, however, Christmas pine trees available in the marketplace so that our children were able to enjoy a tree lighted with a few candles. The Russians simply replaced the Christ child and Santa Claus with "Father Frost" who, like the 'Weihnachtsmann' [Father Christmas], arrived on a sled hauling a tree and handed out gifts.

During the settling in period, good friends and a number of young BMW engineers had the idea to further their educations by giving each other presentations on technical subjects. Everybody had an expertise, and I was to contribute something of my knowledge of electrical machinery. We took this very seriously and I thoroughly appreciated having to review some of the fundamental principles. Numerous and many-sided seminars were held in our German technical community. We arranged for church services, dancing sessions, ordinary social events, as well as technical and literary discussions. We were left to our own devices to bring a modicum of normality to our lives. Unfortunately, we succeeded for only a short a time. The Russian authorities were bound to step in.

As we met in these various ways, we wondered how such social organization was viewed from the Russian perspective. It occurred to us to wonder whether we were living in some sort of enclosed zoo. We were somewhat free to do as we wished and felt somewhat "free" because our bounded world was reasonably large. There was always the reality that we cannot escape, that we were observed, and always watched. Nobody knew who the watcher was, but he was always there. In 1951, our freedom to meet in various ways came to an end. In particular, we suffered heartbreaking stops to our educational and entertainment activities. That hit us hard. It seems that a casual conversation with a Russian apparently revealed that our puppet plays were written in a "bourgeois" style [with class distinctions]: not allowed in communism! Regular meetings concerned with technical discussion topics were frowned upon. Literary subjects were not sufficiently focused on "progressive", communist books.

The Russians learned a lot by observing us as we lived in our enclosure. I was sure that the lessons would have been missed had we been aware of being watched!

Chapter 19

THE WAITING YEARS

[At some level, the higher-level decision makers in Moscow must have examined the totality of the abduction of thousands of Germans and their maintenance in terms cost and benefit. Measuring the cost can be done in rubles sent to Kuybyshev to pay German engineers and, perhaps, a measure of reputational damage to be paid by the Soviet Union in some distant future. The benefit is more difficult to measure. In the final analysis, the point of the abduction was to transfer technological skills to Russia and the completion of assigned projects. No matter how the accomplishment of that task is measured, there must have come a time when maintaining some of the people involved are just a cost and the logical thing to do is to send them home. Ah, yes, logic was required.

This chapter will involve names of locations in Russia associated with jet engine projects. The process of returning to Germany will take Pfügel and his colleagues to various locations identified in the overview map in the Introduction.

Again in Kurt Pflügel's voice:]

Ever since our arrival in Upra, the same question hung consistently over us: How much longer will we have to work here, detained against our will? At the speech at the Club "celebrating" our arrival Col. Olechnovich talked only of the work ahead. Never did he mention going home. Nothing we heard or saw in the years that followed would kindle a desire to stay here one more day. In our minds, the yearning for a return always maintained questions regarding whether and when would we be allowed to go home. The various government ministries in Moscow, the Ostzone, and the GDR were silent on the subject. The insecurity regarding our future fostered by the official silence was a greater disappointment than having been brought here.

It was a hard test of nerves. The Ostzone minister Geisler even said publicly that there were no such people as us, deported against our will and working here. We were supposedly here voluntarily and working under contracts. We always clung to thin news and signs that there might be an end to this nightmare. The ups and downs of reading vague tea leaves was for many a mental anguish. We felt as in a rudderless boat, adrift and hoping to stay afloat.

The construction work in building the Finn houses (1946–7) was done by German war prisoners. The following year (1948), we were allowed to talk to them as their changing status allowed them to work in House 35. They were convinced that they would be returning home that year. If that was true, we would surely follow. In 1950, I received news from Munich that a close relative who was working as director of an industrial concern in Germany. He had been abducted to Baku [capital of Azerbaijan] after the war and was released. There was also news that an engineer from Dornier working for the French was allowed to go to Germany on vacation. ... on vacation!

We took all such news as signs of hope and suppressed all news that did not nurture such hopes. Many of us had correspondence connections to Dessau and to the other collective concerned with airplane construction located north of Moscow [Baade's OKB-1]. We kept hoping for news that a date might have been set. The reports of rumors grew in 1949 and more so in the following year. Every rumor was unsettling. The optimism naturally rose as the economic conditions improved. For example, behind House 35, there was an unfinished building that, after several false starts, was finally completed and in it was a store where kitchen utensils could be purchased. We were thrilled to be able to purchase a small sheet-metal tub. A new group of Russian engineers moved into this building, and we thought that they might be our replacements.

Then, in 1950, our hearts beat faster, again full of hope. Nine men with suitcases stepped out of the bus from Kuybyshev. They looked different and were differently dressed. A collection of German children playing nearby approached them. The men were astounded: these children spoke German! It appeared that they landed among Germans. One of the men asked: "Does a Mr. Pflügel live here?" – "Yes, of course!" What was the connection of these men to one of us? ... to me? It turns out they were former German war prisoners. They were led by a Dr. Chr. [Dr. Manfred-Rudolf Christian according to some sources.] Another was a long-time engineer friend of mine. The men's last assignment during the war (March 1945) was to defend the Oder [River] line. Back then, all expendable men were called up, even these engineers. When they were captured and found to be potentially useful to the Russians, they were brought to a holding prison in Krasnogorsk near Moscow. The following year, 53 men were moved to a new camp in Kurakino (also near Moscow) to build a turboprop aircraft engine under the direction of Dr. Chr. In 1948 a smaller group of nine of these men were moved to Kazan (a city on the Volga 220 miles north of Kuybyshev) to build a test model of this engine. [Kazan was the site of Engine Production Plant No. 16 where BMW 003 engines were manufactured as RD-20s.] Promises were made the following year that all prisoners were to be repatriated. At about the same time, their engine project was canceled so that the German prisoners thought they were headed home. After all, they had lost their jobs and would no longer be needed.

No such luck, in 1950, these Kazan engineers were transferred to Kuybyshev with the false belief that they would be joining other Germans going home. Their trip was on one of the large boats traveling on the Volga. They were ticketed "first class", with good food and very pleasant service attention in the dining room. The good times were finally here! The meeting with the Upra children was momentous: what a happening for them and what great news for us! Among the group of nine were two of particular interest to me, my friend E. and an engineer from Mannheim, M. The connection to that German city became a quick and close bond between us.

[Brandner writes in his memoir of the technical failure of 6,000 HP turboprop engines. They were going to be used in coupled pairs to make 12,000 HP engine nacelles. Four such nacelles were going to be used on the Tu-95 bomber. That failure caused Kuznetzov to decide to build a whole new engine of 12,000 HP and hoped, therewith, to win the prestigious Stalin Prize. Kuznetsov needed the German specialists a while longer and that included the ones transferred from Kazan.]

The turmoil that followed their arrival was a momentous event for the whole German community. Everybody was excited and what happened in the end? Not much. It took four more years for us to be allowed to go home. The new men were to be distributed into various working sections of our enterprise. They hesitated, of course, because they had been promised returns home since 1949. They were not associated with the BMW factory but were former soldiers and should be handled as such. It took a lot of acrimonious arguments and conferences with the state police and, within a week, all but Dr. Chr. gave in. The need to be earning money overcame the attainment of freedom. Dr. Chr. held out longer. In the end, however, he also capitulated and was put to work on some special project not connected with us.

The summer of 1950 came and passed, rather beautifully from a weather viewpoint. The new men were integrated into our community, and we even took chances to spend times camping in the wild landscape of the Volga and swimming in it. We had, in effect, given up hope that we might return home. Rumors were all we had to hang on to. There were no announcements from the factory and few new words in the rumor mill. Words like "tomorrow", "soon", "some time" took on a variety of meanings depending on your degree of optimism.

Train 1 – 22 September 1950

One day in September, a group of people were pulled, randomly it seems, from their workplaces to report immediately to the Club. No one knew why. The people assembled there were told that they would shortly be returned to Germany. They were denied further access to the factory. The group chosen consisted of about 200 families or about 600 people. The jubilation was as extreme as the disappointment of those who would not be going. More rumors followed. Additional groups would follow soon, it was said. The departure was well organized with a lot of help from the folks who stayed behind. Everybody helped to pack boxes and load them on the train. On 22 September, the first train left the Krasnaja Glinka station with tearful eyes on the faces of those remaining on the platform.

We were not among the "happy ones." Disappointment was the order of the days that followed. The Askania people left also, not to go home but to a new workplace near Moscow [Tushino, see Chapter 26]. Some of them had the misfortune of letting themselves be talked into signing employment contracts that would keep them in Russia longer. Fortunately for us, we did not sign such contracts and were, in fact, able to return sooner than they did.

[The repatriation of the Askania specialists did not take place until between 1956 and 1958, some eleven years after the abduction.]

When the repatriation got started in the fall of 1950, the nine Kazan engineers protested to clarify that they were POWs and should not be held any longer. That led to a tragic turn in the spring of 1951 for Dr. Chr. and his 24-year-old son. They had the courage to protest openly in front of the Upra factory. Dr. Chr. was never shy in withholding expression of his opinions. He gave us, by example, encouragement to resist unjust persecution of our community.

One night, that spring, the door to Dr. Chr.'s apartment broke open revealing armed men from the state police. He and his son were dragged out of their beds. Their stuff was rummaged through and searched. Dr. Chr. was arrested and hauled off in a car. He disappeared. We could not believe it. For months, his son inquired with the justice officials in Kuybyshev about the whereabouts of his father. Even his excellent command of the Russian language did him no good. The rumors at the factory were that he participated in some anti-Soviet activities. The Russians officials countered that he had been framed somehow. We were angry. After a couple of months, his son learned that he was sentenced to a prison camp in Siberia. All this time he sat in the local Kuybyshev prison while being brutally interrogated. It appears that a diplomatic action on the part of Konrad Adenauer[1] resulted in his eventual release and return to Germany.

A similar story goes with one of our people who had returned to the GDR. We heard that he was arrested for apparently meeting with a former Junkers employee living in West Germany. He was imprisoned in northern Russia and had since disappeared.

The promised end: 1 July 1952

In late 1950, those of us left behind were invited to the Club to hear a speech by an Air Ministry general. He thanked the attendees for their work and stated that by 1 July 1952, all specialists would be home again. That was the first time anyone had uttered a firm date. Does that mean two more years? Naturally, everyone was hopeful that they would be out on the next train, whenever that was. His speech included mention of the great honor bestowed upon us because we were privileged to learn how our participation benefitted the social construction of the community! The social construction? Really? We were "allowed" to stay! ... and invited to sign a "thank you declaration" to Stalin laid out on the table. We had other ideas about putting our names to such a document and those who could, escaped the room via a side door, without signing.

We celebrated Christmas and New Year confident that it would be our last in Russia. Divergent views grew within the left-behinds over the next few months. The optimists thought they would be leaving in May and the pessimists in the fall. A wave of deal-making stirred. All that was to be left behind: furniture, rugs, clothes, sewing machines, dishware, etc. was offered for sale to the Russians. They had never had opportunities to buy the things that were suddenly available. Sales were brisk and the convertibility of rubles to Ostmarks led to a flood of fund transfers to bank accounts in the GDR. The specialists understood that they would enjoy a preferred status for buying new things in

1 Adenauer was the first elected chancellor of the new Federal Republic of (West) Germany, the BRD, in 1949.

Germany when they got home. Traveling "light" was the order of the day with the anticipation of enjoying new stuff in their future homes. It was an exciting time.

What we missed noticing in all this excitement was the fact the work assignments were growing in volume and more intense. We had achieved the first performance steps of the engines as we were tasked to build, and now higher performance was the goal [the new 12,000 HP engine]. It looked like we were at the start gate again but, in our minds and hearts, were already on the train going home.

The waiting continued through the summer of 1951. No word of a new departure date. The warm season and the newly acquired self-confidence within the group led to the courage to test the physical boundaries of our world. Such tests were primarily to further out beaches and islands of the Volga and a welcome escape from Russian eyes and their hard demeanor. Naturally, there were warnings and postings on the black board about boundary violations, but we ignored them. The trips to the river and woods provided a new and welcomed equilibrium to life.

Train 2 – 18 December 1951

Finally, just as in 1950, another partial assembly of Germans was called to the Club. The promise of assembling another batch of departees was kept. But I was not among them, neither were the friends living in our apartment, nor the remaining eight Kazan engineers. We held together as a group and drew comfort from the fact that 1 July 1952 was not far off. The rows of desks in the office were emptier. The train left on 18 December. Only 190 days to go.

In the spring, we were asked to put together pieces to go into a memory book focused on our time in the USSR. GDR officials planned to give us this book on our return to Germany as part of welcome home festivities. A few of us wrote a few pages about what little good or enjoyable there was to be enjoyed but the response was generally mute. I wrote a few paragraphs about the beauty of nature. We heard that previous groups returning were welcomed but they were quite unhappy with the official reception. It seems that the GDR people expected the returnees to speak in glorious terms of the experience. They didn't. Their experiences were life-changing to be sure but certainly not "glorious."

It was time to decide what to sell and gather crates for the things to go home with us. Our mood went in ups and ... unbearable downs. Promises, consolations, depression were all part of our days. Soon, soon, not yet. We experienced these emotions over and over and nearly became as fatalistic as the common Russian normally is. We counted the days like the children do before Christmas. A group of my colleagues pushed a couple of us to confer with the Russian management to confirm the date of 1 July 1952. The director, Mr. Kuznetsov was surprised and astounded. He said he knew nothing of the deadline.[1] The Germans must have erred. The translator must have made a mistake. The optimists were smitten, and the pessimists saw themselves as vindicated. On the walls of the office, we devised a new calendar where the month of June had a 31st day, a spot for the 32nd, the 33rd, etc. Had the Soviet Union changed the transport plan? Things were very dark indeed.

Hopes for a return that fall collapsed. There were contacts with the GDR diplomats in Moscow. We hoped they would speak on our behalf to the Soviet government or at least find out what can be learned about a date. The appeal by the GDR diplomats was made in the name of a Mr. "Wartmann" [Waiting man]. The reply from the Soviets was for us to wait some more! We waited some more and were told that lists and welcome celebrations back in Germany were being prepared. It was just a question of time, a lot of time.

Stalin died on 3 March 1953. The Russian engineers were shaken and emotionally down with tear-filled eyes after they left a memorial service in the factory. For us, the meaning of the event raised more questions about our futures. What are our chances now?

Sigrid's perspective

[The story cannot be told from just the perspective of the father when thoughts expressed by the children are available. My contact to his daughter Sigrid in early 2023 shed a bright light on the experience from her point of view. A previous attempt at locating the oldest daughter Christa failed and I learned from 89-year "young" Sigrid that her older sister had recently passed away. The conversations that ensued led to the following as a picture painted by one of the young people in Upra. Sigrid was born in 1934 and hence was about 18 in 1952. The following paragraphs are in her voice.]

In 1952 I did the Russian Abitur [high school graduation] at our German school, where we lived in a kind of ghetto and were relatively sheltered as children. Looking ahead to a possible return to Germany, it seemed wise to expand my language skills to include English. I was

1 Kuznetsov knew he had made the date impossible when he started the new NK-12 engine project.

able to enter the teacher's college in Kuybyshev and took English language courses for about a year.

There, I was confronted by the reality of the Soviet environment outside our "protection system." I lived with a German classmate and three Russian students in one room of a dormitory. Since we Germans were suspicious [and suspected] foreigners, we were constantly monitored and became a kind of outcasts. My command of Russian was not great. All the lessons in the classes were in Russian. We had to learn the writings of Marx, Lenin, and Stalin in Russian. I didn't understand a word of it and resorted to memorization.

On Sundays we were allowed to go home to be with our parents. The time had come when I could no longer get academic help from my father or even enter discussion with him because I could not translate what I had learned from the complicated writings into German. An important connection to my trusted father was now broken. My parents did not know the circumstances of my living in that school. I felt abandoned and helpless.

One of the students in our room, Valya, was a Chuvash [member of a small indigenous group of people in that part of Russia]. She was forbidden to learn anything about her own culture and to speak Chuvash at school. Our shared circumstances allowed us to understand one another. We were able to communicate honestly. In general, however, we were not allowed to have close contact with Russian students. Mostly, they were enthusiastic "Komsomols" and needed to be shielded from foreign influences! [The word is an abbreviation/contraction for "All Union Leninist Communist League of Youth."] These young communists were not people with whom heartfelt discussions were safe and inconsequential.

My German roommate and I had the good fortune to have met a Volga German student studying Russian literature. Her family had been resettled in the Kazakh city of Tashkent. Contact between us was quickly banned so that our time together was brief. We apparently knew too much.

I became very depressed and didn't know what to do. As a way of dealing with reality, I was allowed to participate in artistic gymnastics. In that activity, I met and got to know a Russian woman, Vera, who also felt very much like an orphan because she was far from her parents and from home. Our gymnastics lessons brought us a little joy and we always looked forward to them and to being together.

In retrospect, it was very important for me to have been in Russia and to have gotten to know a small number of Russian people. During the war, and even later during the occupation, they were our enemies, barbarians, etc. We were the same to them. During the times outside our "protection" zone, I learned more about the Russian as a person in his reality. I met Russian soldiers who studied there, and we communicated, albeit on a shallow level. I got to know a political dictatorship first-hand. In the school, I was not shielded by the "reality-protection" fence that surrounded the adults of our community, our ghetto.

My parents did not know or understand that this was such a dangerous and difficult time for me. [The danger was in the form of ostracizations and worse, if you said the wrong thing to the wrong person or were overheard saying the wrong thing by the wrong person.] Similar boundaries were faced by my brother. He studied at a technical college in Kuybyshev for a short time where he could only live in a room with German schoolmates. The circumstances for my older sister were even harder. She often abstained from attending high school and had partly removed herself from the emotional care of my parents. My parents didn't know, for example, how often she skipped school and hid in the basement. At the time I did not know either. I learned about her travails much later. We led very different and difficult lives in Russia.

Train 3 – summer 1953

[Back in Kurt's voice.]

June. A new decision announcement came from Moscow. It was barely comprehensible and at odds with our guesses about possible roads ahead. It said that the people in Moscow understood our plight of being kept in the dark and then they surprised us with new realities: a new group of returnees is to depart shortly for Dessau. Even the leader of our group [Brandner?] will be allowed to go home. A second group is to be transferred to a place in the northern section of the Volga, near the city of Kalinin [today Tver].

We [the Pflügels] were again left behind with many others to await a possible second train to Germany. The news service said that some of the specialists could not go home because they had to spend some time outside the technical field where they had been working. We interpreted that as being a kind of quarantine for the mind. It was a bad sign that the last train to Dessau had only third-class coaches with hard wooden seating. The previous train [train 2] had only first-class coaches. We soon heard the news that the people on train 3 were removed from the train and forced to a camp on a lake island surrounded by barbed wire. [The island was Gorodomya on Lake Seliger, about 200 miles northwest of Moscow.]

We, our fellow apartment dwellers, and the few remaining people, including the Kazan engineers, prepared for a hopefully last summer in Russia. We were now a fairly small community. The Russians suddenly became much friendlier and gave us more elbow room. That summer, more free times on the Volga were enjoyed, apprehensively perhaps, but enjoyed, nevertheless.

Our children were old enough to proceed with their education within the Russian system. The academic calendar was forcing decisions to be made. Possibilities in Germany were still too remote to be able to plan for anything there. Anticipating our departure, however, we made the rounds to the places we knew, the cemetery, and the special places of nature in the forest. The order for the travel arrangements finally came on 9 November 1953. Things were moving fast. [By design,] there was no opportunity to say our good-byes to the Russians with whom social interactions had improved. We were barred from the factory. The frustration and uncertainty of the last few months had, at long last, been put to rest.

Did we make it, … finally? No. We were separated into two groups. One group would be going to the Ostzone and the other to somewhere that cannot yet be revealed. Those staying behind will be allowed to send their families to Germany. What?! Separate the families after all this time! I am told I must stay because my group is scheduled to leave Upra a little later. When??? The turns came as shocks. The men and our wives could not believe what we were hearing. Our heads were spinning, but we had a decision to make. When the war ended, my wife and I made a pact to not separate and to endure together all that came our way. Two important aspects had to be considered. First, we were told that those who stay will soon follow. Could we believe this vague promise? The second: our children were old enough (18–22) to deserve an education in Germany. There was no time to lose. With heavy hearts, we decided to part and go on separate ways. For only a short time, we hoped. Mutti and the children will go to Germany and I … , I didn't really know what was to become of me and the remaining men.

Train 4 – 25 November 1953

We did not have much furniture left and now we had to separate my stuff from that for the family. Their departure date was on the 25th. All night, Mutti spent baking and repairing my clothing. The snow was deep that next morning when the heavy wooden boxes were hauled to the truck and thence to the station. Mutti was mentally and physically exhausted. Almost all families agreed to separate and go on the train to Germany. On the other hand, the women in couples without children stayed with their husbands. Even the son of Dr. Chr., the sole remaining former POW, was allowed to go. Through the thickly iced windows, on which openings were scraped for a better view, the families waved to the men standing on the platform: statues with fur caps and uplifted collars, snow blowing around them. It was by far, the lowest point of all my days in Russia.

Just before the train left, Mr. B. [Brandner] came running up to the group of men. He had been traveling with a delegation of Russians to inspect a new worksite and had just returned to the station on a different train. He called out: "Everything is in order; you will soon be catching up with them! We will have a meeting tonight."

Strangely, on our way back to the nearly empty apartments, the low-lying midday winter sun was accompanied by two beautiful pink and gold sun dogs amidst a few thin clouds.

Chapter 20

ON SEPARATE WAYS

[Continuing in the voice of Kurt Pflügel.]

That evening Brandner gathered in his residence what remained of his once substantial group of colleagues. He recounted his trip to the small town of Savelovo, a town north of Moscow, near Kimry on the Volga. "Everything is beautifully arranged with good housing, and we will reunite with our comrades who left this summer", he said. [They were the comrades on the Gorodomya island surrounded by barbed wire who left on train 3.] He assured us that we would not stay long in Savelovo. We did not believe him.

Train 5 (just the men) – 1 December 1953

On the first of December, we finally left Upra with small boxes containing what little we had. We were put on a first-class sleeping coach contrasting again with the earlier third-class train to Germany. Our destination was Moscow. The men finally had time for themselves and filled it with discussion about why we, now fewer than 100 people, must take this special trip. There were lots of possible reasons why we were not released. It could be about this technical quarantine idea because the entirety of the most important men was either sequestered on that island or on this train. All the people in this group were either the lead engineers or had advanced academic degrees. The shop people, the machine operators, metal workers, etc., had been sent home. This collection of us could be just bureaucratic mismanagement, or it could be that the men chosen were felt to have connections to West Germany and might therefore be harder to keep in the GDR? The Kazan engineers, for example, belonged in that category. Perhaps former Nazi party membership was in play? Or a record of politically unacceptable behavior? Or were we those who had to work with the folders marked "secret" to do our work? – which meant that we knew secrets. It was all pure speculation.

We arrived at the little station in Savelovo and were greeted by some of the families and friends transferred here from the Gorodomya island compound. We quickly learned from them what happened after our separation earlier that summer. They told of being offloaded from the train to a steamship and ferried to a thickly forested lake island with a wide sandy beach. On the island, a road led to an open gate and barbed wire fencing: they knew they were trapped. They were taken to a group of masonry and wooden houses and learned that about 60 families had been living there in isolation for about seven years.[1] The specialists on the island all that time were the ones who worked on the V-2 rockets in Peenemünde. Some were experts in optics who had worked for Zeiss. They too were awaiting a departure for home and were bitterly disappointed when they saw the new arrivals because it meant that their own departure would be delayed. It seems the islanders did not endure great work-related difficulties. They were kept busy on almost meaningless projects that had nothing to do with their expertise. [They were in intellectual isolation. It was Soviet policy that work on ballistic missiles was to be done secretly by Soviet engineers to the greatest extent possible.]

The bad and good news for the islanders was that nine of the families were to be transferred to the new location (Savelovo) and the other 50 would be returned to Germany and presumably were. Purely by coincidence, when the nine families left the island and arrived in Savelovo, their train halted next to another train full of jubilant Germans on their way home. [The origin of this group is not stated but could have been from the Junkers airplane building collective, probably OKB-1.] The arrivals from the island hoped, of course, to transfer to that train and join them going home. No such luck. Their time had not come.

We learned that the last 100 or so engineers from that other Junkers [airplane construction] collective were also going to be transferred here [to Savelovo] from their present location nearby. Something big was brewing. We were told to spend another night in our sleeping coach compartment, and we would move into our new quarters in the morning.

---

1 These V-2 engineers and technicians were used to set up the first launches of Russian V-2s (as OKB-456) and then removed from further work in rocketry. The Russians took it over and maintained all further work in strict secrecy while the Germans did little to nothing significant for the duration of their captivity.

Savelovo is a small town with the town of Kimry on the opposite shore of the Volga. The river is wide and constitutes the northern end of the navigable Volga to the Caspian Sea. It seems we were destined to be bound to the Volga! A factory was the town focus. A multistory stone structure appeared to be connected to this factory as were a series of new two-story houses with two entrances each. The new arrivals from Upra, from the island, and from OKB-1 were distributed into the dwellings. My fellow Mannheimer and I chose to live together in one of these new two-room houses. The rooms were of good size (160 sq. ft. each) and associated with them was a WC and a kitchen. One of our rooms had a balcony. With carpeting on the floor, the place was quite livable, and I wished our quarters in Upra had been nearly this good. A nice heating unit kept the place sufficiently warm. For community use there was a small house with a bath and shower. We moved in.

After a few days, we were called to the "Zavod." A section of the factory was for the Germans. There was office space and two adjacent large rooms with writing desks set up. It seemed we were entering a new phase of our stay in Russia. No Russian officer stepped up to begin a recitation of facts concerning our future. Instead, Herr B. [Brunolf Baade] leader of the Junkers Aircraft people in the OKB-1 located in nearby Dubna spoke to address us. [In Pflügel's text, the location is Podberesja.] We were told that our work for the Soviet Union was over. We were pulled together to Savelovo for a new assignment with our work to benefit the GDR, the government of the former Ostzone. The project was the construction of a jet airliner, together with building the facility to make that possible. The airplanes were to be built in the GDR and sold for export. The middle of April [1954] was projected as the date when the work in Savelovo would be finished, and we could count on returning to Germany. The Russians were no longer part of the project and would be concerned only with the transition management.

The deadline seemed achievable. The seven years of work with the Russians was certainly sufficient experience to allow the development of an airplane and engine configuration so that groundwork for the project in Germany could be defined and started before we arrived there. We had as an immediate goal, the construction of a [plywood] mockup of the airplane. Baade himself was to lead this effort.

The team was apparently what remained of the people abducted to the Soviet Union in 1946. It consisted of men from the former German air industry reassembled here from various places in Russia. In large part, the men are from the aircraft and engine divisions of Junkers. Lightweight structures engineers from Arado, Heinkel and Siebel were part of the team as were the jet engine people from BMW who were caught in Stassfurt. Smaller groups and individuals were engineers who came as refugees from the Sudetenland and former POWs like Dr. Chr.'s people from Kazan. Groups with expertise associated with facilities in other locations were also included in the reassembly. Examples were the engine test facilities in Rechlin (that is why I was still on the team), the air weapons school in Halle, and others.

To our surprise, a new man was introduced to the team. He had been held in relative isolation as a particularly important "catch" by the Soviets. He was the former research director of the DVL [German acronym for German Flight Research Institute located in Berlin], Herr Prof. Dr. Dipl. Ing. Günther Bock [identified in Pflügel's writing as G. Bo. together with all those academic titles]. Was this his end of a lonesome stay in Russia and was he to play an important role in our new project? It shortly came out that while Baade oversaw the overall project, Bock would direct the airframe structural design and Brandner the propulsion group. [An image of Brandner, Baade, and Bock is shown in the plate section, taken at about this time.]

Another Christmas in Russia.

Bock's travails

In the summer of 1945, Günther Bock was captured by the Red Army in their occupation zone like others who had not fled to the West. Several interrogations by Russian officers led to his arrest and transport to East Prussia a month later. While being transported further east and just before entering Russia, he was able to send a coded message to his wife that he was alive. His first prison cell was in Moscow's notorious Lubyanka prison. There he was in "safe storage," as he liked to say, until the authorities decided what to do with him. Nine idle months followed, just passing the time. Conditions in prison were not all that bad for him. He sensed that others there had it far worse. The stay substantially diminished his fragile health so that when the Russians finally decided to put him to work, they allowed him a few weeks to recover in a sanatorium [very nice of them!].

[During the negotiations that led to the creation of this trio of leading German engineers and the focus on a German airplane project, philosophical differences between these principals came to light. Baade, having gained a negative opinion of Americans, became an enthusiastic communist. Bock, for his own reasons, became disillusioned and disgusted with events in the Western World. Both men, despite their experiences at the hands of the Russians, held sympathetic beliefs in the communist ideology as practiced by the Russians. Brandner, on the other hand, was keen to return to his home in a still occupied but undivided Austria and to the West generally. While supporting the general idea of the German airliner project, he did all he could to escape the grip of Russian control of his life. He also believed that the project was unfeasible because it depended on close cooperation with the USSR to supply materials and to purchase the airplanes. He succeeded in separating himself from the project after arguing that it should be based in West Germany. In this argument, he did not prevail, and the project landed firmly in East Germany. Brandner left the project, and, in short order, Bock followed.]

In order to make the coming time in Savelovo without our families more attractive, we received salary increases. That bonus made the winter months tolerable. I knew my family was safely in Berlin and they had even made a trip to the Rhineland to visit family members. I was allowed to send about half my earnings to Berlin and my wife reported that it was adequate to meet her needs. Life was looking better. Our social life improved with occasional men's parties and celebrations. We even put together a men's chorus. Kimry across the river was a nice, old Russian town, certainly nicer than Upra. A small city might be a better description. As winter settled in, the river froze over so that trucks and horse-drawn sleds were seen doing commerce on the ice or just enjoying the space.

The letters from the Ostzone were fuel for rumors and led to lively discussions. We learned, for example, that we were to be transferred to a new location in Pirna [near Dresden] to continue our work. We also heard that we were expected to sign binding employment contracts. As with a similar offer made in Upra, that proposal was not well received. The fear was that we would be tied to this new enterprise without the chance to explore other opportunities when those became apparent. We turned down signing because, more than anything else, we wanted our freedom after all these years of captivity. High GDR officials came to discuss the contract matter and move it along, exercising considerable pressure. We were not interested in signing until we actually were in Germany, the GDR in this case. My secret weapon was a letter from my former employer [BBC in Mannheim, in the American zone] saying I had a job waiting when I came back [to West Germany]. Somehow, I avoided signing. Perhaps, using the heavy workload as an excuse was an effective argument.

Our lives were noticeably less restricted than they were in Upra. It appears that we were meant to have good memories of our time in Savelovo. The spring came as did wonderful times spent exploring the nearby natural regions, the forests, etc., the cultural and historical sites.

Especially interesting was a tour of an old church built by the men from three neighboring villages before the Revolution. Several times we were taken to Moscow to enjoy an opera, to shop, and enjoy the sights but always accompanied by official supervision. The city exuded a certain air of sterility and absence of life. I was left with the distinct impression that Moscow was designed and run to be the showpiece for Russians and foreign delegations. [Tourist trips to Moscow as we might imagine them today were still in a distant future.]

The contrast between Moscow and the circumstances of the peasant villages around Savelovo, just 60 miles from the city, was stark. Despite all attempts at displays of success and modernity, there were always the long queues for the necessities of life. Prices were high in relation to incomes and the standard of living was consequently mediocre. Items on display in store windows often looked like they were imported from Germany. They were not. Russian factories existed just for making stuff that looks like it was made elsewhere. The copies of Leica cameras and of Bosch refrigerators were excellent and undistinguishable from the real articles. Even copies of new-looking Opel cars could be seen on the streets of the city. These items were mass produced but never in quantities to satisfy the needs or for affordable prices. It also appears that whatever product is produced is made in only one variant model. [Wasn't it Henry Ford who said "a customer can have a car painted any color he wants – as long as it's black"?]

During our tour of Moscow University, we ran into colleagues from the Askania Group. They were employed in Moscow in what they described as a golden cage. They had signed employment contracts and could only dream of releases to return to Germany.

Train 6 – 26 June 1954: the last train!

While laboring in Savelovo, the date for our departure was pushed back week by week. One bit of news from Moscow announced that nothing stood in our way to return to West Germany. Really? West Germany? Was that promise believable? A list was drawn up to note the desired places where in Germany the specialists will want to go. Few dared to put down the actual place. Russian or East German knowledge of that location might become a trap. Activity and rumors around the workplace intensified and appeared to point to a more serious event happening at the end of June. We were leaving! To celebrate, we were invited for a steamboat ride on an undeveloped arm of the Volga and on that trip, I wrote my last letter to Berlin. About 300 men from Junkers and BMW finally left the train station in Savelovo on 26 June 1954.

The mood was apprehensive. We knew that the GDR wanted to keep us together in Pirna and put us to work as a team. As such, we felt that we were exposed to a recall to Russia, and we pondered often and secretly how we might escape being heaped into whatever Pirna was going to be.

East Germany – the GDR

Into Germany via the required change of trains at the Belarus border. Our baggage volume had increased (I owned a new refrigerator) while we were in Savelovo because we had the money to spend. In fact, we brought so much cash over the border that we exceeded the maximum allowed, but nobody seemed to have paid any attention. Our moods were improving as curiosity regarding our reception grew. On the train, we were finally told that our trip had a destination, Dresden. The well-equipped and attractive dining car was a harbinger for a new beginning.

The welcoming committee in Dresden consisted of a few of our colleagues' family members. The bus ride to nearby Pirna took us to its headquarters where we overnighted in local lodgings. The welcome speeches the next day were followed by a tour of a display of amazing things we had not seen in years: all manner of goods ranging from new clothes to automobiles. We were free to order any of the offered items. The officials went all out to impress us. Their sincerity was, however, put into a bit of doubt when we learned from the native people around us (the service staff) that they had never seen any of the displayed items in any store, ever.

Awkward interviews and bizarre expressions of welcome and sincere envy about our experiences led to a separation of our group into smaller ones according to desired destination. Everyone in our group was offered a job at Pirna. I hesitated because my family lived in Berlin, and I was a bit out of place in this new venture as an electrical engineer. I ventured to state that job opportunities for me were better in Berlin. Many in our group finally laid out their cards: they stated that they had no interest in working here and preferred to work in other cities in the GDR. To my amazement, there was a group destined for travel to West Berlin and another to West Germany. The Kazan engineers were among the latter. The breathing got easier, and the breakup of the group was underway. For seven years we lived and worked together, and the parting could have been difficult, but it was not. The new reality was that we were going home!

A bus ride later I was in East Berlin in the arms of my wife and children.

The next morning, to my great surprise, our Upra friend from Mannheim stood at the door. Beaming, he showed me his second-class train ticket to Mannheim. "We [he and his family] are on our way!" he said, assuring us that the gate to West Germany was open and I should follow. I allowed myself the pleasure of harboring hope that there might actually be an end to our ordeal.

The bus carrying my friend to West Germany did not leave Pirna to reach its destination without a few scary hours. Late that night as it approached the entry post to East Berlin, the gate was down, and no one was to be let through. The guards encouraged everyone to step into a nearby restaurant "to have dinner." The bus riders refused and got back onto the bus. Following a few arguments with more officials, the bus took off again. After about an hour of driving in near total darkness, they arrived at a chain-link wire gate with the name "Airport Schönefeld"[1] posted. The bus riders revolted: it was a trap to take us back to Russia!! They locked themselves in the bus and dared not exit from it. The official East German escort personnel were speechless. They had never seen resistance expressed to government officials. Had everyone gone mad? After a while, more officialdom came to the rescue arguing that it was all an unfortunate misunderstanding. The explanations were doubted but, happily, they successfully crossed this barrier and all further checkpoints into the West.

Police state

[Kurt Pflügel was fortunate to have his wife's single-minded determination regarding their destination in Germany. It was advantageous that he was relatively high ranked in terms of importance to the Russians in Upra so that they helped him reach West Germany with the promises they made.

More ordinary individuals might not have been so fortunate. The early 1950s were the tense days of not only the Cold War but of consolidation of power by the communist Social Unity Party (in German, SED) to form the GDR out of the Soviet Occupation Zone. State security is always a major concern for single party rule in any country and the German machinery to maintain it was brutal and efficient. An agency called the Ministerium für Staatssicherheit, called "Stasi" for short, controlled the lives of all GDR citizens. Dossiers were maintained for anyone suspected of independent thought that had the potential of conflicting with official thinking. These files were created for anyone who aspired to have an important position in education,

1 Schönefeld became the official airport for the city of Berlin in the reunited Germany.

industry, rights to open a small business, even for association with the church.[1] Interviews were arranged where the candidate spoke "freely" about topics raised and the discussion put him on a scale from "harmless" to "dangerous" as far as the state was concerned. Citizens were deputized to be undercover agents keeping track of others and reported deviant activity to headquarters. In other words, everybody spied on everybody else, and trust was in short supply. Such records were instrumental in securing employment, constraining the freedom to travel, even determining personal safety, etc.

Prior to the building of the Berlin Wall in 1961, the entire city of Berlin was a control zone for the Stasi. Trains were stopped on their way into any part of Berlin and within East Berlin to check if the travelers were on the controlled lists, and if they were, it was likely that bad things were likely: arrest, prison, and disappearance. In the western sectors of the city, dealing with people on the control list was more clandestine, including kidnapping to uncertain futures, etc. Trains were the common way to travel because automobiles were not widely available to the average person and roads were strictly controlled. The trains from various places within the GDR never entered East Berlin through the western sectors. They were rerouted around the western sectors to enter the part of the city called "Berlin, Hauptstadt der DDR," Berlin capital city of the GDR.

The GDR authorities realized that travel to the West and interactions with Westerners were undesired possibilities so that entry to East Berlin involved significant checking. It turns out that before the war, Berlin had an extensive urban and suburban railway system called the S-Bahn. Managing the system was thought by the Allies to be best done as a single entity so that an administration in one of the sectors would be responsible for running it. That task fell to the Soviets and later to the GDR. Since this rail system was present in the West and in the East, it was a way to get from one to the other. However, the system was also thickly populated with spies and nasty agents to thwart such movements. The reality was that sitting anywhere on an S-Bahn train was not the same as being in West Berlin or easily able to reach it. Bad things did occur, but prior to the erection of the Wall and the shutdown of service across it through the tunnels of the S-Bahn, many people successfully escaped from the GDR.

If the stories about successful and unsuccessful escapes to the West were all written down, they would fill whole libraries. Unfortunately,

1 Both Protestant and Catholic. The church community could not be eradicated by the SED. In 1989, the Leipzig church community was central to the movement that brought the GDR and the Wall down.

most such memories died with the individuals who went through those experiences. Their lifetimes are nearly over as this is written. However, there are published records, and this telling is not meant as a compendium of all that is written but rather is an anecdotal look back at some of what is available. The stories by Pflügel and his daughter Christa in the next chapter and by Singer are examples of such travails. In his book, Singer describes a discovery, made after almost five decades, that there was a group of students who also had difficulties with East German authorities' interviews for church work. They did not escape to the West and were eventually convicted. They died for their moral views. Today, there is an official memorial the Donskoye cemetery in Moscow in their honor. Undoubtedly, there are more such stories. They are hard to live with and impossible to forget.]

Chapter 21

TO BERLIN WITHOUT FATHER

[This story of the family's trip back to Germany without their father is told by the oldest daughter Christa, as recorded by her father.]

After tearful goodbyes from the men standing on the platform with snow swirling about them, we roll through the same countryside we saw seven years ago and vaguely remember. This time we were going in the opposite, a happier direction. We harbored the hope to be able to reunite soon with our fathers. That was the promise the officials made.

The trip was slow. We often woke up in the middle of the night to find the train stopped and everything was still. We looked forward to the hot water that was available from the steam locomotive at stations when we stopped. We used the water to wash up and make tea. Up to Brest-Litovsk we traveled in a third-class sleeping coach and a compartment just large enough to accommodate our family. With sheets isolating a corner of the compartment, we managed to be able to wash and change with a modicum of privacy. We took our meals in the dining halls of the larger stations when the train stopped for a time.

[Brest-Litovsk is now in Belarus on the border with Poland. A peace treaty with the Central Powers (Germany) was signed there in March 1918 ending Russia's participation in WWI.]

Unlike on the trip to Russia, the necessary transfer of our boxes and furnishings between the freight cars was not done by Russian soldiers: we had to do it! Naturally, for exorbitant prices Russian civilians were ready to help. We could not afford their fees and did it ourselves. In the process Dieter caught a very severe cold.

While this was going on, some families were subjected to invasive searches by armed Russian officials. They apparently had a list of travelers they suspected of being capable of smuggling something out. These examinations were of everything they had, even the insides of radios and sealed cans containing food. We were spared. The officials knew, for example, that I was an avid photographer, and I could have taken pictures of some forbidden subjects [bridges and street intersections, for example]. Earlier that summer, a Russian and Mr. E. came by to "admire" my photo collection. I am convinced that it was an inspection to see if my pictures were indeed [politically or militarily] harmless.

On arriving in Frankfurt/Oder our sick and exhausted family thought: Finally, freedom! We are in Germany! Home! No such luck. On the platform, The People's Police [Volkspolizei, aka the Vopos] with shouldered guns would not let anyone out of the train cars. Pleas went nowhere, even those for a little dog with an urgent need were denied.

Welcome to the Deutsche Demokratische Republik!

We finally arrived in Leipzig to speeches about how privileged we were to be allowed to get to know the praised land where socialism reigns supreme! At the hotel where we were to spend the night, a commission had been set up to make arrangements for travel to our final destinations. Transition monies were provided. All cities in the GDR were open to us, except Berlin because we had neither an available accommodation nor relatives there. Our appeal for going there was denied and the alternative suggested was Dresden. We were particularly concerned about care for my handicapped sister Renate who needed residential treatment with competent medical care, care she was denied during our seven years in Russia. Understandably, the many and sudden changes in the circumstances brought about by this trip were very hard on her emotional state.

The arguments for going to Berlin were for naught. We were brought to a small pension in the outskirts of Dresden where we could stay, temporarily. The complete destruction of the city wrought by the mid-February 1945 firebombing was emotionally shocking. It looked like little had been done in the eight years since then.

We looked like "wild" people, people from a wilderness, with well-used, home-made coats, home-sewn backpacks, and some inappropriate summer clothes protecting us from the cold November air. We looked odd. People stared at us and when my mother ordered a bottle of red wine to go with dinner that evening, the waiter asked if we could pay for it. He later apologized when he was clued in on our circumstances. We three oldest explored the city that Sunday and on Monday, it was time for Mutti to figure out how we could go about to not appear like vagabonds. She had no idea about the economic conditions in the GDR and when asking about a wool dress to buy, the response was: "I think you might be thinking you are in another [occupation] zone!" We did find things to wear, but distinctly odd things. Mutti tried desperately to make us look civilized using what she found. At the cash registers to pay for our purchases, we always got quizzical looks, answered by whispering discreetly to the checkout person: "We just got out of Russia!" and the typical response was a blank look with a dose of pity.

After a few days, we moved back to the city of Dresden into cold and miserable quarters. The next objective was seeing about getting into education streams for us children. It was mid-winter and academics for others were in full swing. Dieter was told he could not get into the technical university. He would have to wait until the start of next year. Sigrid's relatively good command of the Russian language brought out the strong suggestion that she teach it in a local school. I indicated that I had a strong interest and experience in photography. Official advisors came back with the idea that a good photographer needs to learn about real life. They wanted to send me to a farm to get life experiences! Mutti was flabbergasted. She brought all this up at one of the meetings with the Oberbürgermeister [mayor] who had arranged for a meeting of the returnees to address outstanding concerns. Mutti suggested again that we be allowed to go to Berlin, and he agreed to investigate the matter. The response came two days later: the two girls could go to Berlin to study and will be required to live in a "home." Everyone else must stay in Dresden. Mutti refused to allow the family to be split up. She proposed to represent the family interests in person to the officials in Berlin. Amazingly, they agreed. [They were out of officially sanctioned options.]

Mutti and I took off to East Berlin with the intention of staying with friends we knew from Upra. We went to the Interior Ministry which flatly declined our request to allow the whole family to move to the city. Our last hope was a visit to the Russian military commandant of the city. Other Upra returnees had had luck in dealing with that office. The friend with whom we stayed was a translator. She came with us to help with her excellent command of Russian. By pure chance, Mutti met a Russian man she knew as we entered the building. With his help, we arranged for a meeting to present our concerns to the commandant's adjutant after lunch. As we did, the discussion was joined by a senior officer in civilian clothing. To our surprise, he listened sympathetically and asked all kinds of questions. He asked me whether I was in the communist German youth movement [Freie Deutsche Jugend: FDJ]? No, I said, I was in Russia and, as a German, was not allowed to join the Russian equivalent organization. Is your father in the Party? Of course, he had to be because he is a public employee, a "Beamter." It appeared to please him that I could answer all his questions in perfect Russian. Toward the end of the discussions, he revealed that he was the highest ranked Soviet officer in the city. We were also told we should keep that fact a secret. He turned to his adjutant who called the Berlin city officials and demanded a place to live for the "poor" Pflügel family. These officials were probably outraged and sour because, just the day before, they and the Interior Ministry had denied the very same request. Under Russian pressure, the request was officially approved, and they reluctantly assigned us a supervisor who would have to deal with the details of our issues. That man probably grew a gray hair or two dealing with our single-minded and determined mother.

We did it!! There was still enough time for me to apply for and obtain for a student position at the state-owned film institute (DEFA, in Berlin) where I presented all the necessary credentials. We returned happily to Dresden and stayed there until after Christmas.

No date had been set for our move to Berlin. The living situation in Dresden became unbearable from many viewpoints and Mutti decided to pack up the whole family and go unannounced. When we arrived, she called the city magistrate and demanded to speak to the supervisor in charge of our case. So summoned, he came to the meet us. He was very surprised and quite upset because the plan was for the family members to arrive individually when he called for them. After much arguing, he finally agreed to do his best in finding a place for the whole family. For the meantime, he suggested we can stay in the Hotel Adlon[1] located at the Brandenburg Gate: two rooms with bath. That turned out to be very expensive for us. To add to our woes, the Interior Ministry canceled our stipends because "we took matters in our own hands." Our ration coupons were quickly used up. The prices for food paid with cash rather than ration tickets were generally very high. We survived by eating easily obtainable food like hot dogs [Würstchen] in our rooms using a hotplate that had to be kept hidden from hotel staff. We managed.

Our location gave us opportunities to receive local friends and relatives from Essen [West Germany]. Our western connections helped us out financially with D-marks with which we improved our wardrobe and the food supply. We were also able to visit places like Rechlin and even West Berlin. Our private discussions in the hotel

1 Today, the hotel is for the rich and famous, Michael Jackson holding his kid out the window for one!

room about West Berlin were always held in the bathroom whispering with the water running. We were always afraid that we were being monitored.

In April, we finally moved to a larger apartment adjacent to the Treptower Park, the site of the gigantic Soviet War Memorial, complete with cannons, tanks, and heroic Soviet figures.

Our scant furniture did not go far to cover our needs so that we purchased some and got some repaired at state expense, using the move from Russia as the reason for the damage. The area near our apartment was supervised by a block warden and the house itself was managed by a woman whose husband was a Volkspolizei officer. We had to register every visitor from the West with them and they, in turn, kept watch on the visitors and us. We stayed very quiet because it was imperative that we avoid raising suspicions about our [illegal and very consequential (if revealed)] intentions to these agents. Part of life in the building were obligatory schooling sessions of the residents emphasizing the wonderful advantages of communism. No one, not the schooling leaders nor our fellow building inhabitants ever asked us about our experiences in the Soviet Union – even though they knew of our having come from there.

For me, Berlin life was exciting! Really modern clothes! I was free from schooling that summer and free to explore, within limits. My first foray into West Berlin was like landing in paradise: Brötchen mit Leberwurst, Camembert, and other things I had only dreamed about. An election was held that summer with only one question on the ballot: "Which do you prefer: the EWG or peace?" [EWG is a German acronym for "European Economic Community," in other words, "do you prefer the Western economic system to peace?"] Yes or No. There was no other option on the ballot.

I was expected to join the FDJ, the communist youth movement and went through the formalities, albeit without enthusiasm. One day I was eager to miss a particular all-day event and did so by scheduling a trip to Rechlin with a friend. I wanted to revisit the town of my childhood. It was disappointing, as most such trips tend to be. I met with former friends and met a lot of adults who knew our family. Most irritating for me was the fact that everyone addressed me with the familiar "Du" rather than what I knew to be appropriate, the more formal "Sie." I was old enough to be addressed by "Sie." I never felt as if I was a so-called "comrade." [This manner of addressing people was a part of the new communist, non-existent egalitarianism, mimicking somewhat the absence of distinction between formal and informal "you" in English.] I was introduced to town officials by the friend who accompanied me on this trip, and they expressed envy at my having had the opportunity to spend time in Russia! It was difficult to know how to respond.

A few trips to familiar places and an old part of my life slipped firmly into the past. Funny, how when in the West, I felt socialistic and when in East, I felt capitalistic! Where did I belong? Who am I?

Chapter 22

HAPPY ENDINGS

[In the voice of the father, Kurt Pflügel.]

In Berlin back with my family, now what? My Mannheim friend and colleague who also came back from Russia had a train ticket to go West. It is my turn to find a way. I knew that the (GDR) Labor Ministry was responsible for dealing with the returnees, but they were known to be difficult. To get around them, I turned to the former Aviation Ministry office where I often came to work during my time in Rechlin. I cited as my reasons for going to West Germany that my wife came from there and all her family members currently live there. It was only the fortunes of war that caused me to be in Rechlin. No dice. I mentioned the assurances we were given by the Russians in Savelovo: The ability to return anywhere in Germany. That did it. The authorities would inform other agencies. Something changed! We did it! ... We reached the end of a nightmare.

It seems clear to me now that my wife's insistence on moving to East Berlin was the key to our journey out of the Ostzone. Had we stayed in Dresden or anywhere else in the GDR, it is unlikely we could have left. Staying in East Berlin allowed for contacts with Westerners, but it also exposed us to more control and scrutiny by the many East German state agencies based there. [Among these was, of course, the notorious "Stasi" spy network.]

With exit visas in hand, we did not linger longer than we had to. The East German bureaucracy took the next few weeks to put things in order. The offer to return to work at the firm where I was employed before and during the war was sweet indeed. Things got complicated, however, and delayed our departure. An exit visa from East Germany also required an entry visa to West Germany. Such permissions were provided by the Federal Republic only to those who had documentation that a job was waiting and a place to live was available. [There was a housing shortage. Was there also a shortage of jobs?] All this bureaucracy was not easy to overcome before an actual departure. I now understand why so many of my Upra colleagues chose to skip it by crossing the border illegally.

On 12 August 1954, I returned to Mannheim, the city I left 11 years earlier. My family stayed behind for a few weeks to oversee the move. Once in the West, the children prepared to go to places where their studies were to begin. We eagerly looked forward to finding a good facility for our handicapped Renate. In September, our furnishings arrived in Mannheim and the paperwork was finally complete. We were free at last!

We spent seven years in Russia as a family of six and, together, we returned to West Germany. It was time, however, for the children to go their own ways and each had a plan for a way forward. The return to a new home and settling into a renewed social life provided many opportunities to tell the stories of our experience in Russia. I could honestly say that I did not know much about Russia. I had seen just a small part of it. The experience led to much reflection of the war's effect on people, in Russia and in the GDR. Wrapped up in such thoughts is the stark contrast between the communist economic system and the free market in the West.

*

This is the end of Kurt Pflügel's translated writing. All that follows is my voice.

A clear reality is that while men wrote this history, the wives and mothers were powerful and indispensable forces to assure a physical and emotional survival. Who can write their story? Who will? Holding together a family with four children, one of whom was handicapped, under very trying circumstances was job number one for Mutti, the mother in the Pflügel family. Daughter Sigrid said it well: "Ohne sie ging es nicht" referring to her mother's inner and physical strengths. "Without her, it would not have been possible ..."

Writing about a painful experience may be therapeutic but it reopens the wound. Kurt Pflügel chose to go through it for his own reasons. These might have included setting the historical record straight. For that aspect, we are grateful. The pain may, however, be sufficient to want to repress it. His wife (Mutti), who certainly felt that she was deprived of a large part of a normal, ordinary adulthood, fell into the camp of wanting to forget the deprivation associated with the seven years in the Soviet Union. She went as far as actively and strongly discouraging her husband from writing what is reproduced here. He prevailed – as most who need to release pent-up emotions do. According to Sigrid, she never read his writing while he was alive and did so only after he died. Her reasons and reaction to it will remain unknowable, but the process speaks to questions about reliving past experiences, both good and unpleasant ones and, possibly, about bringing her husband's spirit back into her life.

Chapter 23

THE NAMES

The Haida-Clan website cited earlier was a source for some of the information I gathered for this book including providing names, lots of names. Listed are the men who were taken as technical specialists. Also compiled are the names of the wives and the children. Who compiled them I do not know but it is good that the lists exist. The older generation has largely passed away so that it is the children, dragged or born there, who are keeping the memory of the Russian abduction alive. The website includes the words of Russian authorities who, after years of denying the occurrence of these events, are finding delicate wordings to justify them. It is hard not to conclude that a significant part of the motivation was that, from their perspective, someone, anyone, had to pay for the deprivation, misery, and death brought to the Russian people by Germany during the war.

It is easy to comprehend numbers like a hundred, a thousand, or ten thousand and feel the magnitude of whatever is described. The event sinks in much deeper when names are connected to such numbers because it brings the force of humanity to the event, conjures up the suffering, and puts emptiness in plain view. Normally, one does not think much about the humanity when studying a battle between, for example, Romans and Gauls. In a history book, there might only be the names of the generals involved and who won or lost the battle. Many more with names forever lost, lost lives, limbs, or sanity. Consider for a moment the power of a memorial where the victims have names. The women persecuted in the Salem Witch Trials, the Jews named and some lost forever in Holocaust memorials all over the world, the victims of the World Trade Center attack on 11 September 2001, or the Vietnam Memorial Site, just a few of the examples of sites built by the living to evoke memories of the dead. They are often commemorated by names when names are known. The citation of these names is supremely powerful in drawing in, to a memorial site, the visitor who is willing to be transported back to a friendship or a love, now gone.

The thousands of people abducted to Russia by the government of the Soviet Union have names. The children have the names their mothers and fathers passed on to them together with the names that were chosen for them. Most survived the Russian ordeal, damaged in health perhaps, and some died of cold, despair, or the usual reasons that body and soul part company.

The Haida-Clan names are German names of people who were part of the story and horror of WWII. They were, in all likelihood, patriots willing, or perhaps reluctant, to do what was required by those in power. As a person with a love for technology and responsible for a family, it was relatively easy and perhaps necessary to isolate oneself from the moral morass that war can be. To what extent were they even aware of what their government did? Were they the Nazis who did the horrible things ascribed to Germany as a whole when Hitler was in power? Unlikely. The horrid things were done by an empowered minority in a sea of a politically impotent majority. Were they Nazi Party members? Some surely were, for living in that time in Germany required it for economic, even physical, survival. Did they believe in the Nazi ideology that some men are superior to others? Perhaps. We will likely never know and, if you believe in enlightenment and redemption, they might have changed abhorrent views to something better.

The pages that follow is a random selection from among the thousands of the technical specialists, men mostly who, on the original file, are in alphabetical order. The birthyear is also noted. In showing it, I wish to illustrate the humanity of this abduction. Its magnitude is harder to display, save with just hollow numbers.

....

Nandzig, Willi (1914) Neudecker, Ferdinand (1900) Neufeld, Fritz (1901) Neuholz, Arthur (1903) Neumann, Ewald (1917) Neumann, Otto (1906) Naumann, Otto (1907) Neumann, Paul (1902) Nickel, Achim (?) Nikolai, Otto (1918) Nidack, Gerhard(1919) Niepmann, Gerald (1919) Noack, Erich (1909) Noack, Hans (1923)

Oppermann, Karl-Heinrich (1912) Oppermann, Otto (1895) Orlamünder, Georg (1913)

Panneck, Ernst (1914) Patlesky, Georg (1912) Paul, Erich (1907) Paul, Ernst (1905) Pawlowitsch, Alex. (1915) Pechta, ? (?) Peisker, Georg (1904) Pertermann, Werner (1920) Pertuch, Rudolf (1906) Pfeiffer, Dr. Alfred (1900) Pflügel, Kurt (1903) Pfützner, Hans (1907) Pieper,

Rudolf (1900) Pietrus, Bernhard (1909) Pietsch, Wilhelm (1911) Pingel, Heinrich (1921) Pinther, Rolf (1907) Pleß, Erich (1917) Plischke, Erich (1910) Pohl, Georg (1908) Pöll, Gudrun (1911) Pöll, Wilhelm (1913) Pooch, Konrad (1915) Prestel, Karl (1906) Preuschen, Lore (?) Priegnitz, Gerhard (1920) Probst, Otto (1914) Prüß, Walter (1900) Purgold, Alfred (1904)

Raab, Hans (1905) Rademacher, Otto (1913) Radewald, Franz (1901) Radtke, Helmut (1921) Redenz, Joachim (1914) Redlich, Paul (1905) Rein, Gerhardt (1912) Reinhardt, Alfred (1901) Richter, Erich (1909) Richter, Walter (1910) Richter, Wilhelm (1893) Riedel, Erhard (1916) Rittau, Willi (1912) Rogge, Walter (1914) Ropohl, Willi (1906) Rosemann, Willi (1908) Rosenberg, Kurt (1905) Rösicke, Walter (1920) Rössler, Reinhold (1911) Roßner, Werner (1911) Rossow, Otto (1917) Rümmler, Rudolf (1913)

Sablinski, Kurt (1913) Salzmann, Albert (1918) Schaedler, Josef (1911) Schär, Hans (1913) Schaupp, Karl (1907) Scheibe, Dr. Alfred (1896) Scheibe, Herbert (1910) Scheinost, Dr. Rudolf (1907) Schellhöh, Hermann (1906) Schenke, Karl (1915) Scheumann, Walter (1903) Schicht, Alfred (1903) Schiepek, Rudolf (1919) Schildhauer, Otto (1902) Schildhauer, Paul (1893) Schlechte, Walter (1903) Schlimper, Kurt (1909) Schlüchtermann, Ernst (1907) Schmalfuß, Karl (1908) Schmarje, Karl-Johann (1906) Schmelzer, Alfred (1909) Schmerse, Alfred (1909) Schmidt, Erich (1907) Schmidt, Franz (1902) Schmidt, Friedrich (1907) Schmidt, Gerhard (1918) Schmidt, Helmut (1909) Schmidt, Otto (1908) Schmidt, Otto (1909) Schmidt, Dr. Rudolf (1908) Schmidtchen, Kurt (1917) Schmitz, ? (?) Schmoll, Paul (1910) Schmukalla, Werner (1913) Schneider, Fritz (1923) Schneider, Heinrich (1909) Schneider, Horst W. (1918) Schneider, Mathias (1891) Schnetz, Dr. Heinz (1911) Schöbel, Albert (1902) Schömann, Otto (1905) Schöne, Otto (1898) Schönfeld, Franz (1903) Schönfeld, Kurt (1912) Schott, Eduard (1910) Schott, Erhard (1901) Schott, Friedrich (1913) Schotte, Herbert (1910) Schreier, Wilhelm (1914) Schreuner, Karl (1912) Schröck, Richard (1891) Schröder, Ernst (1912) Schröder, Willi (1905) Schröder,Dr. Hans-Joach. (1906) Schrödter, Paul (1908) Schrödter, Willi (1916) Schubert, Heinrich (1909) Schüler, Heinz (1920) Schulte, Erich (1909) Schultze, Rudolf (1908) Schulz, Georg (1900) Schulze, Dr. Gustav E.R. (1911) Schützan, Willi (1909) Schwab, Ernst (1913) Schwabe, Dr. Gerhard (1904) Schwarzer, Kurt (1911) Schwarzer, Max (1903) Schwarzkopf, Karl (1913) Schwertfeger, Walter (1901) Seeck, Franz (1901) Seele, Wilhelm (1912) Sehorsch, Hermann (1912) Seidel, Herbert (1908) Seifert, Herbert (1910) Seitz, Rudolf (1897) Selzer, Philip (1914) Sembt, Hilde (1910) Senst, Walter (1908) Siding, Gert (1905) Siebert, Erich (1904) Siering,

Hermann (1895) Sievert, Helmut (1898) Simon, Martin (1910) Simon, Oskar (1912) Singer, Heinrich (1894) Slotczyk, Oskar (1910) Söcknick, Ernst (1908) Sohr, Gerhard (1910) Sommerlatt, Arthur (1902) Sonntag, Otto (1898) Spata, Georg (1909) Speck, Willi (1904) Sperlich, Josef (1899) Staadt, Friedrich (1899) Stadelmann, Wilhelm (1909) Steinacker, Gustav (1907) Steinäcker, Wolfgang (1919) Steinbach, Otto (1903) Steinmann, Max (1913) Stephan, Fritz (1907) Stephan, Richard (1923) Steuck, Ernst (1909) Steudel, Hans (1883) Stich, Paul (1921) Stierwald, Hugo (1909) Stoiber, Otto (1901) Stolze, Karl (1907) Stoyck, Ernst (1909) Straußberg, Hermann (1894) Stubel, Hermann (1907) Suchy, Paul (1911)

Tangermann, Walter (1903) Tempel, Helmut (1909) Tempelhoff, Karl (1904) Teuchert, Ernst (1919) Theuer, Heinrich (1920) Thiemicke, Margot (1921) Thomas, Karl (1897) Tillmann, Johann (1892) Todt, Georg (1904) Topp, Rudolf (1907) Tornow, Rudolf (1915) Treiber, Johann (1902) Trimbuch, Herbert (1910) Trojahn, Curt (1910) Tuchelt, Franz (1900) Twardogorski, Karl (1911) Twerdy, Walter (1903)

Uhde, Kurt (1905) Ulmitz, Wilhelm (1912) Unger, Gotthardt (1916) Urban, Stefan (1914) Utrecht, Paul (1892)

Vahldieck, Werner (1920) Vester, Walter (1913) Vogel, Kurt (1909) Vogel, Walter (1902) Vogt, Rudolf (1913) Vogts, Dr. Josef (1906) Voigt, Alfred (1906) Voigt, Otto (1908) Vollheim, Wilhelm (1903) Vollmering, Berthold (1900)

Wachs, Herbert (1914) Wachtmann, Karl, Wagner, Erich (1905), Wagner, Willi (1900) Wagner, Willi (1915) Waldmann, Emil (1911) Walther, Heinz (1917) Walther, Willi (1908) Waltmann, Clemens (1904) Wandersleb, Egmund (1909) Watolla, Otto (1912) Wattroth, Rudolf (1909) Watzke,Franz (1897) Weber, Kurt (1907) Weckwert, Horst (1920) Wegner, Alfred (1898) Weidenhammer, Reinhard (1901) Weiser, Theo (1902) Weiß, Werner (1913) Weißbach, Alfred (1912) Weitsch, Paul (1906) Wenz, Karl (1886) Wenzel, Kurt (1921) Werner, Felix (1914) Werner, Reinhold (1919) Werwitz, Alfred (1901) Wesely, Rudolf (1916) West, Daniel (1909) Westermaier, Josef (1904) Westphal, Heinz (1913) Weyer, Theo (1911) Wiedecke, Walter (1903) Wiederhold, Max (1882) Wiemann, Kurt (1915) Wiese, Heinz (1924) Wiesenmüller, Gerhard (1911) Wilhelmi, Friedrich (1909) Wille, Ernst (1909) Winguth, Rudolf (1912) Winkler, Erwin (1903) Winkler, Herbert (1909) Winter, Willi (1909) Witt, Arnold (1921) Wittig, Karl (1900) Wittke, Kurt (1912) Wodtke, Emil (1896) Wolf, Alois (1918) Wolf, Gustav (1918) Wölfer, Hans-Joachim (1920) Wolfermann, Hermann (1914) Wollmann, Kurt (1908) Worm, Walter (1909) Würembeck, Hermann(1906) Wurmstedt, Karl (1906) Wüstenhagen, Gustav (1904)

... and many, many more ... including a list of the family members. Where possible, the names of female children are connected with the names they took on as marriage partners.

As you look over the names and wonder, consider the likelihood that they were victims. The state is always more powerful than the individual, but the hope should always be that the individual can hold the state to foster a belief in human dignity. Punishing one group, as these men, women, and children were, to right the wrong done by others has never brought peace. It is not justice; it is simply revenge.

It is true that the Soviets wanted to bring their aviation to a more advanced state. They did it in a way that could have been more humane. As it was, they succeeded in joining the jet age, but the process took place behind an Iron Curtain which kept them always a step behind developments in the West. There is and was always industrial espionage and reverse engineering in play, but even that is always a defensive position, a position where the other is ahead.

As a German American, I take some comfort in most processes that finished WWII. The guilty people were largely found and punished; some by victims precisely at the moment the tide changed and others by legal processes that were open, not perfect perhaps, but in a way that connected crime and punishment. Some criminals escaped justice to be sure. They have their consciences to live with and the constant fear that justice or a revenge seeker may be stalking them. To constantly look over one's shoulder is a form of punishment.

The names on the nearby pages are taken at random; the totality is of many more. Judging from the birthyears, they have undoubtedly passed away as this is written. Even their children are aged as one born (say in 1954) when this story ended, would be aged 70 in the first quarter of the 21st century. The age issue makes interaction with those who experienced this story difficult. Even among the living, memory is damaged by age, by the time passed, and there may well be the desire to not remember. Names change by marriage. Telephone numbers, street, and email addresses go out of date. A list and the words that witnesses have written are all that will soon be left of that history.

Chapter 24

TECHNOLOGY TRANSFER ENDINGS – WEST AND EAST

By the early to mid 1950s, the evolutionary ups and downs associated with the new jet engine technology that Germany contributed to the world during and after WWII had largely settled down. The jet engine was real, practical, and useful for propelling airplanes. It was in military use by all involved in the Cold War and its hotter sub-wars. It was also promising to gain a solid foothold in civil aviation.

In the West

Jet engine technology was at the point where jets with thrust levels of about 6,000 lbs. were widely available. This was a far cry from what was practical in 1945 and much better performance was yet to come. For example, in France the new ATAR engines were installed on military airplanes. In Britain, the Rolls-Royce Nene, designed in the 1940s, became more powerful and the basis for other engines built in that country and in the US. In the US, the General Electric J47 showed the way to a new generation of airplanes. The swept wing idea introduced by the German, later American, aerodynamicist Adolf Busemann was also a great contribution to allow aircraft to fly at speeds close to the speed of sound. By the mid-1950s the Jet Age had effectively arrived. The German input to these engines was quickly diluted and augmented by engineers in and from other countries. An important aspect of the technology transfer after 1945 was the demonstration that the jet engine was practical. The British took their own approach and they too, showed the way.

Specific story endings for the technology transfer process initiated by the Allies can be summed up in terms of the institutions created or redirected as a result. In France, there was the very successful creation of a world-class builder of modern engines: Safran that started as SNECMA and Turboméca in earlier times. In Great Britain, the new jet engine brought to Rolls-Royce by Frank Whittle not only spawned interest by other big engine-building companies (Armstrong Siddeley, Bristol, de Havilland, Vickers, for examples) but decidedly redirected the compressor technology from Whittle's radial flow designs to the axial flow configuration introduced by the German engineers. In the US, the existing big engine companies embraced the technology with competitive enthusiasm. There was money to be made! General Electric, Westinghouse, Allison, Pratt & Whitney, and others turned their talents to satisfy American military wants. Even the small team of Junkers engineers headed by Anselm Franz built AVCO-Lycoming into a competent producer of gas turbine engines. Its medium sized gas turbines found wide applications in military and commercial aviation. While the ownership of Lycoming has changed over the years, the engine manufacturing by the successors continues from its German roots.

The technical and historical consequences from *Operation Paperclip* people were not limited to jet engines. Notably, the American space program with its monumental Apollo component is directly attributable to the involvement and leadership of Wernher von Braun. He was not the only German brought to the US to build rockets. Credit must also be given to other Germans brought to Fort Sill and to the many American colleagues who made the successful moon landings happen. Individuals too numerous to mention made their marks in established fields in the US. Some mentioned earlier in this story belong to that group. The Soviets also took advantage of what the German V-2 rocket engineers had learned. The specialists exploited cited in the Pflügel story[1] were part of the foundation of the Soviet space program. A new competition into space was initiated by the first and successful launch of a satellite, the beeping Sputnik, into orbit around earth in 1957.

There will always be a cloud hanging over *Operation Paperclip* regarding the activities of individuals in Nazi Germany during the war. Were they serious enough to warrant being labeled "inadmissible to the United States?" Individual officers interviewing people had

1 From the discussion of V-2 engineers kept on the lake island (in Chapter 20), it appears that the Soviet rocket program involved another group. Indeed, that group was located at OKB-1, near Moscow. Later Russian follow-on work with rockets involved Nikolai Kuznetsov and his team's experience with turbomachinery which led to the development of the very capable NK-33 rocket engines that were going to be used in the race to the moon. After the dissolution of the Soviet Union, the basic design features of this rocket were adopted for propelling American and European rockets. More powerful engines of this genre served for many of the satellite launching vehicles in the following decades.

to make decisions or pass the examinations on to higher authorities. To what extent were the moral aspects of activity during the war overlooked because the person was now militarily valuable as a help in fighting for the West in the Cold War? For example, von Braun was an officer in the SS. Where does that fit into the balance? We will probably never know because he and his judges are long gone. The written record will always be less than the oral arguments that were surely made. The dilemma facing a person having to decide another's fate was real and always critical in determining the future of the Germans in Allied hands. It is safe to say that while the production of jet engines involved involuntary and potentially abused labor, the design and engineering was connected to Naziism only in the sense that it took place in Germany during WWII. The engineers were largely apolitical, and the Allies established that reality to their satisfaction.

East of the Iron Curtain – Russia

It would be inaccurate to say that the Soviet effort to build jet engines was limited to the Upra-Kuybyshev complex. There were other institutions involved. The facilities for producing the replicas of Jumo 004 and BMW 003 are such examples. Some were OKBs. So, what was the state of Russian technology in the mid-1950s when our story ended?

The Kuybyshev effort under Brandner successfully developed a powerful turboprop engine, the NK-12. The initials are those of Nikolai Kuznetsov, the institute's Russian leader. The engine was an evolution and realization of the Jumo 022 gas turbine engine that existed only on paper in 1945. These engines were used to drive large contra-rotating propellers and the availability of this engine permitted the Soviet Union to proceed with the building of an intercontinental bomber. The Tupolev Tu-95 was the late answer to the American B-36 to achieve parity in the Cold War. Parity was thought to be required as a deterrent to (nuclear) war: a kind of equilibrium as long as the Soviet Union and the West, specifically the Americans, had the ability to destroy one another. The theory was MAD: Mutually Assured Destruction.

The big bomber

With the Tu-95 having large gas turbine engines, it also dawned on the US Air Force that the B-36 with its overtaxed piston engines was obsolete. The Air Force had reached that conclusion even before the Tu-95 became a reality. The Boeing Company that built the first medium high-speed bomber with swept wings, the B-47, took on the task to design and eventually build a jet replacement for the B-36 in response to a request from the USAF. That airplane became the B-52. It is interesting that one of a number of Boeing design iterations for this airplane in 1948 (number 646–35 before the design became final) resembled the Tu-95: a swept wing, four-engine turboprop-powered airplane. Was espionage involved in fixing the design of the Tu-95 to resemble this early version of the B-52?

The arms race was in full swing, and the US chose to better the Tu-95 with the B-52 powered with jet engines, not turboprops. Although faster, the jet-powered bomber design iterations always had difficulties with having enough range to carry out the contemplated intercontinental missions. In that sense, the B-52 was deficient to the Tu-95 because of the considerably greater fuel consumption by the jet engines compared to the turboprops. The American solution to the range concerns was in-flight refueling. That mission aspect required a tanker airplane bring fuel to the B-52 where it was needed. The speed mismatch between the relatively slow piston-engine powered tankers (KC-97) available then and the fast B-52 was functionally awkward. While refueling, the B-52 had to fly slowly (as slowly as it could) while the tanker had throttles at full power to fly as fast as it could. Logically, this speed disparity led to the development of a faster, jet-engine-powered tanker (the KC-135) and a commercial derivative (the 707), both built by the Boeing Company. In the United States, the commercial jet age had begun.

The B-52 required engines that were more powerful than the General Electric J47 used on the B-47. Pratt & Whitney was eager to get into the jet engine business after having been excluded from it during the war. The company tied its fortune to the engines for the B-52. The J57 jet engine that resulted was a technically significant improvement and put the company on its way to becoming a major engine builder in the decades that followed.

The Soviet response to the commercial jets that were flying and sketched on the drawing-boards was the conversion of the Tu-95 to become the loud and short-lived Tu-114 airliner. The noise had to do with the powerful propellers and was felt inside the cabin and outside the airplane, notably in the airport environment. Naturally, Soviet airplane design OKBs went to work on real jet airliners. The Tu-104, for example, was put in service in the mid-1950s, at about the same time as the de Havilland Comet. The first Tu-104s looked like bombers with bombsight or perhaps navigation windows (it is good to be able to see where one is going) in the nose. The construction of these airplanes was apparently a military budget item potentially serving either of two purposes: carrying about a hundred people to another city or destroying it. The Soviet commercial jet age had begun in earnest with an accident-prone airplane. The engines for them were always determinants of their economic performance.

On the military side, both the Tu-95 and the B-52 are, after many decades, still in service. So, it appears that the German Upra engineers had a long-term impact on aviation history.

Over time, the Soviet airliners changed to be less directed at military purposes and served the airlines and countries of the communist world relatively well. How well in the 21st century? One needs only look at the airplane fleets operated in the Russian Federation (Aeroflot and Russian regional airlines) and by the national airlines of countries in the former Soviet sphere of influence. To a very large degree, they operate Western airplanes with Western engines, and it must be said that as this is written, the invasion of Ukraine will play a role in the future.

The centralized planning regimen associated with the Soviet Union is closely linked to that country's success, or lack thereof, in the world of commercial aviation. Political decisions are rarely as good as economic ones made in an open market.

Chapter 25

BRUNOLF BAADE: ENDINGS "BETWEEN" EAST AND WEST

East Germany (the GDR, in German DDR) was not between East and West in a political sense or a geographical one but certainly was on the eastern side of the boundary between them. In this communist state, aviation history is primarily the story of the engine enterprise we saw operating in Kuybyshev under Ferdinand Brandner and the airplane building by Brunolf Baade. These two individuals set the stage for a noble but disastrous journey into civilian commercial aviation. The plan was to use the capabilities of the engineers at the Upra facility after the Germans sequestered there had outlived their usefulness for the Russians.

The story of Brunolf Baade is an unfortunate one. It centers on the only attempt to enter commercial aviation by East Germany before the Berlin Wall fell in 1989. In 1952 the GDR government officials decided to get into the aviation business because, it was felt, that the long and extensive German history in aviation was theirs to advance. The other problem to be solved was providing jobs for the returnees from Russia and, most importantly, earn money by selling airplanes.

Baade tied his fortune to the Soviets because of the negative interview experience with American interrogators in 1945 (see Chapter 8). He was made chief designer at the OKB-1 (Alexeyev) design bureau near Moscow. The team that was brought to him, or brought there with him, was tasked with designing several military airplane types. The last one of these was a jet-powered bomber for the Soviet Air Force. The airplane that came out of this design exercise was called the Model 150. It had two engines suspended from wing struts and a swept wing mounted high on the fuselage. The US and France built airplanes with a similar configuration, albeit somewhat later. The most distinctive feature was the tandem landing gear under the fuselage with outrigger wheels at the wing tips for stability on the ground. This aspect of the configuration was an emulation of the American B-47 bomber and the French Vautour bomber using the ATAR 101 engines developed by the Groupe "O" team. The Russian Model 150 airplane first flew in October 1952 and was involved in a serious landing accident in May 1953. The 150 program was subsequently cancelled, in part because another airplane (the Tupolev Tu-16) was making better progress toward reality.

The GDR set up a state-owned airplane construction company whose mission was, first, to build Soviet military aircraft under license in the old under-used Junkers factory in Dessau. Second, it hoped to set up a commercial airliner building business to earn hard currencies for the GDR by selling the aircraft abroad. Before the first goal was finalized, the Berlin uprising in June of 1953 led the Soviets to change their minds about supporting the military airplane construction aspect of the GDR plans. East Germany might be too unreliable or too close to the West from the perspective of a future conflict. The GDR's response was to refocus on the second goal, manufacturing a civilian airliner. The site was not to be in Dessau but in Dresden where the VEB[1] Flugzeugwerke Dresden (FWD / Werk 801) was created. The basic work that Baade had invested in the Model 150 airplane was just what was needed to lay out an airliner, renamed the Baade 152. The airliner maintained the overall configuration of the Soviet bomber, except for the substitution of four smaller (and soon to be available) engines made by VEB Entwicklungsbau Pirna / Werk 802.

The bomber was adapted by Baade so that 24 passengers could be transported 1,600 miles. The capacity was quickly raised to 48–72 passengers by design improvements. The first example of the 152 still carried the glass nose so that a military use could be made of the airplane. That nose was quickly replaced in later airplanes by a conventional one, probably to project a more peace-loving look. The expectation was that the Soviet Union would buy 100 of these airliners, and more could be sold on the world market. To say that these expectations were unrealistic would be an understatement.

The first example of the (quite incomplete) airliner was rolled out on 1 May 1958, coinciding with the usual Mayday hoopla carried out east of the Iron Curtain. The engines were of Russian manufacture

1 VEB is a German acronym for Volkseigener Betrieb, publicly-owned enterprise. When Germany was reunited after the Berlin Wall fell, these VEBs were the low-hanging fruit picked up by agile, mostly western entrepreneurs as the unified government sought to rid itself of the once state-owned enterprises.

(Tumanski RD-9Bs) because the Pirna 014 engine was not ready. The first flight was on 8 December 1958 and a second flight was made on 3 March 1959. That second flight was made under great pressure from political elements because it was announced with fanfare for that date. The final part of the flight involved a low flypast over the Dresden airport runway with cameras rolling. The airplane was staged to be "clean", i.e., flaps and landing gear retracted so that it would appear as if in normal flight. The limited experience of the flight crew executing this cinematographic maneuver caused them to fly too slowly. They crashed the airplane in view of a large audience, killing the four men aboard. Today in Dresden, there is a heroic-looking cemetery plot with laudatory headstones for the individuals who lost their lives in that mishap. Notably missing is a plaque dedicated to the absence of wisdom associated with taking an insufficiently checked-out airplane out on a politically inspired stunt.

Several more 152s were built and no. 4 was modified to have a conventional tricycle landing gear because takeoff handling with the earlier configuration was too difficult in practice. The airplane was equipped with Pirna 014 engines and flew on 26 August 1960. A second flight a couple of weeks later revealed fuel system problems that caused all 152s to be grounded on 7 October. These and other technical defects were serious. Staff discord among themselves as well as with the government on how to fix them finally caused the GDR to cancel the project. The writing was on the wall that this project was not going to succeed. A year earlier the Soviets canceled their interest in buying the airplane. They were building their own jet airliners, the Tu-104 mentioned earlier and more successful airplanes: the Antonov An-24, the Tupolev Tu-124, and the Ilyushin Il-18. In the West, jet airliners were also flying: the DeHavilland Comet (first flight 1949), the Sud Caravelle (1955), and the Boeing 707 (1957). It was increasingly hard for government and Pirna people in the GDR to imagine how the 152 was going to compete with these Russian and Western airplanes. One major shortcoming was that the airplane was too small.

February 21st 1961 marked the end of all activity associated with the production of the 152 airliner. The facility was put to use as a maintenance base for the Soviet-built military aircraft of the GDR air force and the East German national airline Interflug. The Pirna engine factory was repurposed while Pirna 014 engine production continued at another VEB state enterprise for a short period of time. The word "short" applies here because the world, including the Soviet Union, was producing significantly bigger and better engines.

There is evidence in the literature (*Flug Revue*, 3 October 2019) that some of the airplane builders scattered to workplaces in the West. The degree to which the GDR government tolerated such an outmigration is hard to assess. In August of that year (1961), it built the infamous Berlin Wall specifically to thwart the drain of manpower to the West through that city. Travel by East Germans to East Berlin and, from there, to West Berlin had been possible and somewhat safe. Once in West Berlin, there were safe travel options to West Germany, primarily by air. The Berlin Wall plugged the last point of leakage of people out of the GDR. The intra-German border was already quite effective in blocking migration with armed guards ordered to kill would-be escapees and installation of horrific passive measures, such as victim triggered guns, to prevent crossing the border. It was, after all, a crime to leave the GDR.

Baade stayed in East Germany and became a professor at the University of Dresden. A more complete life story about the man is available (in German) on the website by the freelance journalist Holger Lorenz cited in the Bibliography. Baade died in 1969 a few months after he retired, in part, due to the poor health he brought back from his time in Russia. He was an interesting man who lived in an interesting time.

It is a sad testimonial to the events that the most capable contributors for the Baade airplane project, including Kurt Pflügel in our story, were the ones held for the longest time, while people lower in the industrial skill hierarchy started going home to East Germany years earlier. The Askania specialists stayed even longer. Resettlement to West Germany was granted to some while others used risky means of doing it illegally.

History has a way of revealing the truth about events that may have happened many years ago. In 1996 and 2006, the Russian Federation celebrated the work of the Kuybyshev engine works over the achievements of the previous 50 and 60 years, respectively. Note that the official starting year was 1946 and not 1941 when aircraft engine construction was relocated there from Moscow to protect it during WWII. According to German visitors present (in what was then a more open Russian Federation), not a single word was officially uttered in the speeches regarding the reality that German engineers and families were involved in setting up or developing this factory. However, a memorial plaque that speaks closer to the truth is located on the site:

> For the skilled workers, engineers, technicians and researchers of Junkers, BMW and Askania, who were forcibly sent to work in the USSR in the autumn of 1946, as compensation that the German people, in accordance with the Potsdam Agreement, were obliged to provide to the

> peoples of the Soviet Union for the inestimable damage caused during the Second World War.
>
> In the village of "Management" of the Kuybyshev region (now Samara), in an empty room, they organized a factory for the production of engines with the help of equipment and machine tools delivered by the Red Army from Germany. For 7 years, 600 men and women with their own hands, using their special knowledge, have developed, and established the most modern and powerful production of jet engines.
>
> In 1996 and 2006, celebrations were organized in Samara in honor of the fiftieth anniversary and sixtieth anniversary of the founding of the plant. Since not a word was said about the significant contribution of German specialists to the organization and development of this enterprise, this memorial plaque should contribute to the preservation of the names of these German specialists as part of the history of German-Russian relations and the expression of respect and gratitude for their work.

That truth is out but the sad fact remains that the Russian Federation, like the Soviet Union, deals only with facts that reflect well on its view of history. The thought might be that the Russian population can be made to see only such interpretations. In Russia, official "truths" limit what one can write, say publicly, or even privately, but can anyone control what one thinks?

Chapter 26

ASKANIA TALENT ON HOLD

The airplane builders were safely back in Germany in 1954, although many were forced to stay in the GDR. The engineers working within the Askania group of experts in avionics (guidance and control of flight vehicles) had a longer stay in Russia. Beginning in 1950, they were moved to a facility in Tushino, about 8 miles NW of Moscow's city center and within today's ring road around the city. The writing in this chapter is that of Karl Breuninger, whose father Helmut was part of the Askania group. It is a translated and edited version of memoir notes for talks that Karl has given on the experience in Russia. His father also kept notes, some of which are quoted here.

The story is interesting because of its part in the Cold War and what the Soviet Union was able to get out of the German captives. Whereas the airplane builders had transmitted what they knew to Soviet engineers and were returned, the Askania people stayed longer for reasons that will become clear in the text.

My contribution is limited to clarifying comments in square brackets. Images associated with this chapter were provided by Karl Breuninger.

1950–1955 in Tushino near Moscow

The Askania Group (OKB-3) was engaged in various developments of autopilot systems. The tasks set by the Soviets were successfully completed. It was still a time shortly after the war when opportunities in Germany that involved technically challenging work were very limited and likely unavailable. Consequently, some of specialists wanted to solve challenging tasks they saw as doable and made appropriate proposals to the Soviet leadership.

The transfer from Upra to Moscow (Helmut Breuninger)

An hour after the start of work on the morning of 13 September 1950, I was told to go home – immediately. In two hours, I was to be in front of house 45, where a bus would be waiting. I was told that I, together with seven others, will be taken to the airfield to fly to Moscow, our new workplace. Our families and the rest of OKB-3 (except those to be repatriated that month) would follow a little later by train. Mrs. Möller (and her cat) came along on the airplane trip because her husband was too dependent on her with his mutilated hands from his failed suicide attempt (see Chapter 17). The rest of the OKB-3 and the families arrived in Moscow on the 24th.

At the time, the Cold War between East and West was in full swing. The Americans regularly undertook spy overflights of the entire Soviet Union and, at an altitude of 20km (65,000 ft), flew over the country undisturbed because no Soviet anti-aircraft weapons were available to reach this altitude. The Soviets monitored these spy planes and could do nothing about them. They also feared an attack by American bombers that might drop atomic bombs. Through their spies, they were aware of the American simulation wargame exercise called "*Operation Dropshot*" [a total destruction scenario] that had the Soviets worried.

In response, Stalin decided to put on a defensive belt around Moscow in the summer of 1950 consisting of two rings of surface-to-air anti-aircraft missile systems to be built as quickly as possible. At the time, no such a system existed anywhere and involved three aspects: detection of enemy flying objects, rocket launchers, and guidance of the missiles. To solve the various tasks, two development teams were set up: a Soviet one and another German. For the German group, rocket specialists, guidance, and high-frequency specialists were assembled from the German groups present in various places in the Soviet Union.

This new German team consisted of four groups: the Askania people from Upra (44 experts under the direction of Waldemar Möller), 13 high-frequency specialists from Monino, seven rocket experts from the island of Gorodomya (under Johann (Hans) Hoch) and 35 German political prisoners.

In the USSR, "political prisoners" meant all sorts of things; most of them were "Nazis" and were arrested in 1945 and deported to the USSR. It was there that the authorities realized that among political prisoners were people with technical expertise. They slowly tapped into it. Some of these prisoners were neither Nazis nor free individuals but endured tragic fates in Nazi concentration camps. For example, one man spent time in the Dachau and Buchenwald camps, while another did so because he was married to a Jew, and a third was a former SPD [Sozialdemokratische Partei Deutschlands, a political party banned in Nazi times] man. That such people would also end up in Soviet prisons was a tragedy. The entirety of this group was called the "Blue Ones" because, until 1951, they were taken from prison to work in a blue bus.

In total, there were 99 professionals transferred to Moscow. The abducted specialists (groups 1–3) lived provisionally in the Kuntsevo District in three guarded masonry houses surrounded by a prison-like enclosure. From the summer of 1951 onward, they were moved together with Group 4 into a purpose-built compound in Tushino consisting of Finnish houses [quite similar to the houses in Upra] and German houses supplied by the GDR as reparations. The German houses were built on lots covering an area of about 1,000 sq. ft. They were of a common design, generally having a floor area of about 500 sq. ft. [about the size of a modern two-car garage]. Walls with a central chimney divided the space into four rooms, the largest being a living room, a smaller bedroom, a kitchen, and combination hallway and WC. Additional unheated space was an enclosed veranda and mudroom. Some of the furniture at our no. 31 First-of-May Street home, consisted of wooden packing boxes that once held parts for V-1 guided missiles.

The compound was surrounded by a wooden fence about 9 ft. tall. In it was a commandant's office (with guards), a shop, a clubhouse, and a house that was used as a school for the early grades. Since the compound was built by German prisoners of war, the local population believed that we were also prisoners of war. This view was later shared by many in West Germany when we returned. [In a way, it was true.]

The specialists went to work every day in a special bus to the Sokol district of Moscow. The Soviet head of the OKB-1 was the physicist Sergei Beria (son of Lavrenty Beria, the notorious head of the Soviet secret police ... until the father was executed for treason in 1953). Sergei Beria had been in charge of the rocket specialists under Helmut Gröttrup[1] and Hans Hoch on Gorodomya Island (see Chapters 19 and 20). Gröttrup was sent back to the GDR in 1953, while Hans Hoch "was allowed" to work on the missile defense system in Tushino. It appears the Soviet appreciated his work. Initially, the parallel Soviet group lived in buildings adjacent to ours. The two groups did not know about each other and worked in competition on the Berkut [transl. Golden Eagle] anti-aircraft missile system.

1 Gröttrup was the chief expert on flight controls of the A-4 (V-2) ballistic missile in Peenemünde.

The German specialists worked without a contract until February 1951, when they were presented with contracts. These stipulated a return to Germany by 1955, after successful completion of the work. A minority of 13 refused to sign: 12 mechanics and 1 design engineer. Ultimately, whether people signed or not did not matter, the document had no impact on the eventual release date. As a form of punishment, the salaries of the objectors were somewhat lower than those of specialists who signed.

The "Blues Ones" had no family members [in Russia] because they were captured as individuals. Some decided to let their family members residing in the GDR join them. Upon their arrival, they faced the present reality. It contrasted starkly with the picture of a so-called "promised land" Soviet Union as painted by the GDR propaganda. It was a shock, especially for the older children who were deposited directly into Russian schools.

Life was strictly controlled. Adults were not allowed to leave the compound without being accompanied by a security monitor. For shopping, theatre visits, etc. even walks in the city or in nature, a Russian official had to come along. To bring a visit "outside" about, they had to register a request with the commandant's office a few days in advance and could include a companion. When adults were admitted to the hospital, a monitor was placed in the hospital room, even though he was healthy. The idea was to prevent contact with the other Russians in the hospital. In cases involving childbirth or a contagious disease, of course, no suitable monitor was found. I recall my father was unsupervised in the hospital when he had a case of jaundice and my mother enjoyed similarly private time at the birth of my sister in January 1953. While the cultural offerings of Moscow and even trips to the countryside could be enjoyed, the monitor was ever-present. Germans who did not know Russian had to rely on the translation services of the monitors. These were not uniformly good but were passable. Over the years, some of the Germans developed close relationships with the monitors who were trained to be emotionally "distant."

By way of contrast, the children could leave the compound, unaccompanied, at any time. I was consequently sent on errands to places nearby, even on the coldest days of winter. My journeys outside the compound routinely involved trips to a small farm for milk and other needs as necessary.

Numerous children of different ages lived in the compound, so that playgroups were quickly formed. These helped cement ties between the adults who often took care of more than their own children when the need or wish arose. Within these social groups, the books that made it to Russia were passed around and well appreciated. Among them were the popular fictional tales about early America by the German author Karl May. Some of the families owned televisions and, occasionally, I felt fortunate to be allowed to watch local programs. A few families also kept dogs or cats and many kept gardens to produce lettuce, strawberries, currants, and potatoes.

The projects

In the spring of 1953, a flying test airplane was successfully shot down at the Kapustin Yar test site near Stalingrad, proving the feasibility of the "German" solution to the airplane interception challenge. Others in our group dealt with air-to-air missiles and with guidance systems for missiles for use by planes against ships. The Soviet leadership was so satisfied that two German specialists received the Stalin Prize, which was associated with a lot of money and the possibility of free travel in the USSR for life. In general, it should be said that German specialists were never involved in the final completion of various projects. Their contribution was preparatory work for Soviet development teams, with project management in the hands of the Soviets. The tasks to be completed were typically assigned to more than one German group and set up as a competition. After the execution of L. Beria in July 1953 and the subsequent deposition of his son, the Germans were withdrawn from the secret projects by the new leadership and refocused on documentation of their past work, the establishment of means for mass production, and testing. To bury the name Beria and the association with him, the project Berkut became S-25. In 1956, 3,360 launch pads for the S-25 anti-aircraft missile were stationed around Moscow.

This defense system [resembling somewhat the American Nike], was later upgraded and called S-75. This is the rocket that shot down an American U-2[1] spy plane on 1 May 1960, over the Urals near Sverdlovsk flying at an altitude of more than 65,000 ft. and caused a tense Cold War incident. Since many of the German specialists had returned to West Germany by then, they were thoroughly questioned about their knowledge of the system by American authorities. But that is getting ahead of our story. The four-year employment contracts signed in 1951 were expiring. At the beginning of 1955, everyone hoped to return home soon, but nothing moved.

1 The CIA pilot, Francis Gary Powers, was captured. He was later released in a trade for Soviet operatives in a prisoner exchange on 2 February 1962. His story is told in books and film.

Words by Helmut Breuninger:

On February 16th 1955 a number of specialists, including myself, were summoned to a meeting in the Club; It lasted about an hour and a half. It was headed by a Russian colonel assisted by a translator. The purpose of the meeting was to make it clear to us that the repatriation will not take place at the end of the month, when the four years of the contract expired. We were told we could not be repatriated, because the contract was not signed by everyone. Sarcastically, we were asked: why are you in such a hurry to get home? The rhetorical answer provided was that this case is in the hands of the government and a decision will come soon. *What kind of decision?* A few months later, June 30th, another meeting at the Club where 10 Soviet representatives on the podium declared: they are being transferred to the small resort town of Agudzera near Sokhumi around 15 July 1955, where they were to work in an institute together with us (!), the German specialists! Our stay in the Soviet Union was to be extended until December 1957. We could then return to Germany, if we still wished! The German wives waiting outside heard this and stormed the meeting room, something unheard of in the Soviet Union.

[It is probable that this move to a new place near the Black Sea was a kind of technical quarantine for the specialists and perhaps a way of keeping them under Soviet control, should the technology transfer not have been successful or sufficiently complete. In any case, the Soviets likely hoped that with a transfer to a pleasant sub-tropical location, the specialists could be kept happy about their lengthened stay in Russia.]

Following the meeting in the Club, it was decided to mount a street protest the following day, a Friday, July 1st. That next morning the people gathered punctually at the entrance to the workplace but did not proceed inside. Two or three representatives went in to make a statement which essentially called for a discussion with German government officials before any relocation was executed. We got a promise from the Soviet side for a contact opportunity with (East) German representatives before leaving for the south. We decided to return to work the next day. The strikers were not paid for that day and a compensation plan was organized: vacationers and sick people who received a salary that day had to pay something to the strikers.

The Soviet people around us learned a lot from observing this event, especially from the freely mobile children. That same Friday morning, the women made their usual trip to the market in a large bus. It was a bit dusty on its back side and a child wrote into the dust with his finger: "Свобода немецким специалистам" (Freedom for German specialists). With this inscription, the bus drove to the market square of Tushino. There, the accompanying state security people noticed that many people were gathering behind our parked bus to admire the inscription. It was immediately wiped away, of course.

> Back at home, Karl asked me for paper, colored pencils, and ink of all kinds, and I asked him why he needed it. He grinned and said, 'You don't need to know.' I gave him what he wanted. The children were about to put into practice what they had learned at school. He was taught that in the capitalist states, when the freedom of the workers is suppressed, the children put slogans on house walls and billboards such as: Peace, freedom, etc. Here and now, they saw our freedom being suppressed and reacted accordingly. They wrote slogans in Russian on pieces of paper, such as: "Not to Sokhumi, but to Germany!". They stuck the pieces of paper through cracks in the fence to Russian children outside who glued them to lampposts. For a short time, the papers with their slogans were said to have been emblazoned on almost all lamp posts from Komsomolskaya Ulitza (Communist Youth Movement Street) along Molotov Street to near the underpass under the Moscow Canal. Their discovery by the State Security Service (KGB) resulted in a speedy removal. As parents, we were told to stress to the children the virtue of refraining from such (counter-revolutionary) activities. We assured the officials of our intention to talk to the children and added that this event was the result of Soviet education and was the proper reaction to a suppression of freedom. For some time thereafter, the perimeter fence was guarded day and night by special patrols.

On 3 August, my father and others were summoned to a meeting with a representative of the GDR. Everyone was able to freely state their wishes regarding their place of residence in Germany. Since both German states were recognized by the Soviet Union, my father opted for West Germany because he had no family ties to anywhere in the GDR. Ten others followed with similar preferences and two specialists declared themselves to be Austrians.

Appeals for release were made to the Premier of the Soviet Union, N.K. Bulganin, stating objection to the USSR's violation of the terms of their contract. The letter politely demanded return to Germany, personal freedom, and respect guarantees of these measures by lower-level Soviet authorities. The appeal was signed by all German specialists. There was no response.

On 3 September we were informed that the stay of the German specialists would end the following year, 1956, and the scheduled departure for Sokhumi was to be the 12th. The fathers were to be employed in an "open" institute doing unclassified work. For that setting, a representative of the GDR was assigned to look after the German group.

In parallel to these events, we note that Austria gained its independence in May 1955.[1] The Austrian Hans Hoch ceremoniously hoisted a home-made Austrian flag in his garden, high enough for the Russians outside our compound to see. He was asked by the commandant's office to remove it immediately, as such demonstrations were prohibited in the Soviet Union. Unfortunately, shortly after this event, Mr. Hoch fell ill with appendicitis, was operated on, but died from complications a few days later (15 July).

The Chancellor of West Germany, Konrad Adenauer, arrived in Moscow on 12 September for a state visit. This was the same day we and our furniture were picked up to go south on a special train. Surely the timing was arranged to avoid contact between us and Adenauer's delegation. We reached Sokhumi on 16 September. The German students who were in Moscow at the time succeeded in contacting the delegation with little consequential result.

Mrs. Hoch stayed behind in Tushino with her three children and the Soviets promised her a speedy return to Austria. By then Mrs. Hoch had lost faith in the Soviet bureaucracy and took matters into her own hands by contacting the Austrian Embassy. She succeeded in getting her family of four home to Krems (Lower Austria) in November. Prior to his death, Mr. Hoch had taken financial precautions by having his father buy a house in that city with salary money he had transferred to Austria. The purchased and presently vacated house had served as the seat of the Soviet military commandant's office until Austrian independence in May 1955. The spell was broken; the first people of our anti-aircraft missile group had returned home, specifically to the "West".

My uncle Raimund visited Mrs. Hoch in 1956 and was briefed on our living conditions in the Soviet Union. He wrote two letters making personal appeals. The first to the Chairman of the Council of Ministers of the USSR for which he received only a postal acknowledgement of delivery. The second to the Soviet Embassy in West Germany. He noted that the "state of war" between Russia and Germany had officially ended on 25 January 1955 and that there were to be positive consequences for the detainees associated with this new state of affairs. The answer from the Soviet embassy in Bonn came back:

> Dear Mr. [Raimund] Breuninger,
>
> We hereby confirm receipt of your letter regarding the acceleration of your brother's departure from the USSR to the Federal Republic of Germany.

1 For the promise of neutrality, Allied occupation was ended.

We inform you that for the question of leaving the Soviet Union for the Federal Republic of Germany, your brother must personally contact the appropriate Soviet authorities.

With regard to the question of legal provisions concerning the transfer of money from the USSR to the Federal Republic of Germany, your brother may also receive explanations from the Soviet financial authorities at his place of residence.

Yours faithfully

Secretary of the Consular Section

September 1955 – February 1958 in Agudzera near Sokhumi

In Sokhumi [the capital city of today's autonomous Republic of Abkhazia, Georgia] we were quartered in a compound in nearby Agudzera, where the Germans of the group working with Nobel Prize winner Prof. Gustav Hertz[1] had lived and worked until the spring of 1955. The specialists' workplace was located right next to the residence compound. A legacy of the departed Germans was a collection of stray dogs and cats. We adopted a beautiful black house cat.

Our family settled in a Finn house (3 rooms) with a very large garden. There were also some two-story stone houses where several families and bachelors lived. The compound was fenced, albeit lightly, with an inconspicuous wire fence. Every German was given an identity card with which he could leave the compound. Within a radius of about two miles, we were able to move about freely and the adults were later allowed to take the public bus to Sokhumi unaccompanied. We were able to go to the local bazaar outside the compound and to the Black Sea (about ½ mile walk) for swimming. For us children, it was a paradise. The weather in Sokhumi is subtropical with warm winters and hot, humid summers. Snow was very rare and then only for a few days.

The specialists here were engaged in unclassified tasks: continuation of documentation of past work and construction of test equipment. They had access to foreign scientific literature from the West and thus got an overview of the level of developments in the "hostile" foreign countries.

There was no special school for Germans in Agudzera and we had to go to the Soviet school in Gulripschi. Some of the parents with younger

1 Hertz was a good catch for the Soviets. He was awarded the Nobel Prize in physics in 1925 as well as the Stalin Prize in 1951 for his contribution to uranium enrichment. Hertz was among a group of German physicists who believed that the US should not be the only power to have nuclear weapons. They willingly accepted offers to work in the Soviet Union.

children refused and taught them privately at home. Technically, we were in the Soviet Republic of Georgia where schools were divided into two parts: one part for Georgians where all subjects were taught in Georgian and Russian was taught as a foreign language. The other part was for all other nationalities. Russian was the language of instruction there, and Georgian, along with German, was a foreign language. Our knowledge of Russian was barely sufficient for the lessons so that our parents organized tutoring.

Group excursions into the wider countryside were organized and undertaken as were individual trips. Our fathers were monitored by the "headhunter" from the GDR, whose task it was to make attractive job and housing offers to the specialists. He also tried to persuade the aspirational "West Germans" and "Austrians" to opt for going to the GDR. The summer of 1956 brought the first signs that the first small groups would go home. We, as West Germans, were offered the prospect of leaving in October via the GDR. We packed a lot of our things in suitcases and wooden boxes. An official from customs came and checked everything, especially books and photos. Photos with prohibited subjects were retained. These included photographs of road intersections, bridges, city squares, train stations, etc.

We waited for the trucks to arrive on the appointed date while sitting on the boxes. In our group were many GDR people. Their belongings were picked up, ours were not. Then came the shock: West Germans and Austrians had to stay, everyone else could go home! One reason appears to have been that one specialist in the first group took advantage of an opportunity to flee from the GDR to the West and presumably informed the Western intelligence services about our plight and who we were. It now appeared that the Soviet confidence in the GDR's ability to keep people from going to the West was without merit. They had to rethink the problem.

Money transfers from our group had been allowed to be made to banks in the GDR. It became apparent that this money would never find its way into a bank in the West where many of us hoped to settle. The solution was to buy stuff available at the HO [Handelsorganisation, a trade organization in the GDR] and have the purchases shipped to West Germany. That was a permitted practical way of transferring our wealth to the West. Included in the bounty were a 12-piece porcelain tableware from Meissen [famous porcelain works located in the GDR] for a couple getting married, clothes, books, technical toys (a steam engine and a hot air engine), and an EXAKTA single lens reflex camera. From the GDR, we were also able to receive in Sokhumi the chemicals required to develop photographic film. Everyone with that interest made their first self-developed color slides.

The GDR "representative" who had recently left was replaced by a new one who, in January 1957, informed us that we would stay in the Soviet Union until the end of 1958. The children had to go back to school after half a year of waiting in anticipation of a trip home and, of course, catch up. In our house, we continued to live among packed boxes and suitcases.

On 3 November 1957, the dog Laika was launched into space by Sputnik-2. A month earlier, the first Sputnik had surprised the world with its radio signal. The Russian students were naturally very proud of these achievements. During school breaks, there were heated debates about how long she would survive. One day I reported dryly: "She's dead!" I had heard this news from listening to the radio station "Voice of America." Listening to such enemy radio broadcasts was strictly forbidden. If that fact had been passed on to school officials, a penalty would have come my way. Fortunately, my classmates didn't betray me. The Western broadcasts in the Russian language were jammed in the Soviet Union, but those sent in German or English were sometimes not. By these means, we were able to follow the events of the Hungarian uprising in October 1956 and other world news.

The second GDR headhunter/monitor left us, replaced by a third one. He, too, tried to lure Western aspirants to return to the GDR, and, in some cases, he succeeded. My parents and others refused and tried to firm up the way to the FRG with valid West German passports. Going through various official channels did not bring success in obtaining them. The first step in this process was current photos sent to Germany where valid passports were issued. That done, they were sent via diplomatic mail to the German Embassy Moscow who then tried to send the passports directly to us.

Words by Helmut Breuninger:

> The passports that the FRG embassy had sent at the end of September 1956 had disappeared without a trace. The embassy then tried a new way. Rather than send a passport directly to an address in Russia, they sent a second one intended for a colleague named Heilbron located here in Russia (whose first passport has also mysteriously disappeared) to Heilbron's relatives in the Federal Republic. The relatives then sent it on as a registered letter to Mr. Heilbron in Russia. That worked and it worked several times for others.
>
> On 27 March 1957 I wrote to my brother: "Wilhelm can send you two booklets. You will then have something to send us ... I don't

> have the king's (in German König) booklets anymore." Wilhelm was the first name of the West German ambassador and meant the West German embassy in Moscow. By "booklet" we meant passports. "You then have something for us" meant: "Send them to us then." "König" was the surname of the GDR ambassador in Moscow, meaning that I no longer had the GDR passports. On May 5th I wrote: "For now, I am only interested in one of the booklets. You can keep the other one until after I've read the first one." Meaning that my brother should first send only my passport, and when I have confirmed its arrival, send the other one for my wife and children. The two passports arrived safely on July 1 and 22 respectively. That's how we obtained our FRG passports."

In January 1958 it was suddenly announced that we could go home to West Germany, the GDR or Austria. We sold or gave away our furniture to friendly Russians and took with us only personal belongings (clothes, books, toys, photos, and memorabilia).

We were divided into two groups, the Breuninger family was in the first one and left Sokhumi on 8 February. In Moscow we changed to the long-distance train to Berlin and reached Frankfurt/Oder [German/Polish border] on 12 February. There, the returnees to West Germany were taken off and transferred to a special train to Marienborn/Helmstedt on the [intra-German] zone border crossing. From there a bus took us to the Friedland reception camp,[1] where radio, television, newsreels, and the major newspaper journalists awaited us. The "West Berliners" remained on the Moscow-Berlin train and went on to East Berlin. They were then taken by bus to West Berlin, where they were also greeted by journalists.

In the Friedland camp we received a small amount of welcome money (about 50 DM). My uncle Raimund showed up unexpectedly and, two days later, we took the train to my grandfather in Heidenheim/Brenz. There, two families took us in, one my father and me and the other my mother with my sister Emma.

We had reached the end of our forced stay in the Soviet Union.

We then faced having to find our way around everyday life in West Germany. From April 1958 on we lived in Ulm with, oddly enough, two families who had lived with us in Sokhumi. They left for the GDR in 1956 and then fled to West Germany quite quickly. The father of one of the two families was a "Blue One" who had not seen his wife and son for 10 years. Their reunion was not easy.

---

1 A refugee transfer camp in Lower Saxony that had operated continuously since 1945.

Having been in 7th grade in Russia, I entered the 6th grade in Baden-Württemberg. Initially, I was regarded as exotic or an Ivan [a negative portrayal of a Russian] by my classmates.

Before we were back in West Germany, my uncle Raimund, living in Bavaria (AOZ), was contacted, with all the intrigue elements characteristic of the Cold War, by what seemed to be US Army or CIA agents making a request to let them know, as soon as possible, when my father was back in West Germany. They had interrogated others who fled the GDR to the West and knew my father was likely to be coming also. They also knew that my father was well respected in his field of expertise and were consequently anxious to talk to him. For almost half a year, my father and many of the other returned specialists were questioned in detail by the US intelligence agents. Statements were compared and checked for contradictions. During these interviews, my father was on-leave from Telefunken where he rejoined several former colleagues who had come back from the Soviet Union a couple of years earlier (1956). During the interrogation period he received a good salary from the Americans, and they presumably learned what they sought. For us, life turned toward more normal. [... and the Cold War went on, tensely at times. Highlights on the timeline include the Berlin Wall, missiles in Cuba, an uprising in Czechoslovakia, just to mention a few of the events that punctuated the 1960s.]

Chapter 27

FERDINAND BRANDNER

The Brandner story continued after he left Russia and arrived in Dresden. It seems that the demanding and constrained work in Russia together with the stated ability to return to any place he wished obliterated any desire to stay and work in the aviation industry set up by the GDR. In 1954 he returned to his family in Austria. That country (occupied but without division by the Iron Curtain) would be firmly in the West in 1955 after some postwar uncertainty[1] around an initial Russian occupation. Eight years under the Soviets must have been enough for Brandner. His Nazi political leanings did not align with the communist ideology and continuing work at the VEB Pirna was unthinkable, in part, as was stated earlier, because the new airplane project was constrained by unsurmountable obstacles centered around the Soviet Union's dominance over the GDR.

After Brandner left Dresden, the engine people remaining in Pirna got a new director and established the plant whose function was to build the Pirna 014 turbojet. This engine first ran on a testbed in 1959 and on the Baade 152 airliner during the next year.

Brandner was also not fond of the Anglo-Americans. On his return to Austria, he declined to meet with English intelligence officials to talk about Russian engines. This was a time when he wanted to be clear of any involvement in engine building. For a time, he got involved in a firm building power machinery and later, technical management of the Austrian national airline, AUA. These activities were, however, too far from his interests. His views softened and to get closer to the engine business, he agreed to meet with the British. Sir Roy Fedden and Dr. Stern, who visited Oestrich in Stassfurt in 1945, came to see

1 The uncertainty centered on whether Austria was going to be administered by communists as were other countries behind the Iron Curtain. Austria remained in the West, with restrictions.

Brandner in Austria where they were presumably brought up to date about Russian activities.

After the time outside the engine business, Brandner re-entered it by becoming head of BMW Triebwerkbau GmbH (a forerunner of the today's MTU,[1] a West-German builder of jet engines and their components) in 1957. Unrealistically, he was determined to work only on engines unrelated to military applications and solely for the benefit of BMW. However, these were the intense days of the Cold War and jet engine work was not only driven by military applications but in cooperation with other NATO countries as in, for example, joint German-British projects. Because of his Austrian citizenship he could not hold a leading position in such projects. The 1955 agreements about the fate of Austria with the Soviet Union's Nikita Khrushchev precluded Austrian membership in NATO and prohibited Austrians from participating in projects. An application for German citizenship to circumvent this issue was denied on the basis of his Russian and, perhaps, his prewar and German wartime histories. In short, he was forced out of BMW in 1958. This left him embittered because the door on his working on aviation engines in the West was firmly closed. Reflecting on his state of affairs, he turned to the past for blame. In his writing,[2] he faults the Western Allies for having left many [most?] of the engine engineers behind in the Soviet Occupation Zone. More importantly, he blames them for not protesting the Russian abduction of the German engineers at the appropriate meetings of the Four Powers.

However, not all doors were shut to him. The Middle East was in turmoil since the creation of the state of Israel. For its part, Israel was building up to be a formidable military power and modern military airplanes were going to be needed by the Arab nations as a counter move. Brandner and other German engineers, primarily contacts with whom he had worked, were available. In 1959, they were recruited by the Nasser Government in Egypt. Brandner was invited to lead the construction of a jet engine for an Egyptian supersonic jet fighter (the Helwan HA-300). This project is interesting because it was started in Francisco Franco's fascist Spain with airplane designer Willy Messerschmitt[3] (who was on the *Operation Paperclip* list) as the principal leader. This project was abandoned by Spain for technical and financial reasons and sold to Egypt with Messerschmitt remaining at its head.

1 A part of Rolls-Royce Holdings.

2 H. Zoeller, personal communication.

3 The Messerschmitt Company, unable to build airplanes, built single-door microcars between 1955 and 1964.

Egypt wanted its own capable military airplane for a possible future war in the Middle East when it could not rely on Western sources. With Messerschmitt designing and building the airplane, an Egyptian engine was needed and Brandner was the man to build one.

This secret project run by German engineers came to light in the press and was terminated in May 1969 by pressuring the technical people out and blocking necessary industrial support from the West. An important reason was Brandner's Nazi past and the political atmosphere around the balance of power in the Middle East. The main objections to the project were expressed by Federal Republic of Germany (West Germany) and the state of Israel.

The cancellation of the Egyptian airplane and engine project forced Egypt to buy military aircraft from the Soviet Union and deprived Brandner from working in his field away from under both Western and Soviet influences. The title of his book, translated into English says it well: "Life between Fronts." Brandner's having been checkmated led to his Nazi outlook being revealed. It was well illustrated in a *Der Spiegel* (38, 10.09.1967) interview in 1967 where, he blames the "difficulties" in Egypt (the Six-Day War was in June of that year) on "Jewish companies in the US." With Western and Soviet work options at a dead-end, only China remained as an outlet for his technical interests. After leaving Egypt, he lectured (1972–3) on engine developments at Beijing University and dedicated his later years to the writing of a memoir published in 1973. He died in 1986 in Salzburg.

Chapter 28

OUT OF THE ASHES

What is "technology"? In essence it is a learned way of doing things using tools and materials found in nature. In that sense, technology has always played a role in the history of mankind. Life has always been challenging and technology was often a critical aspect of survival. Millenia ago, men and women might have used a stick, a tool, to cook a piece of meat over a fire that took ingenuity to create when nature did not provide one. Chipping a stone into a cutting or scraping tool took more ingenuity and skill. It has always been true that some needs could only be met by using the mind and hands to create an object that allows carrying out a task. As the motto of the Massachusetts Institute of Technology states, it takes mind and hands: "mens et manus."

In the present age, the nature of technology has not changed. What has changed is that its complexity has increased manifold. Being effective requires building on what others have learned and perhaps put in practice. Technology is now everywhere around us. We need it to make a vaccine, to build an electric power system, a factory to manufacture just about anything: an airplane, a jet engine, a computer, or ....

Complex systems require the skills of many, and this story is about the men who made one such complex system, the jet engine. History shows that many have contributed in many ways though most will never be adequately recognized for what they added to the totality of a practical product.

An interesting question raised by the stories associated with *Operation Paperclip* as implemented by the US at the end of WWII is: in whom rests the knowledge to build something, when it is known that someone has succeeded, and one may wish to replicate it? Is it the chief engineer and his main assistants or is it the collective skill of all who integrated their skills, the hundreds of engineers and technicians in this case?

The answer lies in the self-confidence or arrogance inherent in the conviction that one is smart enough and has the resources to create a new and perhaps better jet engine. All one needs is the knowledge that it can be done and, perhaps, a few people with ideas to guide your efforts. That was the approach taken by the US government in 1945: get a few of the technical leaders to the US and we will take it from there.

The British approach to the available engineering knowledge of the Germans in 1945 was another good example of self-confidence. At the time, the British thought that they knew all there was to know about jet engines! Besides, they might not want to leave the impression that the German engineering was useful. War has a way of spawning such views.

The French approach was pragmatic. The French had a rich history in aviation. In particular, they contributed many important ideas necessary to make flight and the jet engine a reality. Unfortunately, France had to deal with the history of the European continent during the war. The country was occupied by Nazi Germany from 1940 to 1944 and whatever efforts were proceeding toward the jet engine were halted. At war's end, they needed a whole team of engineers and technicians to catch up and do it quickly. They succeeded.

The Russians also used the technique of involving as complete a team of engineers as were available, to start their industry. They used a violence of sorts to achieve it. For the Russians, it was very unfortunate that the Americans and the British had helped themselves to the leading engineers and much of the critical documentation. The left-over people and what they knew were harvested by them and then, when the knowledge was firmly in Russian hands and minds, the German specialists were expelled and returned home to ordinary lives. They were damaged perhaps and certainly no longer at the leading edges of their fields. In many, if not most, instances, they were further condemned to lives under a new autocracy in the GDR that was communist East Germany. Their work in Russia was meekly acknowledged by those who should have done better.

Such approaches to technology transfer applied to a wide variety of fields and were not limited to the jet engine. In that domain, however, the ideas involved were later developed to the point where modern engines barely resemble the ones built in the 1940s, in size and performance. All nations making up the WWII Allies succeeded in establishing robust industries around the new aircraft propulsion technology. By choice and necessity, the methods differed, and success was not only variable but difficult to state. Perhaps survival of industrial enterprises after three-quarters of a century is one way.

Another is that society as a whole is the beneficiary of the technology. Today, you can buy a reasonably priced ticket to fly safely anywhere on this blue planet. That is a measure of success.

When one looks at the state of the jet aviation industry in any country today and considers what it takes to be industrially successful, the conclusion must be that it takes more than ideas. It requires an industrial base that can provide the basic materials and high-tech fabrication methods that must be built into a product that will sell and perform well on the world market. It also requires a degree of openness regarding the engineering that goes into a complicated system like an airplane so that an appropriate understanding of performance in the user's setting is evident. It seems clear that in that sense, the Soviet Union, and its successor the Russian Federation, as engine builders, failed. They may be able to build engines that power impressive military airplanes, but such a capability does not speak to the necessary underlying quality issues that must be built into technology to make it state-of-the-art and truly competitive. Success in that arena requires an open marketplace for ideas and processes and the freedom to allow good ideas to advance and poor ones to fail.

The story of Russian aviation is rich, but it is nearly always in second place on the world stage when a government bureaucracy tells the airplane builders what to copy or to attempt to build better. Being second best always requires extensive industrial espionage to keep an eye on what those ahead are doing. Examples are few in the commercial aviation world where Russian airplanes would be sought by the world's airlines. Decisions made by political committees are rarely as good as those made by motivated people and entities based on economics. The experience of the Tu-144, the Russian "Concordeski," is a supremely good example of the flawed belief that good ideas flow down from the heads of government. Consider further that you probably never made a purchase decision for any object "made in Russia," save perhaps a set of the lovely Matryoshka dolls!

My reading of events relating to the story developed here revealed an interesting artifact about the way Russians view history. Only information or ideas that contribute to a positive image of Russia are allowed to be printed in Russian history books. Kurt Plügel's writing provides an insightful example: Russian students did not learn history accurately. What? The 18th-century Tsarina Catherine the Great was German? Such a myopic viewpoint also applies to this story. Consider that decades after the abduction events, Russian writers (in the Haida-Clan text, for example) who deal with that history refer to the presence of the Germans with words like "in November 1946, the German specialists came to work with our engineers..." The use of the gentle words "came" and "work with..." whitewashes a brutal reality.

It could have been different ...

A tragic and strategic error might have been made by the US government when it chose to deal with only a small number of the important engineers at Junkers and BMW. The failure of the US Army to offer evacuation to the West, if only to the western occupation zones, for a larger fraction of the technical people from BMW and Junkers had two consequences. First, it condemned the engineers and their families left in the Soviet Occupation Zone to seven, some as many as eleven, years of involuntary service and confinement in the Soviet Union. The second consequence was that moving a larger group of technical people to the West might have deprived the Soviet Union of the immediate access to the technology they needed to keep up with the Western Allies as the Cold War arms race took shape. That second point must be tempered with the thought expressed above: technology is not limited by political boundaries. In time, all that anyone needs to develop it is to know that it can be done because it has been done. In time, the Russians would have had workable jet engines, no matter how the Americans dealt with the German jet engineers.

The jet engine technology was not the only sector that played a role in the Cold War. Rockets and missiles were also involved. Kurt Plügel makes reference in his writing that some specialists from the V 2 ballistic rocket operations in Peenemünde were taken to the Soviet Union. Had none of these transfers to Russia taken place, who knows how the Cold War would have evolved? In the race to space, the Soviets certainly grabbed the headlines first, stumbled, and lost not only the race to the moon but almost all effective participation at the leading edge in the world's use of space for a greater understanding of the planet and the needs of life on it.

EPILOGUE – THE ROLE OF THE US ARMY

My interest in writing this story is tightly coupled to the jet engine development history in which my German engineer father was a participant during WWII. The ending of the war led to a cascade of events that might have turned out very differently for me had the US Army, and the US government more generally, handled the events that ultimately made me an American citizen differently. In a sense, this writing is an exploration of a personal alternative history, the tale of an unfortunate doppelgänger.

War is a complicated affair because many actors are involved as individuals and as agencies. The story of my own journey through the events of WWII during its last days had a happy ending. The words of Kurt Pflügel are a stark and terrifying reminder that my days through the postwar years could have been spent in Russia. On that road, it is unlikely that I would have written this story, nor would I have smithed these words in English.

For me and my family, the interactions with the US Army in 1945–6 (even in 1952) were many. The biography I wrote of my father's work with the jet engine provides some of the details. First, there was the good fortune of being caught by American forces and not by the Soviets. Dessau's location on the west side of the Elbe River where the US Army halted was fortunate indeed. Had the city been on the east of the river, who knows? Second, the American military technical people recognized the Germans who were valuable for their purposes. Fortunately, that included my father. That my father was smart enough to have accomplished what he did is a personal stroke of very good luck. One does not generally get to choose one's father! Third, people like him were offered a chance to evacuate to the American Occupation Zone and he agreed to go. During the trip, the soldier driving our truck became intoxicated and wrecked the truck and nearly took my brother's life with serious injuries. That was an unfortunate interaction associated with one soldier and is not attributable to the Army as an agency. The accident occurred in a place that was to become part of the Soviet Occupation Zone just seven days later! Fourth, to their credit, the Army took responsibility for this accident by evacuating my father (and me) out of the area without delay. They conveyed my injured brother to a nearby hospital. They disguised my mother as a nurse to put off possible Russian interest and thwart the possibility of using her to blackmail my father back into the area and into Russian hands. Lastly, the Army followed through with the promise to reunite my family by retrieving my injured brother and our mother moments before the Soviet zone takeover. Finally, it took care of him in American facilities, and provided work for my father while he was debriefed on his previous work and expertise.

With the accident as the exception, those interactions were largely good happenings. Perhaps less good, and certainly not bad, was the absence of an offer for my father to work in the US shortly after war. Such offers were made to several of his colleagues identified through *Operation Paperclip*. A decision to make an offer would probably have been postponed until my brother was released from American medical care and was able to travel. By then, the war in the Pacific was over and there were new priorities. One might have been the matter that only a limited number of German immigrants could be accommodated within American political parameters. President Truman was concerned about employment for the veterans returning to a postwar America. Had we moved to the US then, my youth would have been much more American and certainly different from the one I lived in France. To the good is that I learned French, then English and learned to love two countries, actually three.

Finally, a last aspect of actions by the US Army. Thanks to the Junkers engineers who did travel and work in the US shortly after the war, an offer came to my father in 1952 to rejoin them. He was needed to help build a medium-sized gas turbine engine for the US Air Force. Curiously, the paperwork stipulated that his stay would be limited to one year, but the company for which he came to work was confident that the stay would be extended. Indeed, it was, as all members of our family stayed to become US citizens. The engines these men built were widely and successfully used in the helicopters of the US Army. I think of that success as payback for the confidence the Army placed in my father in 1945 and the many positive interactions that followed.

I especially appreciate that Americans are decent and true to their word, even in war.

A haunting thought

History moves slowly and steadily but it also responds to singular events, events brought about not by decisions from committees or by a misanthropic tyrant surrounded by others like him but by individuals taking it upon themselves to derail the course of those who have inflicted great harm. One such event was executed by Claus von Stauffenberg on 20 July 1944, with his unsuccessful assassination attempt on Hitler. How would the history you just read be different had he succeeded? Such questions are spiritual nourishment for historians, of course, and this one haunts this writer.

I write this in 2023, I think every day of the war of conquest imposed by a Soviet Union-like state onto millions of Ukrainians. It is hard to believe that things have changed much in Russia and its view of the world around them. I was once hopeful that the overtures the world has made to Russia would allow reasonable minds and hearts in that country to embrace a constructive world view that truly embraces peace and competition and scorns the savagery of innocents by war. I am heartened by the bravery and sacrifice of Ukrainian soldiers and the wisdom and courage of Russian men who choose to not participate in the killing of others by leaving the country. They understand the price that war exacts.

I stay hopeful.

APPENDIX: REUNION IN SAMARA AFTER 47 YEARS

The story told ends in the 1960s, but history continued. The Soviet Union's collapse led to a turbulent time involving openness and repression as well as the political repercussions associated with a perception of lost greatness. Whether the Russian people are culturally rich should never be in question, but political aspirations of empire in the age of nuclear weapons are ingredients for disastrous miscalculations of global proportions.

On a narrower scale, the post-Soviet era has led to German re-examinations of the experiences undergone by those abducted to the Soviet Union. It has also led to returns by some revisiting Germans to their ghetto sites.

The perspectives documented by the abductees, and more often by their children, vary depending on their experiences. Some are bitter and some have put the bad aspects of the experiences behind them. Many avoided revisiting the experience altogether and became mute. Others still, continued to live with the pleasant aspects, specifically the interpersonal relationships that came out of the forced living and working in a ghetto as well, perhaps, as an appreciation for the Russian people and culture. Because the handling of a life-altering experiences can differ so widely, an overall and all-encompassing description can never be written. The reader will have to be satisfied by what is available in the archives, newspapers, memoirs, and video media.

Men and women with bitter experiences can and do heal by pushing the memory of the bad aside and focusing on the good. The writing below is a description of conditions in Russia after the fall of the Soviet Union as seen by one group of revisiting Upra Germans. It is one person's perspective of a visit reflecting, perhaps, the views of his fellow travelers. The writer certainly could not foresee how Russia will change again in the years after their visit.

The entirety of this appendix is the translated writing of Prof. Dr. Sc. Heinz Hartlepp. The form is structured as a trip report to share with the travelers who accompanied him. Hartlepp was one of the younger abductees (b. 1925) and has written more extensively about the postwar period (see Bibliography).

Memories of Samara in 2000 – German Specialists in the USSR from 1946 to 1954

The specialists who went to Russia often came together in reunions after their return to Germany. While regular organized meetings took place in the FRG as the "Brandner family", this was not possible on an organized scale in the GDR. The get-togethers in that part of Germany were limited to close friendship circles in apartments, where individuals were among themselves and could talk unhindered. It was only after the fall of the Berlin Wall in 1989 that open gatherings within the GDR and joint ones with people from East and West became possible. First, thanks to the initiative of Mr. Udo Klähn, the sons and daughters of the specialists in the GDR came together with the church of Pirna Sonnenstein graciously providing a venue in its new parish hall. The first meeting was in 1992. The turnout was very large, with many participants who had spent their school years together in Upra. The last meeting in Pirna of these "Upra children", as they called themselves, took place in the autumn 1999.

The first meeting between former specialists from both East and West was organized by Mr. Jürgen Michels, co-author of the book *Luftfahrt Ost* (see Bibliography). Through the research for this book, he established contact with many of the abductees. Archival material had become available in East Germany that provided the addresses of those who went to Russia. He was assisted by Mr. Jochen Werner (his co-author), who, after the fall of the Berlin Wall, had taken over the archives of the renamed Dresden Aircraft Works. At the time, he was a young graduate engineer in the GDR aviation industry. He wanted to continue work in the field by writing a book about this time. With these connections, almost all specialists could be invited to a meeting at the Technical University Dresden in the autumn of 1995. This first meeting with representatives from everywhere was a great success. In 1996, a Volga cruise was put together with planned day stops in Podberesja, Samara, and Upra, in which about 40 people participated. [Photographs from this trip are posted on the Haida-Clan website.]

This experience inspired Udo Klähn to organize a special trip to Samara for the year 2000. The following writing is about this tour.

The journey began in Berlin-Schönefeld for the flight to Moscow in a Boeing 737 staffed with a Russian crew. We had good flying weather. In Moscow, after leaving the aircraft, the immigration control was problem-free, but involved a long queue because several planes had landed in close succession. Our Russian travel companion, a German-speaking Muscovite, Luba, welcomed us with kind words. Because travelers were not allowed to import rubles into Russia, she exchanged small amounts of our dollars for rubles. A special bus took us to the train station. There, we boarded the Zhiguli Express (with sleeping and restaurant cars) to Samara. The traditional stoves for making tea or coffee could be found in every coach. We remembered them well. They were still heated with wood, providing us with the welcome drinks to augment the snack bags.

Happy and content, we arrived in Samara In the early morning and were taken to the Hotel Rossia. The view from the 9th-floor hotel room was of the Volga River's landing dock and its busy shipping traffic. We first made a pilgrimage through Samara to get used to the idea that we were back in Russia. After a good dinner at the hotel, we took a long stroll on the beautifully designed and busy waterfront promenade. Many discos and dance halls lined the way, emitting music. The happy and vibrant, but very well-mannered, hustle and bustle surprised us and invited us to linger in one of the open-air restaurants with a cold beer. During the day the temperature was just under 40 degrees (C), hot but quite bearable. Happy noise could be heard well after midnight. Surprisingly, we did not meet a single drunk, not even a beggar, as we would have in our time. The promenade and the streets were clean.

The city had changed for the better! The new Samara is almost unrecognizable. Lots of new buildings. And there, among them, a newly built church with gilded domes. At a bank we exchanged more dollars for needed rubles. At another bank, a curious surprise: a sign that read "Rubel nyet" [no rubles] obviously testifying to the fact that there were many foreigners in the city who did not function on the ruble economy. In the old city center, we found a few of the colorful wooden houses we remembered. They have stood the test of time and are still inhabited. Next to them were new buildings. The arterial road north out of town [toward Upra] that once led through fields is now widely built-up with many new shops as well as a new church.

We had a bus at our disposal every day. The first excursion followed a city tour through Samara to Upravlencheski. The route was hardly recognizable. The wide asphalt road was heavily built-up with buildings of all kinds long before we reached Upra. At the entrance to the village, in front of the "Magazin", a new clubhouse was built, still with the traditional standing toilets! That's when we realized we were in Russia. Behind the clubhouse was a beautifully decorated recreation park with sculptures and a fountain. Nearby was a well-equipped outdoor restaurant and open space with plastic chairs and umbrellas adorned with Western logos.

The population of Upra had increased from just under 10,000 to almost 30,000 in the years since we left. The reason for this is the enormous expansion of the factory to about twice its former size. The stroll through the Magazin took us back to the old time. An elderly saleswoman told us that she worked in this store in 1948 and was very happy to have served the Germans who she said were always friendly despite the queues that were often long. There is now a small snack stand in front of the building but few other changes. The stone houses are also still standing as they were. The formerly red brick house facade was stuccoed at some point and has now a new, larger Magazin on the lowest floor.

In front of the red brick house stood a new stone house which was under construction when we left. Little has changed in the quarter of the wooden houses. Even the firewood sheds still leaned awkwardly as before. The houses themselves were refinished in stucco [partly to reduce winter's cold air leaks] and therewith lost some of their former charm. Most of the beautiful balconies have been glazed in to increase living space.

We visited the places where we lived. Receptions by the occupants were enthusiastic and warm. Apparently, the word had spread through the village that the Germans were returning to visit. We learned that the families now owned or occupied the entire apartments and did not have to settle for just one or two rooms as we did.

We were pleased to see that the German cemetery still existed and was obviously looked after. The graves were preserved and surrounded by stones. The wooden crosses we erected about 50 years ago had rotted away, but the Russians set up a larger gravestone marker with the names of the deceased. A more organized Russian cemetery occupied the area near the old random plot collection and near the German cemetery. The typical iron fencing surrounded each grave.

The Finn houses behind the red stone house were gone and the area was rebuilt with a new 5-story residential complex. Wide paved streets with generous sidewalks and green spaces testify to good urban design. The large number of cars suggested increased prosperity, although we noted that earnings were still very low.

In the new Russian school, we were enthusiastically received by the headmistress and some of the teachers. She welcomed the former students, some of whom were older than she was. During the tour of the school, we saw memorabilia in its museum room, such as carefully preserved photo boards and albums recalling the German presence. We recognized ourselves and our classmates in the pictures.

A special feature for me was a large board highlighting "the best" workers in the "Zavod," the company. It probably dated to 1951/52 and displayed the 9x12 cm photos of German employees of the OKB of the time.

There were many interesting conversations with the present teachers. The teachers of our time had passed away. After our school tour, we were generously entertained with coffee, tea, pastries, and sausage rolls. In the school's event room, the deputy of the main engine construction group welcomed us with kind words. A small cultural event followed with dancing and singing performed by students of the higher grades. They had rehearsed the program for us despite their being on school holidays.

On this occasion, I met with Prof. Dr. techn. Vladimir N. Orlov, who worked in the turbine department under Dr. Herbert Cordes since 1947 and who became chief designer after the death of N.D. Kuznetsov. I also met another former colleague, Dr. Kocherov, who had worked in design under Dr. Rudolf Vogts. Orlov, Kocherov, and I recognized each other even at our advanced ages near 75 years. These two Russian colleagues were still employed in the company as consultants. They told me about the decline of the company and its work due to the opening of doors to the West after 1991. Since that time, Russian airline aircraft were equipped with Western engines that allow them to operate on Western airfields. No Russian engines were sold after 1988. They said that the remaining production engines were stored for 10 years hoping for better times but were eventually scrapped. The factory now focuses on supplying small rocket engines for the Americans. They did not want to show me the workplace. It was not well suited for visitors and there were security issues. Sadly, N.D. Kuznetsov lived to witness this decline of his life's work. He died in 1996.

Dr. Kocherov showed me a new book, in which all engine developments of the plant were described with many drawings and pictures. He proudly referred me to the introduction, in which my name is mentioned as a contributing resource.

Times have changed. In 1999, for example, the Americans leased a flight-worthy Tupolev Tu-144 supersonic aircraft to carry out investigations for the development of new supersonic aircraft. German television reported on this unusual transaction. In December 1999, the museum in Speyer (Germany) purchased an Antonov AN-22 heavy lift vehicle for their exhibit. This very large transport aircraft was built in Kiev in 1965 and was transferred to the Speyer airfield under its own power by Russian pilots.

The German specialists were well connected with the AN-22. Its NK-12 engines with their contra-rotating propellers were developed in Upra. After we left in 1954, the Kuznetsov team increased from their power output from 12,000 to 15,000 horsepower and installed the engine(s) as standard propulsion on the AN-22 and other airplanes. A commendable achievement by the Russian engineers we trained and a tremendous source of pride for us.

Another meeting at the school was with two of my former draftswomen, Sinaida and Lidia. They were all that remained of my group, which, at the time, consisted of 13 engineers and draftswomen. The two women heard about our visit to Samara and came to see us.

Sinaida came to our group as an 18-year-old, studied at the university, and married an engineer from our design office who later became a professor and died in 1997. She told me that she never forgot me because I gave her flowers for her birthdays. She said she never again had a boss like me! One of her two daughters is an opera singer in Strasbourg (France), the other is a prima ballerina in Stockholm. Every year she visits them for a month. She happily described a dacha she owns on 2,500 sq m [0.6 acres] of land. Two years ago, she sold her car because the traffic had become so unbearable.

The 78-year-old Lidia was married to a colonel who died 10 years earlier. In anticipation of our meeting, she had donned the many war decorations she earned as a nurse. From the factory archives she gave me a copy of the perspective drawing instructions I wrote in 1952 for the draftsmen. She also gave me a photo of herself at a young age and a Seiko wristwatch. I had to accept these gifts lest these thoughtful women be offended. We knew the customs and social duties. I was deeply impressed that even after 47 years, we were not forgotten. I had to promise Lidia that I would send a letter with pictures, which I did.

Both widows received a monthly pension of 1,000 rubles each, which corresponded to about 100 DM. This was not a widow's pension but was earned through their own work. Sina, as she liked to be called, shared that her apartment rent has recently increased from 135 rubles to 350, but she was coping well enough.

In Samara, we visited the old 4-story Stalin bunker built in 1941 in the middle of the city. We were proudly told that this bunker is 36 m below ground level and is deeper than the Hitler bunker was in Berlin.

Stalin had to cope with a very long staircase. A 3-person elevator was installed recently for persons with special needs. It seems curiously odd that a wealthy foreigner built a large, magnificent villa-like house right next to the Stalin bunker.

In Russia, the difference between rich and poor is huge. This is clearly discernible in the vehicles on the road. The price of a Zhiguli [a modest Russian-made automobile] is just under 80,000 rubles, but the purchase of a Mercedes or BMW required about a million rubles [~100,000 DM or ca. $40,000 at the time]. Locally registered Mercedes and BMW cars were, however, not rare in Samara, running along with the Volga taxis and the older Moskviches we remembered.

We could not fail to revisit the countryside. We spent a whole day on the Volga island where we spent so many summer Sundays. From Krasnaya Glinka we circumnavigated the island in a motorboat and got off at a new pier specially built for the island visitors. During our time, the island served only the recreation needs of the Germans. That has changed with many small recreational weekend houses built by the locals. We laid on the wonderful beach, enjoyed a swim and a very good lunch set up for us by the factory. Overall, the island has remained as it was, even as the water level was higher by about 4 m because of the new dam on the river.

A last excursion took us to the Togliatti automobile plant built by the Italians. We were able to visit the 2 km long assembly line. According to the Russian guide, who spoke very good German, the workers on the assembly line receive a monthly wage of about 5,000 rubles. This was countermanded by a worker on the assembly line we questioned and who told us that her wages were just 2,500 rubles. The plant was very generously laid out with well-kept green areas maintained between the factory buildings. In one of the snack bars adjacent to the assembly, we found a wide range of food offerings and enjoyed a good meal. [To put the Russian wages in perspective, we note that prior the Russian invasion of Crimea in 2014, the exchange rate for one ruble was about $0.03. That has since fallen to ~$0.01.]

On the last day of our visit in Samara, we took a long stroll through the city and the bazaar, which was sheltered under a large new roof. The wares exchanged there have changed but the market character has not.

That evening, we took a smaller Volga steamer to the Zhiguli Gate, dined on a generous buffet, and were able to enjoy views of the Zhiguli Mountains highlighted by a picture-perfect sunset.

Our departure from Samara was again by the Zhiguli Express back to Moscow, where we had time for a city tour prior to our flight to

Berlin. We strolled around the city center including Red Square. We admired the renovation of important street intersections and new buildings. Cleanliness prevailed everywhere and new shops were evident. In a part of Red Square, a peaceful demonstration by about 100 elderly communists with placards and red flags yearned for the old days. They were hardly noticed.

Our journey into the past took us to the new Russia of very friendly people. Undaunted, they are hoping for better times.

BIBLIOGRAPHY

*ISBN numbers and/or Internet links are provided for references that may be difficult to find. Items noted with * do not have an ISBN.*

Augustine, D.L., *Red Prometheus – Engineering and Dictatorship in East Germany, 1945–1990*, MIT Press, 2007.

Brandner, Ferdinand, *Ein Leben Zwischen Fronten – Ingenieur im Schussfeld der Weltpolitik* ('A Life between Fronts – An Engineer in the Crossfire of World Politics'), Verlag Welsermühl, Munich, 1973, ISBN-13 9783853391259 (in German).

Branger, André, Trallero, Daniel, and Claveau, Charles, "The German Team 1945–1947". Published in a special edition of *The Diffuser* (*Le Diffuseur- Bulletin de l'Association des Amis du Patrimoine Historique de Turboméca*) Series no. 5, June 2017 (in French) <aapht@yahoo.fr>

*Breuninger, Karl, "Meine Kindheit in der Sowjet Union Okt. 1946 bis Feb. 1958", 2. Aufl. 2019. <www.karlist.net>

Conner, Margaret, *Hans von Ohain, Elegance in Flight*, American Institute of Aeronautics and Astronautics, Reston, VA, 2001.

Decher, R., *Powering the World's Airliners*, Pen & Sword, Barnsley, UK, 2020.

Decher, R., *Turbulent Journey – the Jumo Engine, Operation Paperclip, and the American Dream*, Schiffer Publications, Atglen PA, 2022.

Eckardt, Dietrich, *Jet Web - Connections in the Development History of Turbojet Engines 1920–1950*, Springer Nature, 2022.

*"Fedden Mission to Germany: Final Report, Part 2", Published by the (British) Ministry of Aircraft Production, undated.

Gersdorff, K. von, Grasmann, K., *Die Deutsche Luftfahrt – Flugmotoren und Strahltriebwerke*, Bernard & Graefe Verlag, München, 1981 (in German)

Hartlepp, Heinz, *Erinnerungen an Samara – Deutsche Luftfahrtspezialisten von Junkers, BMW, und Askania in der Sowjet Union 1946 bis 1954 und die Zeit danach* ('Memories of Samara – German Flight Technology Specialists in the Soviet Union 1946 to 1954 and the Time thereafter'), 2005, ISBN 978-3925505-836.

Kay, Antony L., *Turbojet – History and Development 1930–1960* Vol. 2, Crowood Press, UK, 2007.

Klein, Wilhelm, *Keiner wollte es glauben* (No one could believe it), Göttert Verlag, Diepenau, Germany, 2002. ISBN 3-929793-96-2.

Koop, Allen V., *Stark Decency – German Prisoners of War in a New England Village*, Dartmouth College Press, 1988.Kuwschinow, S., Michels, J., Srelov, J., and

Woronkow, J., *Deutsche Flugzeug-Spezialisten im Sowjetischen Russland. Leben und Arbeit 1945–1954 an den Orten Uprawlentscheski und Kasan*. Published in Russian and Germany, 1996. No publisher indicated.

McCutcheon, Kimble D., "The Junkers Jumo 222", *Torque Meter* Volume 6, Number 3 (Summer 2007).

Michels, Jürgen, and Werner, Jochen, *Luftfahrt Ost 1945–1990 – Geschichte der deutschen Luftfahrt in der Sowjetischen Besatzungszone und der DDR* (History of German Aviation of the Soviet Occupation Zone and the GDR), Bernard & Graefe, Munich, 1994. ISBN 978-3763761098 .

Mick, Christoph, *Forschen für Stalin: Deutsche Fachleute in der sowjetischen Rüstungsindustrie 1945–1958 (Abhandlungen und Berichte)* (German Specialists in the Soviet Armament Industry 1945–1958), Oldenbourg Verlag, 2000, ISBN 3-486-29003-7.

Nouzille, Vincent (20 May 1999). "La folle histoire du Dr Oestrich" ("The crazy history of Dr. Oestrich"), *L'Express*, Paris, France. p. 59 (in French). Retrieved 11 October 2019.

Pearce, William, *Junkers Jumo 222*, Old Machine Press, 2005, <https://oldmachinepress.com/2021/06/05/junkers-jumo-222-aircraft-engine/>

*Pflügel, Kurt, *Schicksale Deutscher Luftfahrt Ingenieure* ("Fates of German Aviation Engineers"), no publisher, 1974?

Renneberg, Monika and Walker, Mark (eds), *Science, Technology, and National Socialism*, Cambridge University Press, 1994.

Singer, Friedemann, *Als Lebende Reparation an der Wolga 1946–1950* ("As a Living Reparation on the Volga 1946–1950"), Books on Demand GmbH, Norderstedt, 2008. ISBN 978-3-8370-6169-7.

Steinke, Sebastian, "Baade 152: Der Pioneer aus dem Osten" ("the Pioneer from the East"), *Flug Revue* (Magazine), 3 October 2019. Web link: https://www.flugrevue.de/klassiker/der-pionier-aus-dem-osten-baade-152/

Web Links

https://www.scientistsandfriends.com/

This site lists, among other items, the 2 January 1947 *Operation Paperclip* list and an article in the October 1946 issue of *Harper's Magazine* entitled "SECRETS BY THE THOUSANDS" by C. Lester Walker.

https://www.flugzeug-lorenz.de/junkers-vips/lebenslauf-brunolf-baade

A review of the life of Brunolf Baade (in German) by freelance journalist Holger Lorenz; info@flugzeug-lorenz.de

http://haida-clan.de/die-upra-kinder.html

Site maintained to keep alive the experience of the Germans abducted to Russia.

http://hugojunkers.bplaced.net/index.html

Website maintained by Horst Zoeller dedicated to the work of Hugo Junkers.

Junkers (OKB-1) Jumo 022 (TW-2) (hugojunkers.bplaced.net)

This link provides information on the engines worked on by the Junkers team in Russia.

Creation of the TV-2 (NK-12) Turboprop Engine (airpages.ru)

https://www.russianspaceweb.com/a4_team_moscow.html
A description of the fates of the V-2 engineers in the Soviet Union after 1945.

INDEX

Places

Bad Kissingen, 17, 41–5, 51
Berlin, East, 68, 164, 186, 213
Berlin, West, 73, 126, 170
Berlin-Friedenau, 66
Berlin Spandau, 2
Bregenz, 60
Brest-Litovsk, 79,164

Dayton, Ohio, 12, 20
Decize, 46–7, 51–8
Dessau, 8–9, 19, 65, 75–9, 104, 115
Dresden, 158, 166
Dubna, 68, 156

Fort Sill, Oklahoma, 51, 179
Frankfurt/Oder,79, 165

Gernrode, 16

Kazan, 145
Krasnaya Glinka, 91
Kuybyshev, 83, 102, 133

Landshut, 19–21
Lindau, 45–7, 51–2

Magdeburg, 2, 40
Moscow, 79, 157, 159, 186–92, 217
Munich, 42–4

Oberursel, 17, 19, 115

Peenemünde, 10, 155, 207
Pirna, 68, 158, 185
Podberesja, *see* Dubna

Rechlin, 68, 106–08

Sachsen-Anhalt, 2, 7, 12, 104
Samara, *see* Kuybyshev
Savelovo 154–6
Sokhumi, 193–9
Spandau, 2
Stassfurt, 9, 39
Stratford, Connecticut, 21–2

Tushino, 146, 188, 193

Ufa, 67, 116

Vietzen 70, 72,

Wimbledon, 43
Wright Field, 12, 20, 26

Zhiguli Gap, 133

People

Adenstedt, Heinrich, 18

Baade, Brunolf, 67–8, 156, 183
Berkner, Hans, 18–19
Bock, Günther, 68, 157
Brandner, Ferdinand, 50, 66, 111–17, 201–03

Breuninger, Helmut, 188–98
Breuninger, Karl, 188–98
Busemann, Adolf, 24, 67

Churchill, Winston, 8, 28, 33

De Lattre de Tassigny, Jean, 63
Decher, Siegfried, 16, 21, 46

Fedden, Roy, 28, 40, 201
Franz, Anselm, 13, 16, 19, 179

Garnier, Michel, 49, 53
Genske, Kurt, 85
Gröttrup, Helmut, 190

Hartlepp, Heinz, 212
Hertel, Heinrich, 46
Hoch, Hans, 189–90

Jumelle, Claude, 52, 54

Karkavelas, Sigrid, *see* Plügel, Sigrid
Klein, Wilhelm, 85, 96–7
Kuznetsov, Nikolai, 111, 116, 145, 149

Lertes, Peter, 113

Marchal, Raymond, 53
Marshall, George, 30–1, 62
Mauch, Hans, 27

Messerschmitt, Willy, 26, 67, 202
Moellmann, Heinz, 21
Möller, Waldemar, 73, 113, 127
Mouton, Pierre, 52–4
Münzberg , Hans-Georg, 46

Nallinger, Friederich, 60, 62

Oestrich, Hermann, 17, 39, 50, 52, 201, 220
Olechnovich, N. M., 84, 109–17, 138
Osenberg, Werner, 12

Patin, Albert, 43–4
Plügel, Christa, 99, 133, 164
Plügel, Kurt, 78, 118
Plügel, Sigrid, xi, 149

Rosskopf, Hans, 44

Schairer, George, 24
Schelp, Helmut, 27
Singer, Heinrich, xi, 112
Stein, Wolfgang, 26, 46
Stern, William, 40
Szydlowski, Joseph, 59

Tillon, Charles, 45, 53

Von Braun, Wernher, 27, 44, 180
Von Karman, Theodore, 24
Von Ohain, Hans, xviii, 19–20, 23